T4-ADM-937

FUNDAMENTALS of CRIMINAL BEHAVIOR and CORRECTIONAL SYSTEMS

Publication Number 861

AMERICAN LECTURE SERIES®

A Publication In

The BANNERSTONE DIVISION *of*
AMERICAN LECTURES IN SOCIAL
AND REHABILITATION PSYCHOLOGY

Consulting Editors
RICHARD E. HARDY, Ed.D.
Chairman, Department of Rehabilitation Counseling
Virginia Commonwealth University
Richmond, Virginia

and

JOHN G. CULL, Ph.D.
Director, Regional Counselor Training Program
Department of Rehabilitation Counseling
Virginia Commonwealth University
Fishersville, Virginia

The American Lecture Series in Social and Rehabilitation Psychology offers books which are concerned with man's role in his milieu. Emphasis is placed on how this role can be made more effective in a time of social conflict and a deteriorating physical environment. The books are oriented toward descriptions of what future roles should be and are not concerned exclusively with the delineation and definition of contemporary behavior. Contributors are concerned to a considerable extent with prediction through the use of a functional view of man as opposed to a descriptive, anatomical point of view.

Books in this series are written mainly for the professional practitioner; however, the academician will find them of considerable value in both undergraduate and graduate courses in the helping services.

FUNDAMENTALS of CRIMINAL BEHAVIOR and CORRECTIONAL SYSTEMS

JOHN G. CULL
Department of Rehabilitation Counseling
Virginia Commonwealth University
Fishersville, Virginia

RICHARD E. HARDY
Department of Rehabilitation Counseling
Virginia Commonwealth University
Richmond, Virginia

CHARLES C THOMAS • PUBLISHER
Springfield • Illinois • U.S.A.

Published and Distributed Throughout the World by
CHARLES C THOMAS • PUBLISHER
BANNERSTONE HOUSE
301-327 East Lawrence Avenue, Springfield, Illinois, U.S.A.

This book is protected by copyright. No part of it may be reproduced in any manner without written permission from the publisher.

© 1973, by CHARLES C THOMAS • PUBLISHER
ISBN 0-398-02637-8
Library of Congress Catalog Card Number: 72-84141

With THOMAS BOOKS *careful attention is given to all details of manufacturing and design. It is the Publisher's desire to present books that are satisfactory as to their physical qualities and artistic possibilities and appropriate for their particular use.* THOMAS BOOKS *will be true to those laws of quality that assure a good name and good will.*

Printed in the United States of America
JJ-23

Contributors

William E. Amos, Ed.D.: Member, United States Board of Parole; and Professorial Lecturer, The George Washington University. Formerly: Chief, Division of Counseling and Testing, United States Department of Labor; Assistant Director, President's Commission on Crime in the District of Columbia; Superintendent of a Co-educational Institution for Delinquents; Special Agent, United States Secret Service; and a public school superintendent in Arkansas. Dr. Amos has authored or edited seven books, numerous articles and has served as a consulting editor for various publishers.

Hubert M. Clements, Ed.D.: Deputy Director of the South Carolina Department of Corrections. Prior to assuming his present position with the South Carolina Department of Corrections, he was Acting Director of the National Institute of Corrections, U. S. Department of Justice; Assistant Director for Research, Planning, and Development of the South Carolina Department of Corrections; Assistant Professor and Coordinator of the Rehabilitation Counselor Training Program at the University of South Carolina; and Assistant Coordinator of the Rehabilitation Counselor Training Program at the University of Georgia. He received his master's and doctorate degrees in counseling and guidance from the University of Georgia at Athens, Georgia.

Craig R. Colvin, M.Ed.: Assistant Professor, Regional Counselor Training Program, Department of Rehabilitation Counseling, School of Community Services, Virginia Commonwealth University; Associate Editor of *Job Placement Division Digest*. He has held positions with the North Carolina Division of Vocational Rehabilitation as a counselor for the mentally retarded as well as holding a general caseload. Also, Mr. Colvin was the State coordinator acting as a liaison representative between Vocational Rehabilitation and the Department of Corrections in North Carolina; he is co-author, *Contemporary Field Work Practices in Rehabilitation*. He has made several contributions to the professional literature.

John G. Cull, Ph.D.: Director, Regional Counselor Training Program and Professor, Department of Rehabilitation Counseling, School of Community Services, Virginia Commonwealth University, Richmond, Virginia; Adjunct Professor in Psychology and Education, School of General

Studies, University of Virginia; Technical Consultant, Rehabilitation Services Administration, Department of Health, Education & Welfare; Lecturer, Medical Department Affiliate Program, Woodrow Wilson Rehabilitation Center; Consulting Editor, American Lecture Series in Social and Rehabilitation Psychology, Charles C Thomas, Publisher; Delegate, White House Conference on Aging. Formerly: Rehabilitation Counselor, Texas Commission for the Blind and Texas Rehabilitation Commission; Director, Division of Research and Program Development, Virginia Department of Vocational Rehabilitation. Co-author and Editor, *Contemporary Field Work Practices in Rehabilitation, Social and Rehabilitation Services for the Blind, Vocational Rehabilitation: Profession and Process,* and *Introduction to Correctional Rehabilitation.* Dr. Cull also has contributed extensively to the professional literature in psychology and rehabilitation.

Mary L. Dean, M.A.: Counseling, Assistant Director, Counseling Center, University of Hartford, West Hartford, Connecticut. Former Director, Project "Teenagers and Law Enforcement"—T.A.L.E.; former teacher and counselor.

Vernon B. Fox, Ph.D.: Professor of Criminology, Florida State University. Founder and Chairman of Criminology at Florida State, 1952-1971. Formerly with the Michigan Department of Corrections in several positions for ten years, the last three years as Deputy Warden in Charge of Individual Treatment at the State Prison of Southern Michigan at Jackson and, simultaneously, as Director of Individual Treatment for the Michigan Department of Corrections. World War II Army veteran. Associate editor for the Criminal Justice series for The Foundation Press. Board of Visitors, United States Army Military Police School, Ft. Gordon, Georgia. American Correctional Association's Committee to Revise the *Manual of Correctional Standards.* Personal papers, memorabilia, and publications in the Vernon B. Fox Collection, Archives of Contemporary History, University of Wyoming. Listed in *Who's Who in America,* 37th edition. Author of *Violence Behind Bars, Guidelines for Corrections Programs in Community and Junior Colleges,* and *Introduction to Corrections.* Over thirty book reviews, including reviewing the French literature for *Federal Probation.* Over sixty articles in professional journals, law reviews, and chapters in edited books.

John Morris Gray, M.A.: Department of the Army Penologist, Office of the Provost Marshal General; Member, Committee on Riots and Disturbances, American Correctional Association. Formerly: Chairman, Committee on the Military Offender, American Correctional Association; Colonel (Retired), Military Police Corps, United States Army Reserve; and Public High School Teacher, Athletics Coach, and Principal. Contributor to *The Military Prison, Theory, Research, and Practice*, edited by Brodsky and Eggleston, SIU Press, Carbondale Illinois, 1970 and co-author *Causes, Preventive Measures and Methods of Controlling Riots and Disturbances in Correctional Institutions*, American Correctional Association, 1970. Mr. Gray has contributed extensively to the professional literature in military correctional programs and treatment.

Richard E. Hardy, Ed.D.: Chairman, Department of Rehabilitation Counseling, School of Community Services, Virginia Commonwealth University, Richmond, Virginia; Technical Consultant, Rehabilitation Services Administration, Department of Health, Education & Welfare; Consulting Editor, American Lecture Series in Social and Rehabilitation Psychology, Charles C Thomas, Publisher; and Associate Editor, *Journal of Voluntary Action Research*. Formerly: Rehabilitation Counselor in Virginia; Chief Psychologist and Supervisor of Training, South Carolina Department of Vocational Rehabilitation; Member of the South Carolina State Board of Examiners in Psychology; Rehabilitation Advisor, Rehabilitation Services Administration, Department of Health, Education & Welfare. Co-Author and Editor, *Social and Rehabilitation Services for the Blind, Vocational Rehabilitation: Profession and Process, The Unfit Majority,* and *Introduction to Correctional Rehabilitation*. Dr. Hardy has contributed extensively to the professional literature in psychology and rehabilitation.

Charles W. Hoehne, Attorney: Assistant Director and General Counsel, Texas State Commission for the Blind; General Counsel, National Council of State Agencies for the Blind. Co-author, *Fundamental Concepts of American Jurisprudence, Synopsis of Texas Legal Rules, Principles and Doctrines* (now in 7th ed.) and *Synopsis of Louisiana Law and Practice* (now in 2nd ed.). Member, State Bar of Texas, American Bar Association, and American Judicature Society. President, Texas Rehabilitation Association (1971-72) and Texas Chapter of American Association of Workers for the Blind (1970-72). A frequent member of or consultant to committees and groups involved in the improvement of state and federal legislation or administrative regulations relating to programs for the handicapped. Mr. Hoehne has been instrumental in the development of cooperative governmental programs for the visually disabled, including what is thought to be the nation's first comprehensive rehabilitation program for visually handicapped individuals incarcerated in correctional institutions. He has contributed a number of articles to the professional literature in rehabilitation.

viii   *Fundamentals of Criminal Behavior and Correctional Systems*

Robert G. Lawson: Assistant Director, Division of General Welfare, State Department of Welfare and Institutions. Formerly: Disability Examiner for Social Security; Rehabilitation Counselor, Virginia State Department of Vocational Rehabilitation; Supervisor of Rehabilitation Unit, Bon Air School for Girls; Supervisor of Special Programs, Education Section, State Department of Welfare and Institutions; and Reading Instructor, Smithdeal Massey Business College and Randolph Macon Business College.

William D. Leeke: Director of the South Carolina Department of Corrections. He is presently a member of the Board of Directors of the American Correctional Association, Chairman of the American Correctional Association's Committee on Riots and Disturbances, President-elect of the Southern States Correctional Association, and President of the Association of State Correctional Administrators. During his more than 15 years in corrections, he has served as Superintendent of the Greenville County Rehabilitation Center, Greenville, South Carolina; Administrative Assistant to the Director of the South Carolina Department of Corrections; Warden of the Central Correctional Institution, Columbia, South Carolina; and Deputy Director of the South Carolina Department of Corrections.

David M. Petersen, Ph.D.: Associate Professor, Department of Sociology, The Ohio State University. Formerly: Instructor, the University of South Florida; Research Sociologist, Narcotic Rehabilitation Unit, U. S. Bureau of Prisons; part-time instructor at the University of Georgia, the University of Maryland, and American University. Co-author, *Targets for Change: Perspectives on an Active Sociology,* and *Ecology, Crime, and Delinquency.* Dr. Petersen has contributed articles to the professional literature on the administration of justice, narcotics addiction, and penology.

Julian B. Roebuck, Ph.D.: Professor, Department of Sociology and Anthropology, Mississippi State University, State College, Mississippi. Formerly: Parole and Classification Officer, U. S. Bureau of Prisons; Research Analyst, District of Columbia Department of Corrections; Consultant to Louisiana Department of Institutions; Supervisor, College Interns, California Department of Corrections. Author, *Criminal Typology: The Legalistic, Physical-Constitutional-Hereditary, Psychological-Psychiatric and Sociological Approaches* (Charles C Thomas, Publisher), *The Etiology of Alcoholism: Constitutional, Psychological, and Sociological Approaches* (in press with Charles C Thomas). Dr. Roebuck has contributed numerous articles to the professional literature in the fields of criminology and deviant behavior.

Contributors

Charles E. Smith, M.D.: Associate Professor, Department of Psychiatry, School of Medicine, University of North Carolina at Chapel Hill; and Senior Psychiatric Consultant, North Carolina Department of Corrections. Past-President, Medical Correctional Association. Member, Advisory Committee, *Federal Probation Quarterly* and member, Professional Counsel, National Council on Crime and Delinquency. Fellow, American Psychiatric Association. Formerly: Chief Medical Officer, Federal Correctional Institution, Ashland, Kentucky; Chief, Psychiatric Service, Medical Center for Federal Prisoners, Springfield, Missouri; Assistant Medical Director and Chief Psychiatrist, Federal Bureau of Prisons; Medical Director and Chief Psychiatrist, Federal Bureau of Prisons, Chief of Service, West Side Division, Saint Elizabeth's Hospital, Washington, D. C. Dr. Smith has made numerous contributions to the professional literature in forensic and prison psychiatry.

Dora B. Somerville, A.C.S.W.: First Illinois woman named to the Parole and Pardon Board of Illinois, recently appointed by Governor as Correctional Program Executive. Member, Illinois Youth Commission 1962-1969, Member, State Minority Group Relations Task Force. Director of Social Service Department of Chicago Municipal Court Psychiatric Institute; Clinic Director, Illinois State Training School for Girls; Director, Child Guidance Clinic, Catholic Youth Organization. Citations from Loyola University for contributions to field of social work, and from Ursuline College for contributions in field of social welfare. Responsible for professional recruitment; liaison with universities, colleges throughout the state; summer student work-trainee programs in Adult and Juvenile divisions of Illinois Department of Corrections; Supervision of accredited intern program for clinical psychologists, social workers, sociologists, and behavioral scientists; administer department's apprentice training program, serve as liaison with Illinois Department of Personnel and other state agencies, as well as pertinent commissions, city and county agencies, and federal government units. She is co-author, *The Delinquent Girl*, Thomas, Publisher.

Wright Stubbs, LL.B.: Counselor, Alcoholic Rehabilitation Center, Austin State Hospital, Austin, Texas. Formerly: practicing attorney in Austin, Texas, for 32 years; Inmate, Texas Department of Corrections, Huntsville, Texas, 1958-1959; paroled, then pardoned after three years. Mr. Stubbs also served as a clerk at the Austin State Hospital prior to assuming his current position.

Charles W. Thomas, Ph.D.: Assistant Professor, Department of Sociology and Anthropology, School of Arts and Sciences, Virginia Commonwealth University, with a joint appointment to the Criminal Justice Institute of the Department of Public Safety and Criminal Justice, School of Community Services, Virginia Commonwealth University. Dr. Thomas has been actively involved in research on adult resocialization among both adult and juvenile offenders confined in Virginia's correctional system.

Clyde B. Vedder, Ph.D.: Professor of Sociology and Corrections, Illinois State University; Member, Governor's Advisory Board, Juvenile Institutions; Member, Governor's State Committee on Aging, Delegate to White House Conference, Washington, D.C. November, 1971, Professional Advisory Committee, John Howard Association, and Illinois Academy of Criminology; Executive Board Member, International Criminological Foundation; Honorary Life Member, Illinois Police Association, Fellow of the American Sociological Society, and Gerontological Association; Chairman, Department of Sociology, University of Houston; Developed Division of Correctional and Police Administration, University of Arizona, Chairman, Governor of Florida's Committee on Juvenile Delinquency, Member, Governor of Florida's Committee on Penal Reform, Governor's Advisory Board, Illinois Youth Commission, Professor, Academic In-Service Training Programs, Florida Department of Corrections, Texas Department of Corrections, Illinois Department of Corrections, Governor's Interim Committee, South Central Interstate Corrections Compact, Florida, Co-Chairman Second Annual Conference, Arizona Crime Prevention and Control, State Chairman, Promotion and Publicity, National Institute on Crime and Delinquency, Arizona. Co-author, *Criminology: Book of Readings,* Dryden Press; *Homosexuality in Corrections, The Delinquent Girl,* Thomas, Publisher; Editor and co-editor, *Gerontology: Book of Readings, Probation and Parole Readings, Penology Readings, Problems of the Aged, Problems of the Middle-Aged;* and author, *The Juvenile Offender,* Random House; and *Juvenile Offenders,* Thomas, Publisher. Dr. Vedder has contributed extensively to the professional literature in criminology, juvenile delinquency and gerontology.

Charles F. Wellford, Ph.D.: Assistant Professor, Division of Criminology, Department of Sociology, University of Maryland; Formerly: Sociologist, National Institute of Law Enforcement and Criminal Justice, U. S. Department of Justice; Research Assistant, Institute of Corrections, Philadelphia, Pennsylvania. Dr. Wellford has contributed numerous articles to the professional literature in criminology and sociology.

Glenn R. Winters, A.B., LL.B.: Executive Director, American Judicature Society; and Editor of the *Journal of the American Judicature Society.* Member, American Bar Association. Also served in A.B.A. in its House of Delegates, as chairman, Committee on Judicial Selection and Tenure; secretary of Section of Judicial Administration; and on council of Section of Criminal Law, and Section of Bar Activities. Director, National Legal Aid and Defender Association (1949-61). Member and past president, Christian Legal Society. Member, Illinois State Bar, State Bar of Michigan, the Missouri Bar, the American Law Institute, the Institute of Judicial Administration, the National Municipal League, The American Academy of Political and Social Science, the National Institute of Social Science, the World Peace Through Law Center. Fellow, International Academy of Law and Science. Author, *Bar Association Organization and Activities* (1954). Editor, *Lagging Justice* (1960), *Selected Readings: The Administration of Justice and Its Improvement* (1969), *Selected Readings: Judicial Selection and Tenure* (1967), *Selected Readings: Fair Trial—Free Press* (1971), *Selected Readings: Congestion and Delay* (1971), *Selected Readings: The Jury System* (1971). Mr. Winters also has contributed extensively to the professional literature in judicial administration and in court reform.

This Book Is Dedicated to

CORBETT REEDY

Deputy Commissioner
Rehabilitation Services Administration
United States Department of Health, Education and Welfare

Formerly

Regional Commissioner
Social and Rehabilitation Services Administration
United States Department of Health, Education and Welfare

Director
Virginia Division of Vocational Rehabilitation

Mr. Reedy is past president of the National Rehabilitation Association. He is a teacher, lecturer and writer in rehabilitation and was one of the founders of the Woodrow Wilson Rehabilitation Center, the first comprehensive vocational rehabilitation center in the United States. He was one of the founders of the first graduate program in Rehabilitation Counseling which is located at Virginia Commonwealth University in Richmond. His planning and foresight led to the development of the VCU Regional Counselor Training Program which was also the first of its kind in the nation.

Preface

When the Maine state prison opened in 1824, its first warden proclaimed:

Prisons should be so constructed that even their aspect might be terrific and appear like what they should be—dark and comfortless abodes of guilt and wretchedness.

No mode or degree of punishment . . . is in its nature so well adapted to purposes of preventing crime or reforming a criminal as close confinement in a solitary cell, in which, cut off from all hope of relief, the convict shall be furnished a hammock on which he may sleep, a block of wood on which he may sit, and with such coarse and wholesome food as may best be suited to a person in a situation designed for grief and penitence, and shall be favored with so much light from the firmament as may enable him to read the New Testament which will be given him as his sole companion and guide to a better life.

There his vices and crimes shall become personified, and appeal to his frightened imagination as co-tenants of his dark and dismal cell. They will surround him as so many hideous spectres and overwhelm him with horror and remorse.

The legacy of such a philosophy of penology remains to haunt us to this day; however, we can look with great hope to the future. We are now hearing new words such as rehabilitation penology, rehabilitation approaches in incarceration, academy for correctional administrators and officers, and so on. These descriptive words reflect the enormous increase in interest in improving our prison programs and doing something about causes of crime in the United States. In recent years, there has been a growing awareness of the problems involved in determining causes of crime, incarcerating individuals in prison systems, administering justice systems, developing rehabilitation objectives and plans for inmates, and working with former inmates once they have been released from prison and are attempting to adjust successfully to the outside world.

Various conferences and planning groups are meeting throughout the country on the subject of improvement of penal programs. Some are sponsored by the federal government. Other smaller meetings are being held by interested citizen groups and voluntary organizations concerned with causes of crime, the prison inmate and reform. So it seems that we are living in the day of planning for reform in penal institutions and treatment of individuals accused and convicted of crime. We will make many mistakes and we have much to learn.

The purpose of this volume is to provide the student and professional practitioner in the areas of rehabilitation and corrections basic information which will be of value in the many decisions that have to be made in planning for the future. We, the authors, are of the opinion that no single authority or discipline can adequately treat an area as complex or multidisciplinary in scope as that of correctional rehabilitation and criminal behavior. National leaders in correctional rehabilitation and other closely related fields have contributed many hours to pulling together their ideas and suggestions on where we should go from here.

This book represents an earnest plea for reform and change and gives suggestions and alternative approaches for such change. It is a compendium of writings by various experienced persons, most of whom are making a contribution daily through active administration, teaching, and providing various professional services to the inmate.

The book has been developed to meet the needs of individuals who are working with inmates or former inmates—prison administrators, rehabilitation counselors, parole officers, officials, police officers, and various professional persons who are attempting to deal with the problem of crime and its effects. It will be most useful in various college programs for students who are concerned with the broad general subject area of correctional rehabilitation and criminal behavior.

In developing this book for publication, we are indebted to a large number of people who have made substantial contributions. We are particularly indebted to the various authors who have submitted manuscripts. We would like to single out for recognition Mrs. Maryann Taliaferro, Administrative Assistant at the Regional Counselor Training Program, Department of Rehabilitation Counseling, Virginia Commonwealth University, Fishersville, Virginia. We are particularly appreciative for the many hours she has spent in assisting in the proofing of manuscripts and typing final drafts.

Richmond, Virginia   JOHN G. CULL
                                        RICHARD E. HARDY

CONTENTS

Page

Contributors v
Preface xv

PART ONE

Chapter

1. CRIME AS A SOCIAL PROBLEM 5
2. CAUSES OF CRIME 23
3. AN OVERVIEW OF CRIMINAL LAW AND CRIMINAL PROCEDURE 32
4. THE JUDICIAL ROLE IN CORRECTIONAL ADMINISTRATION 62
5. CORRECTIONAL SYSTEMS AND PROGRAMS—An Overview 82
6. MILITARY CORRECTIONS 119
7. REVIEW OF RELEVANT RESEARCH IN CORRECTIONAL REHABILITATION 135

PART TWO

8. CRIMINAL TYPOLOGY 155
9. TYPOLOGIES AND TREATMENT 176
10. CHARACTERISTICS OF THE JUVENILE DELINQUENT 216
11. CHARACTERISTICS OF THE FEMALE OFFENDER 225
12. NOT LESS THAN TWO NOR MORE THAN SIX 253
13. EFFECTS OF INCARCERATION 270
14. PSYCHIATRY IN CORRECTION 281
15. THE ROLE OF HIGHER EDUCATION IN THE REHABILITATION OF THE PUBLIC OFFENDER 298

Index 333

FUNDAMENTALS of CRIMINAL BEHAVIOR and CORRECTIONAL SYSTEMS

The following books have appeared in the American Lecture Series in Social and Rehabilitation Psychology:

Vocational Rehabilitation: Profession and Process
John G. Cull, Ph.D., and Richard E. Hardy, Ed.D.

Contemporary Field Work Practices in Rehabilitation
John G. Cull, Ph.D., and Craig R. Colvin, M.Ed.

Social and Rehabilitation Services for the Blind
Richard E. Hardy, Ed.D., and John G. Cull, Ph.D.

Introduction To Correctional Rehabilitation
Richard E. Hardy, Ed.D., and John G. Cull, Ph.D.

Medical and Psychological Aspects of Disability
A. Beatrix Cobb, Ph.D.

Drug Dependence and Rehabilitation Approaches
Richard E. Hardy, Ed.D., and John G. Cull, Ph.D.

PART ONE

Crime as a Social Problem

Causes of Crime

An Overview of Criminal Law and Criminal Procedure

The Judicial Role in Correctional Administration

Correctional Systems and Programs—An Overview

Military Corrections

Review of Relevant Research in Correctional Rehabilitation

Chapter 1
Crime as a Social Problem
VERNON FOX

> Origins of Crime
> Modern Crime
> The Problem of Intervention
> The Contributors to the Crime Problem
> Cultural Aspects of Crime
> Conclusions
> Notes and References

The emergence of crime as a major social problem has taken a long time to develop. To endure and function effectively, any social formation needs the internal controls accepted by the individuals of which it is composed or imposed upon these individuals. The amount of individual deviation from these norms influences the effectiveness and smooth operation of the social system. Crime became a major problem when it grew to sufficient magnitude that it impaired this normal operation of society sufficiently that public opinion made it a political concern.

Crime is a symptom of social and personal pathology that results in a dysfunctional relationship between the individuals and his group to the extent that society is damaged in the process. Being a sociopolitical event, as defined by the culture and society, crime may result from a wide variety of causes. These may range from a social situation that brings a relatively normal individual into conflict with society's laws to a severe emotional disturbance within the personality that prevents the individual from relating effectively with his group.

ORIGINS OF CRIME

As a definition, crime is relatively new in the history of man, having gradually emerged between the Middle Ages and the 18th century. The ancient Latin word, "crimen," did not mean "crime" as it is known today, but was considered to be an "accusation." The concept of "crime," of course, emanated from this "accusation." During its evolution from primitive man through the Middle Ages, personal injuries between people were settled by the individuals or families involved until this type of blood-feud became injurious to society itself. Arbitration courts were then established and people were coerced to use them. The rise of the organized church from the fourth century onward brought the new dimension of divine judgment.

In practice, the social sanctions against individual behavior that damages the group grew into crime. The Romans contributed much to this development with an emphasis on politics, considering the serious accusations or injuries to be treason, false testimony, and betrayal of citizens into the hands of the enemy. Rather than crime, as such, the individual was considered to have declared war upon society and, therefore, to have forfeited his right to belong to it. During the Middle Ages, acts against the church and the king became matters of concern. After the Norman Conquest of England in 1066, there began to be concern for the protection of citizens. Thievery and robbery began to merit social punishments. With the beginnings of rudimentary parliamentary government in the 14th and 15th centuries, legislation to secure the social order resulted in new offenses, such as making war against the king, forbidding serfs to move from their land in search of work, and forbidding people who did not own property from keeping dogs. Murder was not yet a serious offense, as it never had been. During the 16th and 17th centuries, the consolidation of church and state resulted in offenses of treason, heresy, blasphemy, swearing, immorality, adultery, and witchcraft. During the same period, the making of vagabondage an offense was an attempt to deal with a social evil by turning it into a punishable offense. In the 18th century, piracy, banking offenses and forgery became concerns of society.

The emergence of the criminal law between the time of French and American Revolutions and the War of 1812 based legal sanctions on the statutory definitions of crime. This concept had been a long time emerging side by side with the development of law. Law and crime have gone through three broad stages to maturity.[1] The first period is the exploratory theoretical discussion in which an area of truth is isolated and a perspective is communicated. In crime and criminal law, the ancient philosophers, lawgivers, and codes provided this service. The second stage is the work of the craftsman attempting to apply the knowledge gained to particular and practical legal problems. The development of the Napoleonic Codes and the effort of Blackstone and his contemporaries in the codification of English criminal law in the last quarter of the 18th century are examples of this stage in the development of law and crime. The third stage of modern law, as a 20th century development, provides an intellectual autonomy and maturity in which the moral authority of legality is explored, the role of social science is clarified in creating a society based on justice, and the function of law, including criminal law, is examined in establishing and sustaining the framework for society. Crime is the final definition assigned to the legal definitions of behavioral deviations so that the force of society can be applied to the individual to effect conformity with the perpetuation of the existing social formation or its orderly change. Crime is the ultimate definition in social control so far as the individual is concerned.

MODERN CRIME

Unhealthy and undesirable social situations are frequently tolerated for centuries, becoming a major social problem only when they become sufficiently large to attract the concern of the opinion-makers and power structure of the society. Crime is a 20th century problem in this context, first becoming of real concern in the 1920's with the notorious gangs and mobsters of the Prohibition Era, a concern that reached its crescendo with the St. Valentine's Day Massacre in 1929. The United States Bureau of Prisons was reorganized, the Federal Bureau of Investigation began gathering crime statistics, the American Association for Forensic Sciences was begun, and the Wickersham Report on crime in America was released in 1931. The crime problem had reached proportions that attracted the attention and concern of the opinion-makers and political leaders in American society.

Modern crime, while overlapping to some extent, can be classified into (1) conventional street crime, (2) crime without victims; i.e., narcotics, dangerous drugs, alcohol, and vice, (3) professional crime, (4) white collar crime, and (5) organized crime. The majority of crime found in correctional caseloads comes from the conventional or street crime and the crime without victims, such as narcotics and dangerous drugs. Alcohol contributes approximately half the cases detained in county and city jails.

Professional criminals spend most of their time directly engaged in crime. Typically, they spend time developing criminal opportunities, such as "casing" buildings they will burglarize or getting acquainted with people they are going to "con" out of large sums, selling goods they have stolen or procured, and other criminal activities. Professional crime exists because of the "fence" and the "fix."[2]

The fence deals in stolen goods. It can be in pawn shops, clothing stores, used car lots, or any other place that sells a commodity that can be stolen. The fix is a mutually profitable arrangement, whether by payoff or other arrangement, in which the professional criminal is sufficiently immune from law enforcement to enable him to practice with reasonable safety.

White collar crime relates to sharp business practices, "thumb-on-the-scales" sales procedures, and other business approaches that violate law, but which are difficult to detect and prove. White collar offenses most frequently violate antitrust laws, food-and-drug laws, safety and health laws, licensing provisions, housing codes, and many other regulatory statutes. The price-fixing by 29 electrical equipment companies in the mid 1960's resulted in Judge T. Cullen Ganey's declaring while sentencing the defendants:

This is a shocking indictment of a vast section of our economy, for what is really at stake here is the survival of the kind of economy under which this country has grown great, the free enterprise system.[3]

Organized crime supplies illegal goods and services to countless numbers of citizen-customers. Receiving its greatest start in the 1920's during the Prohibition Era while smuggling whiskey and other alcoholic beverages, it has since branched into many other areas, notably narcotics and dangerous drugs, gambling, loan sharking, and various forms of vice.[4] Organizations promoting these activities also have entered legitimate business fields and politics. It was general opinion among the citizenry in the area, for example, when the selection of a new chief of police in a middle-sized city was suspected to have had to be approved by the "crime boss." In fact, persons on the Washington scene, when the Presidential *Task Force Report: Organized Crime* was published by the President's Commission on Law Enforcement and Administration of Justice in 1967, have observed that what it did *not* say was interesting. Control of business concerns has been acquired by investments, accepting business interests in payments of gambling debts, foreclosures on usurious loans, and by various forms of extortion. The public is apathetic because it is not aware of all of the implications. An extra four cents for a loaf of bread, another couple of hundred dollars on financing the construction of a residence, and similar "hidden" overcharges are accepted without much concern. Conviction for organized crime is difficult because its citizen-consumers will not testify and its citizen-victims are afraid to testify. Consequently, crime in some way pervades the lives of Americans everywhere. It has been estimated that if the income from organized crime were taxed, the 10 percent surcharge on the income tax requested by President Johnson in the middle 1960's probably could have been a 10 percent decrease.

The majority of offenders in correctional caseloads, however, are those in conventional or street crimes and in crimes without victims, generally narcotics, dangerous drugs, alcohol, or vice. Because these citizen-offenders make up the correctional caseloads over which society has gained the authority through its court system to intervene in their lives, they become the primary concern of the treatment programs.

There is no way of determining the total number of crimes that are committed in America.[5] The crime that comes to the attention of the police is only that crime observed by them or reported by citizens. The estimated number of major crimes committed in America is about five million.[6] Slightly over one million are reported to police.[7] Only a fraction of these ever get to court and fewer are convicted. About five million lesser offenses are reported to police.[8] Probably more than ten times those reported have actually occurred. Many victims do not report crimes because (1) they think it is a private matter or do not want to harm the offender, (2) police could or would not be effective, (3) they did not want to take the time, (4) they were too confused or did not know how to report, or (5) fear of reprisal.[9] The result has been that the American public has developed an intense fear of crime. For example, a Harris Poll found that 3,000 per 10,000 population fear for their lives by being murdered, while only three per 10,000 population are actually murdered.[10]

Crime has become a significant social problem in America. Law and order has become a major political issue. Beginning with the relatively small appropriation for the Juvenile Delinquency Prevention and Control Act of 1961, Congress has appropriated large sums of money under the Omnibus Crime Control and Safe Streets Act of 1968 and its subsequent amendments. The Juvenile Delinquency Control Act of 1968 and its amendments have also received funds. In addition, agencies not originally committed to criminal justice have had legislation assigning them to this task, such as Vocational Rehabilitation, Model Cities, Department of Labor, many programs in Health, Education and Welfare, and many others.

THE PROBLEM OF INTERVENTION

A social problem which has become as significant as crime and delinquency in America demands the attention of many programs and social institutions. The converse must be true, in that all individuals, agencies of government, and private organizations need to coordinate their efforts to control this problem. It is simply not the province of corrections departments, institutions, and programs, any more than learning is the single province of schools and universities. The problem is to find those programs that (1) work best, (2) cost least, and (3) do the least damage.

To bring the efforts of these agencies to bear on offenders who are generally unwilling to accept confinement and correctional treatment voluntarily, society has to have a system of criminal justice that identifies those people who need correctional programs and gives society the authority to provide them. This system of criminal justice begins with law enforcement, which brings cases to prosecuting authorities. The prosecutors bring the cases with enough evidence to prosecute to court for trial. The courts then determine who will go into the correctional system in whose lives society has the authority to intervene to protect itself by controlling or changing the behavior of citizen-offenders. All this procedure has to be in keeping with constitutional guarantees as interpreted by the United States Supreme Court and implemented in the laws of the respective jurisdiction. Consequently, not everyone who appears to others to be guilty may be convicted of a crime and come into the correctional system. The problem of intervention into the lives of citizens is a complex one.

The estimated number of major crimes committed in 1970, those reported to police, those arrested, charged in court, and the percentage of those found guilty or turned over to juvenile court are shown in Table 1-I.

The number of persons in correctional caseloads, then, are far less than the number who have apparently committed crimes. It has been conjectured that if everyone who committed a major crime were caught and convicted, the load would break down the correctional system, since prisons and juvenile institutions are already crowded and probation and parole caseloads are already overloaded. The number of people who can be in the correctional system at any one time is shown in Table 1-II.

TABLE 1-I
APPROXIMATION OF FLOW IN THE CRIMINAL JUSTICE SYSTEM FOR 1970*

Crime	Estimated No. of Offenses	Reported to Police	Total Estimated Arrests	Charged in Court	Disposition Guilty as Charged	Disposition Lesser Charge	Disposition To Juvenile Court
Murder	15,810	8,898	15,230	1,262	35.2% (444)	20.1% (254)	10.4% (131)
Negligent Homicide	—	3,379	4,190	734	38.4% (281)	10.8% (79)	8.5% (62)
Forcible Rape	37,270	21,038	19,050	2,878	27.7% (797)	15.6% (449)	21.9% (630)
Robbery	348,380	201,897	98,210	14,519	25.2% (3,459)	11.1% (612)	40.1% (5,822)
Aggravated Assault	329,240	186,560	155,060	22,827	36.3% (8,286)	14.5% (3,310)	18.1% (4,132)
Burglary	2,169,300	1,247,541	358,100	62,362	23.1% (14,306)	8.6% (5,371)	55.5% (34,611)
Larceny over $50	1,746,100	1,045,234	748,200	180,756	45.6% (82,425)	3.9% (7,047)	36.0% (65,072)
Auto Theft	921,400	599,222	153,300	22,626	18.7% (4,211)	4.3% (1,119)	62.1% (14,651)

Note: From *Crime in the United States—Uniform Crime Reports—1970.* Washington, D.C., Federal Bureau of Investigation, August 31, 1971. *Based on 4,088 cities; total population 102,316,000.

TABLE 1-II
PERSONS IN CORRECTIONAL CASELOADS

Facility or Program	Number
Jails	160,863*
Probation	684,088†
Prison	221,597‡
Parole	122,142§
	1,268,690

---

*1970 National Jail Census, Law Enforcement Assistance Administration, Washington, D.C.

†Task Force Report: Corrections. The President's Commission on Law Enforcement and the Administration of Justice, Washington, D.C., 1967, p. 27.

‡Ibid., p. 178.

§Ibid., p. 60.

This table does not include criminally insane, many community-based programs, criminal sexual psychopaths, many narcotics patients, and other special categories. A reasonable estimate is that there are probably 4,000,000 ex-prisoners included and probably in excess of 10,000,000 ex-offenders, altogether in the population of the United States, based on length of sentence, recidivism rate, size of the population, and other factors.

In addition, there were about 900,000 cases of juvenile delinquency in 1968, involving 774,000 children.[11] There were 53,000 children in public training schools for delinquents[12] and another 10,000 in private training schools. There is no way of knowing how many juveniles are under official and unofficial probation supervision. Neither is there any way of knowing how many juveniles are under voluntary police supervision with the many Juvenile Aid Bureaus in police departments throughout the country. Suffice it to say that the problem of delinquency and crime has become a major one in American society.

The local jail is the oldest institution in American corrections and constitutes the beginning of the correctional process. The first national jail census by the United States Bureau of Census in cooperation with the Law Enforcement Assistance Administration was published in February, 1971, on data collected in 1970.[13] According to that survey, there were 4,037 jails in the United States holding 160,863 persons. These jails were limited to locally operated jails with the authority to retain adult persons for 48 hours or longer, and did not include many lock-ups, stockades, drunk tanks, and other facilities designed to retain persons for less than two full days. Neither did it include the state-operated jails of Connecticut, Delaware, and Rhode Island. Many criminologists estimate that there are about 15,000 local detention facilities, altogether, but whether they should be counted as part of the "correctional" program could be debated.

Throughout history, the jail has been denounced by social critics as being inadequate, under-staffed, and unable to obtain adequate resources from governmental agencies. The jail, itself, is a social problem. The jail holds accused persons awaiting trial, holds convicted persons serving short-term sentences, holds convicted persons awaiting sentence or execution of sentence, and holds material witnesses that have to be held awaiting a trial. Many jails cannot hold persons for more than 30 days while, at the other extreme, many jails can hold persons for a year. In some cases, persons serving consecutive short-term sentences can remain in jail beyond a year. Even so, while most criminologists and jail administrators know the inadequacies of the jail, prospects for jail reform do not look hopeful.[14]

The problem of intervention into the lives of citizen-offenders in a democracy is, in itself, a major one. An ordinary trial costs the counties around $5,000 and many go far above that, which is a measure of its complexity. Only a minority of offenders are ever brought to trial. Many of those cannot be convicted for a variety of reasons. Consequently, the correctional caseload tends to be made up of probably some of the more serious of the problem people who come into the system of criminal justice, though such a generalization is only a tendency.

THE CONTRIBUTORS TO THE CRIME PROBLEM

The people who contribute to the crime problem to the extent of being convicted and being adjudicated delinquent differ from the other clients who receive the attention of governmental agencies. Welfare clients and mental hospital patients, for example, generally have problems other than those of damaging society by committing offenses. The correctional client damages society by injuring or killing others, stealing or destroying property, or damages himself through drugs and alcohol.

The correctional client "acts out" his stress and emotional needs at the expense of others, thereby offending society. This acting-out behavior may be compensatory, reactive, or any of a series of possible syndromes and patterns of dynamics. Crime is a socio-legal event not susceptible to a medical or clinical diagnosis. The personality engaged in criminal behavior, however, may be diagnosed in a wide variety of patterns that contribute to dysfunctional behavior in society. There is no such thing as a "criminal personality," but there are many personality patterns that can generate criminal behavior. The task of corrections and the approaches concerned with helping socially disabled people "get along" in society without causing trouble necessitates the most sensitive, flexible, and competent professional personnel of any field devoted to the general welfare. The correctional client must be simultaneously controlled and helped so that the external control and supervision can be dropped as soon as possible.

The correctional worker and those who assist him represent "authority" to the correctional clients. The common denominator among all correctional clients, regardless of their offenses, is conflict with authority.

Intelligence does not differ significantly between offenders and the population from which they have been drawn.[15] On the other hand, offenders are generally about three grades retarded academically. While the average grade completed by persons over 25 years of age in the United States in 1960 was 10.6, the estimated grade average of prisoners was about the eighth. In 1968, there were 5,417,000 high school graduates and 2,734,000 school dropouts.[16] The majority of dropouts are not in prisons or correctional caseloads, but the majority of people in prison and correctional caseloads are school dropouts. The correctional client, then, is a person of average native ability, but who is retarded in skills, education, and general assimilation of the culture by probably an average of about three years.

The correctional client does not relate well to others, although he may manipulate them or "con" them. He generally does not establish and maintain strong and permanent bonds with people, but may enjoy a series of short relationships. Protecting himself, he projects blame on "the system," refers to "the caught and the uncaught," and rationalizes his behavior. Because he does not relate well to people, does not invest emotionally in them, he may see a man coming down the street either as a threat or as an opportunity. While there is considerable variation among people, these tendencies tend to appear frequently in correctional caseloads.

It is interesting to note that research on parole prediction and on adjustment within the institution focuses on work habits and employment as probably the most important factor in adjustment on parole or in institutions. This factor is probably the single most important index of adjustment for everybody in society, whether he is an offender or not. The offender is less competent in education and in employment skills and stability than the average person in society. It is apparent that education and employment may be only indices of a broader failure to assimilate culture, but which are more visible and easy to measure than the other factors. Consequently, working with the offender cannot be confined to education, training, and employment, but must include other services, such as counseling and casework to support education and vocational training.

Most of these follow-up studies relating to successful adjustment in the community agree that prognosis for social adjustment is poor:[17]

1. the more intermittent a man's employment record and the more unskilled his jobs
2. the fewer ties he has with wife or family

3. the more he is moved around the country

4. the more he spends in leisure pursuits such as drinking and gambling

5. the more members of his family and circle of friends have convictions

6. the higher the conviction rate in the area where he works or lives

The factors that are associated with failure of success on parole, failure in school, and failure at work, then, involve work habits, occupational and social stability, and the acquisition and internalization of occupational and social skills. All the segments of the criminal justice system and the interested agencies and organizations not specifically in that system must be brought to bear on the problem of crime and delinquency. This can be done partially by working with individual offenders in an effort to "shore up" their occupational and social competencies by remedial and instructional assistance.

The persistence and stability of the deviant personality pattern, once developed, can be seen in the rate of recidivism or repetition of crime. The percent of persons rearrested within four years after their release in 1965 is shown in Table 1-III.

TABLE 1-III

PERCENT OF PERSONS REARRESTED WITHIN FOUR YEARS BY TYPE OF RELEASE IN 1965

Acquitted or dismissed	85%
Mandatory release (expiration of sentence, etc.)	75%
Total releases	63%
Fines	62%
Parole	61%
Suspended Sentence and/or Probation	56%
Fine and Probation	37%

Note: From *Crime in the United States—Uniform Crime Reports—1970*. Washington, D.C., Federal Bureau of Investigation, August 31, 1971, p. 39.

18 Fundamentals of Criminal Behavior and Correctional Systems

The persistence of the deviant behavioral patterns can be seen in the rearrest rate for specific offenses, as shown in Table 1-IV.

TABLE 1-IV
PERCENT OF REPEATERS
BY TYPE OF CRIME IN 1965 REARRESTED WITHIN FOUR YEARS

Auto Theft	80%
Burglary	76%
Narcotics	69%
Assault	68%
Forgery	67%
Total (average)	63%
Larceny	63%
All Others	59%
Robbery	57%
Gambling	48%
Liquor Laws	45%
Fraud	42%
Embezzlement	18%

Note: From Crime in the United States—Uniform Crime Reports—1970. Washington, D.C., Federal Bureau of Investigation, August 31, 1971, p. 40.

The age patterns of the repeaters can be shown in Table 1-V.

TABLE 1-V
PERCENT OF REPEATERS
IN FOUR YEARS BY AGE RELEASED IN 1965

Under 20	74%
20-24	71%
25-29	65%
Total of All Ages (average)	63%
30-39	62%
40-49	53%
50 and over	38%

Note: From Crime in the United States—Uniform Crime Reports—1970. Washington, D.C., Federal Bureau of Investigation, August 31, 1971, p. 41.

The behavior patterns that bring persons into the criminal justice system, then, appear to be persistent and well established. To correct this "life style," the remedial strategies necessary to counterbalance and change these patterns must be equally intense, persistent, and long-enduring.

CULTURAL ASPECTS OF CRIME

Crime is the most cosmopolitan and universal measure of the advance of a culture. The law, including criminal law, identifies problem areas in a society. Certainly, crime and violence identify the areas of social stress in society. The reaction of society then becomes a measure of the values and sophistication of that society.

Sir Winston Churchill said the following to the House of Commons in 1910:

> The mood and temper of the public with regard to the treatment of crime and criminal is one of the most fun filling tasks of the civilization of any country.[18]

This statement was made after Churchill had seen John Galsworthy's play, "Justice." The same theme was included in a decision by the United States Supreme Court in 1961:

> The methods we employ enforcement of our criminal law have aptly been called the measure by which quality of our civilization may be judged.[19]

The same theme ran through Robert F. Kennedy's "Foreword" to a symposium on criminal law published by the *University of Florida Law Review* in 1963.[20]

Crime represents the acting-out disorders of a people. The social, economic, and political philosophies of a society, determine its definitions of crime. Together with its attendant subspecialties, crime is the meeting place of all facets of culture, central in the observation and consideration of deviant behavior, both individually and collectively.

It is no accident that literature of the world has crime central to it more frequently than any other approach, except, perhaps, heterosexual adaptations. Voltaire (*Henriade* and *Oedeipe*, both of which were begun while Voltaire was in the Bastille), Dickens *(Oliver Twist),* Montesquieu *(The Spirit of the Laws),* Shakespeare *(Romeo and Juliet),* and others are well known for their works involving crime. Victor Hugo's *Les Miserables* depicts the conflict between cultural definitions of "good," "bad," and "crime," frequently depicting a conflict between the "good guys" and "bad guys," with the hero being an escaped convict. The average American has difficulty when he contemplates trying to identify the "good guy" and the "bad guy" between Robin Hood and the sheriff. The names of Jesse James, Pancho Villa, and Al Capone have become legendary.

Crime defines the areas where individual freedom is checked by the state for the welfare of society. The correctional process focuses on the elimination of deviations in society by remedial, conditioning, and learning approaches. Sometimes the balance between individual freedom and collective security is tenuous and the marginal people receive treatment because they are the better risks in correctional programs. The hard-core, nonmarginal people in these programs may be left untouched because they are too difficult to reach. Whether the point of diminishing returns is ever reached as these hard-core offenders are brought into correctional programs is dependent upon the orientation and judgment of the formulators and administrators of the programs. Certainly, external control has sometimes been applied beyond the point of diminishing returns in the field of corrections and has been found to be unproductive.

CONCLUSIONS

While the problem of deviation that damages others has always been present in society, it has been within the past 200 years that it has emerged as a social problem demanding heavier governmental intervention. Sharp rises in awareness of the need for correctional services appeared in the 1920's and 1960's. Today, services to the correctional client have been broadened to the extent that almost every phase of human services, public and private, is concerned with delinquency and crime. Certainly, the central place of work habits, occupational skills, and employability in this field places the services of Vocational Rehabilitation centrally in working with the public offender.

The average prisoner does not relate well with others and frequently projects blame on "the system." Associated with this are notoriously poor work habits and unskilled employment capabilities. As many sub-systems of society's agencies for social control and helping people focus on the problem of crime, employability and occupational skills become a central concern. Crime and unemployability are both indices of a general dysfunctional social adjustment. Counseling, academic and vocational education, and vocational rehabilitation are only a few of the endeavors designed to address this broader social problem of crime.

The crime rate will continue to go up because there is no other way for it to go. The already complex society is accelerating in its growth, technology, complexity, and need for even more effective controls. The greater the controls and the more complex and numerous society becomes, the greater will be the number of deviations. Consequently, the correctional process becomes a concern of all society. Because of the effectiveness potential of several "non-correctional" programs, such as Vocational Rehabilitation, their coordinated contribution to the total correctional effort will become more and more valuable as they become more and more involved in the pervasive concerns of social control to achieve a reasonably orderly society.

NOTES AND REFERENCES

1. Selznik Jerome: The sociology of law. In Robert K. Merton, Leonard Broome, and Leonard S. Cottrell, Jr. (Eds.): *Sociology Today*. New York, Basic Books, 1959, pp. 115-127.
2. *The Challenge of Crime in a Free Society*. The President's Commission on Law Enforcement and the Administration of Justice, Washington, D.C., 1967, p. 46.
3. *Ibid.*, p. 48.
4. *Task Force Report: Organized Crime*. The President's Commission on Law Enforcement and the Administration of Justice, Washington, D.C., 1967, p. 126.
5. *Crime in the United States Uniform Crime Report—1968*. Federal Bureau of Investigation, Washington, D.C., 1969, p. 115.
6. *Ibid.*, p. 5.

7. *Ibid.*, p. 105.
8. *Ibid.*, p. 115.
9. *The Challenge of Crime in a Free Society.* The President's Commission on Law Enforcement and the Administration of Justice, Washington, D.C., 1967, p. 22.
10. Jack Rosenthal: The cage of fear in cities beset by crime. *Life,* 67:16-23, July 11, 1969.
11. *Juvenile Court Statistics—1968.* United States Office of Juvenile Delinquency and Youth Development, Washington, D.C., 1970, p. 3.
12. *Statistics on Public Institutions for Delinquent Children—1967.* United States Children's Bureau Statistical Series No. 94, Washington, D.C., 1969, p. 13.
13. *1970 National Jails Census.* National Criminal Justice Information and Statistics, Washington, D.C., February, 1971, p. 19.
14. Hans W. Mattick and Alexander B. Aikman: The Cloacal Region of American Corrections. The Annals, *The Future of Corrections,* 381:109-118, January, 1969.
15. Herman R. Weiss and Robert Sampliner: A study of adolescent felony offenders. *Journal of Criminal Law and Criminology.* 34:337-391, March-April 1944.
16. *Special Labor Force Report,* No. 100, United States Department of Labor, Bureau of Labor Statistics, Washington, D.C., 1969.
17. Nigel Walker: *Sentencing in a Rational Society.* New York, Basic Books, 1971, p. 100.
18. Harry Elmer Barnes and Negley Tetters: *New Horizons in Criminology,* 3rd edition. New York, Prentice Hall, 1959, p. 50 quoted from Evelyn Ruggles' Brise: *The English Prison System,* London, Macmillan, 1910.
19. *Coppedge v. United States,* 369 U. S. 438, 449, 1961.
20. Robert F. Kennedy: Foreword. *University of Florida Law Review, 16:* 143-146, Fall 1963.

Chapter 2

Causes of Crime

RICHARD E. HARDY AND JOHN G. CULL

Rapid Social Change
Self-understanding and Adjustment
Prisons and Their Contribution to Crime
References

This is surely a time in American history when concern of most people has reached an all-time high over crime, violence, and law and order concepts. Over five million crimes were reported to the police in 1971. This number represented an increase of 11 percent over 1970. Persons in many areas, both rural and urban, are fearful of leaving their homes at night because of violence. It has been estimated that more than 31 billion dollars is the annual economic cost of crime.

Theoreticians and researchers have varied in their explanations of what causes crime. Some have discussed problems within the society and its constantly changing nature and increasing complexity. Others have written concerning chromosomes and genealogy as factors related to crime.

The bias of this chapter will be seen quickly. In the minds of the authors there seems to be a definite relationship between poverty and crime (especially those aspects concerning housing, educational opportunity and mental or physical health) and rapid social change and crime. It is not the purpose of this chapter to review and report on the various research projects concerning the causes of crime. The authors simply wish to present some of their opinions to the reader for the reader's evaluation. This chapter is concerned mainly with the psychosocial aspects of the "normal" offender, and not with abnormality.

RAPID SOCIAL CHANGE

Institutions such as the church, the family, governmental structures of service, the university and other educational systems, are changing so rapidly that many persons are losing their anchor points for emotional stability. People look around them and find little or no certainty in their jobs, in their family life, or in traditional and religious beliefs formerly held sacrosanct. All of us are deeply influenced by the effects of the mass media such as television. These media to us depict what the outside world seems to have. The outside world seems to have so much more than so many think they have.

Diminishing Value of Work for Work's Sake ("Making It" the Easy Way)

In the early days of the development of this country, the Protestant Ethic played a most important part in bringing about advancements in agriculture, technology and the social services. The amount of hard work which an individual did was a direct indication in many cases of his status in the community. Work for work's sake was highly respected. The Protestant Ethic is now much less an influencing factor on attitudes of persons toward work than it once was. In fact, by the year 2000 it may well be that family attitudes in teaching children such characteristics as dependability and diligence related to work may be drastically modified. Society is moving toward a much greater leisure time involvement. At the present time the effects of this accelerating movement away from the Protestant Ethic are being felt. This means that convincing persons that the way to success is through hard work of an honest nature is becoming even more difficult. Even vocational specialists such as vocational rehabilitation counselors in state and federal agencies are now talking about deemphasizing the vocational aspect of rehabilitation services which in itself indicates some drastic changes in the philosophy of many persons in the social service area on vocations and work.

With an increased amount of leisure time and a de-emphasis on full work days or full work weeks, there is more time for all types of activities, including unlawful activities. There seems to be a definite emphasis toward getting what we want the easy way. This emphasis is perpetuated and reinforced by many white collar workers who are able to "get around the law" by various methods. An example is the landlord who puts enough pressure on tenants to receive monthly payments for rent but does not maintain his buildings according to city ordinances. Persons often see different applications of the law applied according to socio-economic status of the individual accused. Sentences can vary enormously according to whether an individual brings an attorney with him to court, whether the offense is a traffic violation or a more serious one.

Some Characteristics of the Society Which Lead to Crime

We live in a violent society. One which idolizes prize fighters and war heroes. One in which the western robber of the movies is idolized until he is caught—a world in which heroes such as Ian Fleming's James Bond who is "licensed to kill" is respected because he is more violent and gruesome in his treatment of criminals than they are of him and their other victims. Our young military men are taught to kill. The emphasis on violence does not always end with the discretionary thought of the one who is taught to be violent, and this fact has been indicated also in the battles of Vietnam when innocent villagers have been killed as well as those who were obviously the enemy.

Americans have necessarily had a somewhat violent and, in addition, fighting spirit. This characteristic has been most important in conquering the wilderness of the west and forging a new nation. Our highly competitive physical effort is constantly depicted in television programs of the wild west. Even the bad man often does not seem so bad when he robs or takes what he needs. The so-called bad guy is even respected as long as he is getting away with his activities. The most thrilling scene of a technicolor western movie is often at the beginning of the movie when the train is robbed and the bandits are able to elude the sheriff and his posse.

Our city areas are particularly vulnerable to violence. A factor which always causes increased social interaction of all types, and crime in particular, is overcrowding. When persons are heavily concentrated in our cities in areas of ugliness, which include poor housing and general discomfort, violent and criminal behavior will occur. When people are concentrated in small areas there are more persons of every type. There are more mentally ill persons including psychotics. There are more physically unhealthy persons, including individuals who are uncomfortable due to injuries which have been ill attended or not attended. Many persons are taking drugs which compound already existing problems and create new ones. Stability is not enhanced by overcrowding. We can expect only a higher incidence of various types of behavior including criminal behavior in that overcrowding in the cities is worsening as our population becomes more urban.

SELF-UNDERSTANDING AND ADJUSTMENT

Importance of Peer Groups and Role Models

Pressures for conformity come from all sides. Persons in the ghetto feel pressure to conform to the ways of behaving of persons of the ghetto. These behavior pressures are particularly strong among the adolescent groups, and especially influential among adolescent boys. The emphasis seems to be on beating the "system" somehow and this attitude should not be considered an unhealthy emphasis. It represents the wish of most Americans—to somehow get established and find happiness within a social system which is now in constant turmoil and within a society which is in many ways unhealthy.

In order for the person from the ghetto to beat the system, he must either "fake out" some bureaucratic program such as the Department of Public Welfare and get on the public dole, or behave as two different persons. He must demonstrate one type of behavior which will secure his position within his own peer group and demonstrate another type of behavior which will allow him to secure employment in the outside world. His only other alternative is to leave his peer group and those things which he has felt important in order to enter another man's world. It is much easier for all of us to remain in a world which we have known and adjusted to than it is to modify behavior in order to become members of a different society. Think how difficult it would be for most of us to move into a culture different and distinct from our own. The same types of problems which are equal in complexity exist for persons who are from impoverished areas, either rural or urban, when they face finding employment and security in the world of work.

Another problem which often leads to crime is that of the lack of sufficient role models for individuals to follow. One of the earliest influences on all persons is that of parents, and much of the early child's play involvement is concerned with the work behavior of adults. When adults within the family are not able to work, children simulate the behavior which they exhibit and this behavior is often characterized by frustration and idleness.

Many individuals who find themselves in trouble need to understand their own motivations—reasons for behavior. The most prevalent reason, for instance, for dismissal from employment is that of inability to get along with fellow workers. Certainly a real cause of crime is inability to get along with persons within the family, on the street, within the community. This is often due to personal immaturity. When there is a basic lack of understanding of human nature—the weaknesses and strengths of all of us—there can be a real tendency to misunderstand the intentions of our neighbors. "Rap sessions" held in various community centers may be of substantial value to young persons, and older ones too, who wish to come into a group situation in order to discuss problems which they may be having. In addition, they will find support and interest in them as individuals which they may have never found before. Many persons in crime are involved in order to gain attention or recognition, having failed in other areas of life in the highly competitive society of today.

Idleness and hopelessness can be the handmaidens of crime. When persons attempt time and again to find acceptance within their families, but can find no work and no acceptance and must remain idle, crime often results. The hopelessness of many persons is profound, especially in ghetto areas where they must sit on porches or in apartments with inadequate facilities and are unable to join in meaningful activity. Many middle-class white collar workers have experienced what might be called "Sunday neuroticism"—those hours on weekends when they can find little that they may want to do. Many persons are unable to find meaningful activities for themselves outside of their employment. Many are just plainly bored. When employment opportunities are lacking, chances for crime or delinquent behavior are compounded. When employment is found, and is of a menial and meaningless nature to the individual in terms of what he is able to gain from it intellectually, emotionally, or materially, an inadequate adjustment pattern can be established. When the individual has a job which is not commensurate with his capabilities and interests, and the job does not provide what the person needs in terms of materialistic possessions, then the possibilities for crime are again increased. When skills are limited and the work hard, and the obvious fact is that most other people have more in terms of material possessions, then the thoughts of delinquent behavior again arise.

All of us are susceptible to our own innate aggression. Some of us are able to control it better than others through sublimation. A highly "developed" man is able to live and let live without unduly imposing his will or his hurt upon others. Many have not mastered this.

Many people will say that they are not interested in violence and that this innate aggression and tendency toward violence does not apply to them. Certainly it applies to all of us in various ways. Many like prize fighting, some enjoy bull fighting, many are able to vicariously satisfy their violent cravings through hard work, professionalism, or risky activities in sports, etc. Through the ego (willpower) we can suppress and in general control or handle our tendency toward violence, especially if we understand our own nature—tendencies to behave in various ways.

Where Crime Occurs

When we look at the areas of the cities in which crime is most prevalent, we find in those areas dilapidated and run-down housing facilities, poor plumbing, unsatisfactory health conditions, both mental and physical, a real lack of the esthetic aspects of life, poor streets, poor garbage collection, poor transportation in and out of the area, few offices of governmental state or federal service agencies, few pharmacies or drug stores, poor schools with some of the most ill prepared teachers. All these factors and others lead to poor attitudes, poor adjustments, poor mental and physical health and a feeling of inability to escape.

Questions are often raised in rehabilitation service groups concerning how we motivate people. We do not motivate them in our plush offices through counseling and esoteric information when they have to return to poverty or ghetto areas to live. In fact, they feel in an unreal world when they are in the office of the counselor and it is difficult for them to respect his judgment when they feel he is not fully aware of their world.

It should be remembered that crime is more prevalent in the areas just described, but also exists in all segments of the society and in all geographic areas. The auto mechanic who may steal parts for his automobile from his employer, the highly educated white collar worker who fraudulently files his income tax reports, the businessman who cheats on his expense accounts—all commit crime—and of course, we know that persons in every stratum are involved in drug dependency and abuse. It is important for us to be certain not to brand all persons who live in the ghetto as criminals or prospective criminals. Most people who live in poverty never commit a serious crime.

PRISONS AND THEIR CONTRIBUTION TO CRIME

The purpose of this chapter is not to outline methods of rehabilitation, but to indicate certain causes of crime. We cannot doubt that the prison is a training ground in crime. The prison system must be vastly revamped into a rehabilitative and vocationally oriented training program if we are to cut back the high recidivism rate that exists and the high continued crime rate which is prevalent among those who have "attended" prisons.

Karl Menninger has written a book entitled *The Crime of Punishment*.[2] One of the crimes of punishment is certainly the training which individuals get while in prison—training in being more effective criminals. Imagine yourself a young man who has stolen an automobile and who is imprisoned for several years as a result of maybe a second offense. Your initiation to prison life during your first night consists of your being forced into homosexual behavior by the stronger inmates. This continues far beyond an initiation period and may happen every night when the lights go off in the prison cells. You talk with persons who are third and fourth "timers" who can teach you a great deal about how to be more successful in stealing automobiles and other more expensive items. You get ideas beyond your dreams concerning what possibilities in crime are. There you may meet the leaders in the criminal underworld who will locate jobs for you in crime once you have completed prison training. Violence becomes a way of life. The taking from the weak by the strong is accepted. Those who can defraud others and get away with it are the most highly respected members of this community. The person who can "con" the psychologist or the counselor or the other inmates is also highly respected.

Ramsey Clark in his book *Crime in America*[1] has called prisons factories of crime, and certainly this is an apt description of what takes place within the prison system which is manned in some cases by prison guards with less training and education than the inmates. As long as poorly paid and trained guards and other personnel work in these institutions, we cannot expect for them to be less than training programs in crime. As long as there are large dormitory rooms where many live within prisons where guards do not remain at night there will continue to be mass violence. What has been indicated about prisons also can be said about local jails. Much must be done to improve situations in both.

Karl Menninger has indicated that the use of prisons in punishment only causes more crime. Punishment has actually increased the amount of criminal behavior which the public must bear. There must be massive rehabilitation programs to eliminate these conditions within prisons which are so segregated from the normal community in terms of the basic necessities of life. A very high percentage, approximately 70 percent of those persons who are in the federal prison system, never have a visitor while in prison.

It should be noted that a high percentage, approximately 25 percent, of the prisoners in some state penitentiary systems are mentally retarded. Certainly rehabilitation services, in particular vocational rehabilitation, to those who are physically and mentally impaired can be most helpful.

REFERENCES

1. Clark, Ramsey: *Crime in America.* New York, Simon & Schuster, 1970.
2. Menninger, Karl: *The Crime of Punishment.* New York, Viking Press, 1968.

Chapter 3

An Overview of Criminal Law and Criminal Procedure

Charles W. Hoehne

Diversity of Systems of Criminal Justice
Constitutional Guarantees
Basic Principles of Criminal Law
Basic Principles of Criminal Procedure
Observations and Suggestions
Notes and References

A detailed examination of the many details, complexities, and technicalities of criminal law and criminal procedure obviously is beyond the scope of this chapter; adequate treatment of these topics, if intended for a law student or for an attorney entering into the practice of law, easily would require as much space as has been allocated to the entire book in which this chapter appears. The purposes of this chapter are simply (1) to provide the rehabilitation counselor who will be serving a caseload made up of public offenders with a basic orientation to a topic which will be very much on the minds of his clients; (2) to review and expand upon certain concepts to which the rehabilitation counselor presumably has been previously exposed in civic or government courses; (3) to give the reader some "feel" for the official governmental processes through which certain individuals are judicially determined to be unfit for unfettered participation in the benefits of citizenship and are isolated from the larger body of society; and (4) to provide the rehabilitation counselor with a perspective from which insights which should prove of value to effective rehabilitation, hopefully, may be gleaned.

At the outset, caution needs to be expressed about certain pitfalls which the rehabilitation counselor would be well advised to avoid. First, by the very nature of the milieu in which he will be operating and by virtue of the types of cases he will be serving, the rehabilitation counselor will receive greater exposure to criminal law and criminal procedure than will most individuals who are not involved in these matters on a routine, professional, and regular basis. The rehabilitation counselor may well, in fact, expect to encounter "jailhouse lawyers," who, having studied the topic with great diligence and deep personal interest, may appear to be more knowledgeable of criminal law and criminal procedure than attorneys who are not routinely engaged in practice in this most complex area. The rehabilitation counselor, however, is not a counselor at law, and, for reasons which will become more plain later in this chapter, the rehabilitation counselor who desires to achieve maximum effectiveness in his work will want to avoid pretensions to expertise in this specialized area of law. Similarly, the rehabilitation counselor assigned a caseload of public offenders will be confronted with a most challenging assignment, albeit an assignment which involves unusual difficulties and which entails many frustrations. The perceptive rehabilitation counselor working such a caseload will soon note many structural inadequacies in the system of criminal justice. He will find himself surrounded by a system replete with anomalies, characterized by numerous instances of individual inequities, and admittedly ineffective and incapable of meeting the large expectations and responsibilities imposed upon it—in short, a system crying out for improvement and a situation demanding reform in the loudest possible manner. The rehabilitation counselor, however, will be doing well to assist individuals in achieving rehabilitation; the rehabilitation counselor is not likely to achieve any significant degree of success in rehabilitating the system of criminal justice. The latter responsibility, therefore, is best left to those who have primary accountability and more adequate resources for effecting needed improvements in the system of criminal justice; let the members of the bar, the jurists, the penologists and legislators more fully acquit themselves of their basic responsibilities. The rehabilitation counselor who gets too greatly involved in the rehabilitation of the criminal justice system will not, for a number of reasons, prove successful in acquitting himself of his own immediate responsibility to assist public offenders in achieving effective reentry into the mainstream of society.

On the other hand, if rehabilitation programs directed toward public offenders can be implemented and operated with a significant degree of success, this may well prove to be a compelling factor in bringing about long overdue reform of this country's system of criminal justice.

For purposes of providing the reader with a broad and general overview of criminal law and criminal procedure, the remainder of this chapter treats with five distinct, but closely related, aspects: (1) the diversity of systems of criminal justice; (2) the effect of constitutional guarantees; (3) elementary principles of criminal law; (4) basic principles of criminal procedure; and (5) practical observations on and suggestions about the effective extension of rehabilitation services within the framework of the criminal justice system.

DIVERSITY OF SYSTEMS OF CRIMINAL JUSTICE

In an exact sense, there is nothing which may properly be termed "*the* system of criminal justice within the United States." Rather, what actually exists is at least 51 separate criminal justice systems—the distinct system of each of the states, plus the federal system. The existence of distinct criminal justice systems within the states is obtained as a consequence of the manner in which the federal government came into being or, more particularly, by reason of the manner in which the Constitution was adopted and by reason of specific language contained therein.[1] The federal government has no police power in the strict sense.[2] The police power possessed by the several states before adoption of the Constitution was not by the Constitution delegated to the United States, and, hence, this power is reserved in the states and the people.[3]

Despite the constitutional reservation of "police power" to the states, the federal government has the authority to enact statutes which are penal in nature. However, to enact such statutes validly, the federal government must relate the subject matter of the statute to some power expressly delegated to the United States government by the federal Constitution; e.g. the power to regulate interstate commerce, to wage war, to tax, etc. Thus, the Constitution leaves the police power to the states, but if Congress in exercising a constitutionally granted power, such as the power to wage war, necessarily infringes upon state-reserved police power, and such infringement runs contrary to the law of the state, then, under the supremacy clause of Article 6, clause 2, of the Constitution,[4] the law of the state must give way.[5] As a practical matter, the courts have in recent decades placed a broad and liberal construction upon the extent of the various powers granted to the United States government by the Constitution, thereby greatly expanding the ability of Congress to enact legislation relating to criminal matters.

Not only is there diversity as between the states, and between the states and the federal government, but the situation may be additionally complicated by the enactment of local ordinances by local subdivisions of government within a state.[6]

In addition to formal diversity of the type described above, additional variances also arise because of the way federal laws are enforced in different parts of the nation, because of differences in enforcement within a state, and through the types of sentences which different courts are inclined to prescribe for various offenses. On the other hand, there are certain factors which contribute to a rough form of uniformity in criminal law. A majority of the states, for example, have a system of jurisprudence based upon the common law traditions brought to this country by the English colonists. Offenses recognized as such under the common law tradition of England are generally deemed offenses under the penal codes of a majority of the states. And, of course, in enacting penal statutes, states sometimes draw upon legislation previously enacted in another state. On a somewhat more positive and systematic level, the American Law Institute has for a number of years been involved with the development of a "model penal code" for consideration by the legislatures of the states.

Yet, throughout the country there are striking differences in the legislative and judicial treatment accorded different types of acts and situations. Apparent anomalies may indeed abound within the penal code of a particular state—a product in large part of the fact that laws are enacted during different legislative sessions and, not infrequently, in overreaction to specific cases which are fresh on the minds of indignant legislators.[7] Acts which are regarded as outrageously heinous in one state may be viewed as mildly antisocial in another state, well-publicized cases in point being sodomy or the use of marijuana. A state law prohibiting hitchhiking is likely to be ignored by police and prosecutors in a large metropolitan area, but zealously enforced by a small town constable, city attorney, and justice of the peace who have strong personal biases against young people who wear their hair long.[8] Within the federal judiciary itself, courts of comparable jurisdiction, confronted with cases involving identical sets of facts but sitting in different parts of the country, frequently reach conflicting results.

Not only is diversity occasioned by differences in statutes defining certain offenses, by differences in procedure, by differences in judicial predilection, or by variances in local biases, but diversity is further promoted by the different rules of law stated in prior—sometimes ancient—court decisions considered as binding upon courts confronted with the task of resolving the narrow issues of criminal cases immediately at hand. In 1843, for example, in the celebrated *M'Naghten's Case*,[9] an English jurist laid down the following test for legal insanity:

> ... whether at the time the act in question was committed, the ... [defendant] ... had or had not the use of his understanding, so as to know that he was doing a wrong or wicked act.

Despite the abundance of psychological and psychiatric knowledge which has since been accumulated, a majority of the states still follow the "M'Naghten Test" of ability to distinguish between right and wrong in determining legal insanity. In some of the more venturesome jurisdictions, a few courts have taken cognizance of knowledge acquired in the 129 years since the original pronouncement of the "M'Naghten Test," but a majority of the courts have felt that the change of this test is primarily the concern and responsibility of legislators—and a strong lobby for deranged criminals has not been too greatly in evidence in most states.[10]

In theory, it is possible for defendants to render themselves subject to prosecution under the penal statutes of a number of jurisdictions by committing what would appear on the surface to be one crime. Assume, for example, a fact situation in which two individuals decide, while in "State A," that they will go to "State B" to acquire a quantity of narcotics to be brought back for resale in "State A" and that these individuals are apprehended in "State B" after having made the acquisition and while enroute back to "State A." Conceivably, such individuals might be subject to prosecution for having violated the criminal conspiracy statute of "State A," additionally subject to prosecution for unlawful possession of narcotics under the laws of "State B," and still subject to federal prosecution for failure to pay taxes on the narcotics. Moreover, if they were apprehended while exceeding the posted speed limit in a city in "State B," they could also be made to answer on that charge, and if one of the defendants had brought along his unlicensed and unvaccinated dog, this could represent yet another offense. To carry the hypothetical fact situation even further, if the purchase was made in a dark alley and the dog was permitted to get out of the car and run around while the narcotics were being placed in the car's trunk, there could be still another charge based upon violation of the city's "pen and leash" ordinance. As a matter of practice, however, prosecution by each of the jurisdictions with claims to violated peace and dignity would be unusual; the customary procedure, as will be more fully discussed subsequently in this chapter, would be for the jurisdiction having custody of the alleged criminals to initiate prosecution based upon the more serious of the possible charges, thereby allowing room for "bargaining down" to guilty pleas on less serious charges.

CONSTITUTIONAL GUARANTEES

The more widely publicized developments in criminal justice are based upon court cases involving defendants who have successfully maintained that governmental prosecution has been conducted in a manner which violates different rights reserved to individuals under the Bill of Rights[11] or in a manner contraindicated by procedural requirements of the U. S. Constitution. These requirements and protections,[12] then, represent the basic limitation upon government in applying legal sanctions against those persons whose attitudes, conduct, or activities are generally regarded as undesirable.

In consequence of constitutional law, spectacles common in less stable countries are absent from the United States. Deposed politicians in the United States, for example, unlike persons who lose power in certain other nations, need not bear the hazard of being legislatively declared guilty of treason through a device such as a "bill of attainder."[13] Neither are citizens of the United States in risk of prosecution under "ex post facto" laws which would make a crime out of an act which has been previously committed or which enlarges the punishment for a crime after it is committed or which deems the act a more serious crime than it was when committed.[14]

Of the various constitutional protections afforded individuals, the most important requirement, and the one upon which other express guarantees and specific requirements frequently are pegged, is that of "due process of law." The due process requirement is expressed in the Fifth Amendment to the U. S. Constitution and again in the Fourteenth Amendment.[15] "Due process" entails two distinct concepts: (1) procedural due process and (2) substantive due process.

Simply stated, "procedural due process" means that official proceedings must be conducted according to minimum standards of fairness which are not repugnant to the standards of civilized men.[16] "Substantive due process," on the other hand, precludes unreasonable or arbitrary legislation which would deprive an individual of a basic, substantive personal liberty without procedural due process, including items of the following type which traditionally have been regarded as basic and inherent rights of free men: marriage; freedom of association; freedom in education;

religious freedom; freedom of contract; right to earn a living; right to be free from unreasonable interferences of one's person; and, generally, other related types of privileges which enjoyed protection under the common law tradition of England.[17]

The traditional view has been that the Bill of Rights operated mainly as a limitation on the federal government, with the due process clause of the Fourteenth Amendment making some of the other first ten amendments to the U. S. Constitution operate as limitations upon the states as well. In fairly recent years, however, the trend of federal court decisions was toward making more of the Bill of Rights guarantees function as limitations upon state action. Today, it is settled that all of the more vital protections of the Bill of Rights are, by reason of the due process clause of the Fourteenth Amendment, applicable to state action, with some jurists taking the position that due process makes each item in the Bill of Rights applicable to all state action.[18] There are, however, few absolute limitations upon the ability of government to restrain citizens in their personal liberties, and the decisions reflect a constant process of judicially balancing the rights of individuals against the common good of the larger body of society. Where such limitations upon individual liberties are exerted, the courts insist that the limitations be brought about through procedural due process, that there be adequate judicial safeguards, that the necessity of such limitation be made clear and that, in short, state action be, to use a term frequently encountered in the cases, "fundamentally fair."

Basic rights guaranteed by the Bill of Rights to all citizens and residents of nonbelligerent countries cannot be denied through the enactment of inconsistent statutes. Not all of the guarantees and protections of the Bill of Rights have been deemed so basic as not to be amenable to governmental limitation when the larger needs of society seem to be in potential jeopardy. The First Amendment guarantees[19] have been enforced with considerable enthusiasm by the courts, and statutes which would restrict religion, speech, the press, or peaceful assembly, therefore, have had a hard time in the courts. The rather ambiguously worded

Second Amendment[20] has not generally been construed as conferring absolute rights upon the people,[21] and it has been generally conceded that the states, although not necessarily Congress, have power to control firearms; it may safely be predicted that the question of the effect of the Second Amendment will be a fruitful source of increasing controversy for some time to come. The Third Amendment[22] has not been involved in many court cases, nor does this amendment relate to a subject of great concern to the criminal justice system. Fourth Amendment rights,[23] on the other hand, have been involved in many cases and continue to represent the basis for much litigation; the rehabilitation counselor serving a caseload made up of public offenders will, particularly if working within a correctional institution, undoubtedly be exposed to many inmates involved with appeals based upon allegedly improper searches or seizures or upon warrants hoped defective. While the Fourth Amendment is given a liberal construction,[24] felons confronted with long sentences can be prone to wishful thinking, which leads them to disregard the settled principle that this amendment prohibits only such searches or seizures as are unreasonable and is to be judicially construed in the light of what was deemed an unreasonable search and seizure when it was adopted and in a manner which will conserve public interests as well as the interests and rights of individual citizens.[25]

The guarantees of the Fifth Amendment[26] probably have been the source of more public confusion and controversy than have the provisions of the other amendments making up the Bill of Rights. The most controversial provision in this amendment relates to the prohibition against self-incrimination. The law with regard to self-incrimination, as with another major provision of this amendment (the guarantee against double jeopardy) may be regarded as rather well settled, and one is not likely to find many public offenders involved with appeals based upon alleged violations of these protections. It is more possible that one will run into appeals based upon technical flaws in procedures utilized with respect to the "indictment of a Grand Jury" provision of this amendment.[27] And, as previously noted, the "due process of law" requirement of this amendment is quite important, in that it is this provision which imposes the due process requirement upon the federal government.[28]

Compliance with the requirements of the Sixth Amendment[29] is basic to the validity of the code of criminal procedure adopted in any state. While there have been landmark cases in fairly recent times on the meaning of "Assistance of Counsel," prosecutors and trial courts generally are extremely careful not to run afoul of the requirements of this amendment; reversible error, where it does occur, usually can be charged off against inadvertence, inexperience, or ineptitude. The Seventh Amendment, of course, relates to civil trials and, therefore, is not pertinent to this chapter. The Eighth Amendment[30] rarely is the source of a successful post-conviction appeal; judicial proceedings challenging bail as being excessive occur prior to trial or prior to incarceration, and the prohibition against "cruel and unusual punishment" generally seems to have been interpreted with full reference to the historical context in which this amendment was adopted, so that government seems capable of inflicting practically any punishment short of torturing an offender to death in a public place and then having him drawn and quartered.[31] The Ninth Amendment[32] has only indirect bearing upon criminal law and criminal procedure, and the major effect of the Tenth Amendment upon the criminal justice system throughout the nation has been noted in previous discussion about the diversity of the system.[33]

The foregoing discussion of principles of constitutional law is not intended, obviously, to make the rehabilitation counselor competent to sit for that part of the Bar examination in which constitutional law might be covered. As previously noted, however, criminal law and criminal procedure are based directly upon constitutional principles, and the rehabilitation counselor who expects to enter into work with public offenders can expect to hear at least occasional, if not frequent, reference to principles of the type discussed in this immediate section.

BASIC PRINCIPLES OF CRIMINAL LAW

Specific acts amounting to crimes are increasingly defined in state penal codes, although states may have what are known as "common law crimes." Because of the prohibition on *ex post facto* laws, an act is not a criminal offense unless so denominated prior to the time the act was committed.[34] Some crimes require criminal intent,[35] while other acts represent offenses regardless of the individual's knowledge or ignorance of the law.[36] Generally, though, in order to be lawfully convicted of a crime, an individual must have had the legal capacity to commit an offense; hence, compulsion, insanity, infancy, and, in some instances, even intoxication may be good defenses to charges brought against a defendant,[37] and for certain situations in which criminal intent represents a material element of an offense, it may be a good defense if the accused can establish that he was acting in good faith, though in mistake of fact or mistake of law.

Discussion of principles of criminal law must include discussion of the roles which may be assumed by parties to a crime. The term "principals" includes all who are guilty of acting together in the commission of an offense. A "principal to a crime" may be assisted by an "accomplice;" i.e., one who is not present at the commission of an offense but who, before the act is done, advises, commands, or encourages another to commit the offense. Or assistance may come from an "accessory;" i.e., one who, knowing that an offense has been committed, conceals the offender or gives him other aid in order that he may evade arrest or trial or the execution of his sentence.[38]

Crimes may either be *malum prohibitum,* meaning crimes which may be committed without criminal intent and wherein it is not necessary that criminal intent be proved in order to obtain a conviction,[39] or *malum in se,* meaning crimes in which intent is a material element of the offense, so that the prosecution must prove up all of the elements of the offense, plus specific criminal intent on the part of the accused.

Intentional crimes are proved up through direct evidence, through circumstantial evidence, or by proving that the means used would result in the commission of the crime. There are a number of possible defenses to intent crimes, in addition to the defenses of compulsion, insanity, and infancy which have already been mentioned. In some states, a wife can plead "coverture" (marriage) to mitigate her punishment for helping her husband commit a crime. It may be a complete defense to prove that the act was an "accident," because the fact of accident precludes the possibility of intent. An excuse or alibi, such as proof that the accused was not at the scene of a crime, may be offered in defense to a charge. "Entrapment" may be offered as a defense, the usual test being whether the criminal intent was formulated in the mind of the accused or in the mind of the police officer who "entrapped" (if the latter, this is a complete defense).

There are crimes against the person, including such offenses as murder, voluntary manslaughter, involuntary manslaughter, assault, battery, and rape. The crime may relate to personal property, in which case the offense usually carries a formal label of "theft," "swindling," "larceny," or "receiving stolen property."[40] The criminal act may have been directed at a dwelling, in which case the offense usually will be termed "burglary" or "arson."

Although a specific act may have fallen short of amounting to homicide, assault, theft, arson, or some other offense requiring that criminal conduct be completed, a crime may, nevertheless, have been committed. "Conspiracy"[41] can be a criminal offense. It may be a criminal offense to attempt to commit a certain act, as an escape from an officer holding one in legal custody, lynching, perjury, rape, abortion, burglary, bribery, arson, or theft.[42] Also falling into this category of offense are state and federal statutes prohibiting "solicitation" to commit specific criminal acts or to teach or advocate certain unpopular doctrines; such statutes, however, being limitations upon free speech, are confronted with special problems by reason of the First and Fourteenth Amendments to the U. S. Constitution.

A separate category of crimes may be defined as those acts which represent "offenses against morals." Included in this category would be such offenses as adultery, bigamy, fornication, incest, sodomy, seduction, drunkenness, or vagrancy. Of the public offenders most likely to be encountered by a rehabilitation counselor, those whose crimes most likely would fall under this category would be persons convicted of violations of narcotics statutes.[43]

While the courts are inclined to give a broad and liberal interpretation to the constitutional guarantees provided to accused individuals under the Bill of Rights, the practice is to interpret penal code provisions narrowly and technically. Similarly, a strict construction also is placed upon the procedures through which alleged offenders are prosecuted.

BASIC PRINCIPLES OF CRIMINAL PROCEDURE

The fundamental rights accorded by constitutional law in cases involving criminal prosecutions already have been discussed. It also has been observed that the criminal procedure of the states and of the federal government must conform to constitutional requirements. At this point, then, it becomes appropriate to examine the nature of the process by which an individual accused of a specific crime is prosecuted for his alleged offense. Specific details of this process may vary from state to state, and there will also be some minor differences in procedure in federal courts and state courts; but, because of constitutional requirements the main and essential features of this process are similar in most courts. The discussion in this section is based upon the process as it operates under the Texas Code of Criminal Procedure, the Texas system being fairly representative of the approach of most states with a system of jurisprudence rooted in common law traditions.

Venue[44] is typically established when the site of the alleged offense is ascertained. *Jurisdiction*[45] is determined by the nature of the offense. Venue may be changed from the county in which the offense allegedly was committed if a fair and impartial trial is not possible in that county. If the offense occurred in another state, there may not be an extraterritorial assertion of venue by a state in which the criminal act was performed, even though the state may have custody of the accused, unless some element of the offense, such as the planning function in a conspiracy case, occurred in the state having custody of the accused.

In most serious cases, arrests are made by warrant, unless the accused is caught while committing the offense or immediately thereafter. Prior to the arrest, a complaint normally will be filed with a magistrate of an inferior court (in Texas, a justice of the peace), who issues an arrest warrant. If a police officer is present when an offense is committed, no arrest warrant is necessary. Neither is a warrant required if a statutory provision specifically gives a police officer the right to make an arrest or if arrest is necessary to prevent escape of a felon or if arrest is necessary to prevent certain crimes from being committed. The arrest may be, and in more serious cases frequently is, preceded by an indictment by the grand jury.

Immediately upon arrest, the accused must be given certain required warnings by the arresting officer.[46] Regardless of whether the arrest is with or without issuance of a warrant, the accused must be taken before a magistrate without unnecessary delay. The magistrate is at this time required to advise the accused of certain basic rights.[47] Unless an indictment has been returned by the grand jury, the accused in a felony case is entitled to an examining trial. The objective of the examining trial is to permit the magistrate to examine the truth of the accusation made and, if there is probable cause for believing that the accused committed the offense, to bind him over to the grand jury for further proceedings.

Three alternative courses of action are possible following the examining trial. First, the defendant may be set free.[48] Secondly, if there is probable cause for believing the defendant guilty but if the defendant is not eligible for bail,[49] a commitment order may be issued, sending the accused to jail in the proper county until trial is held. The third alternative is for the defendant to be released on bail. This may consist of any of three different types of appearance bonds: a "personal bond," which, in effect, is no more than a written promise to appear; a "cash bond"; or a "surety bond," which is, in effect, a written contract through which the defendant and the bondsman guarantee to pay a specific amount of money to the court if the accused does not appear to answer the charges against him.

In misdemeanor cases, it is not necessary that the grand jury return an indictment; the misdemeanor case is initiated with the filing of a sworn complaint and "information" with a magistrate. As a result of constitutional requirements, though, felony cases may not be prosecuted until an indictment has been returned by the grand jury. The "information" in a misdemeanor case or the indictment in a felony case represent the pleadings of the state, and once these are complete, the burden of pleading passes to the defendant.

Various pleadings are available to the defendant, including pleadings which amount to an attack on the validity of the indictment or "information" used to initiate the case. To the charges made against him, the defendant may enter one of three pleas: (1) plea of guilty; (2) plea of not guilty; or (3) plea of *nolo contendere*.[50] Under Texas practice, the defendant may, prior to trial, file an application to have the jury determine if he is to be granted probation,[51] and the defendant also may elect to have the jury assess his punishment in the event that he is found guilty by making written request for this at the time he enters his plea to the charges against him.

Once the initial pleadings are completed, additional motions are possible. Either the state or the defendant may move for continuance.[52] Subpoenas may be issued to obtain testimony, and related writs may be used to secure other evidence. Motions may be made to suppress certain evidence. If codefendants are involved and if there is ground for showing that a joint trial would be prejudicial to one of the defendants, a motion for severance[53] may be filed.

After the various possible motions are made and acted upon by the court or waived by the state or the defendant, a jury is selected and the case put to trial. The constitutional requirements of a "fair trial" then come into play.[54] Following the evidence and arguments, instructions are issued by the judge to the jury. The jury then retires to consider the evidence and to arrive at a verdict. If the jury is unable to reach a unanimous decision, the jury is declared "hung," and the case is carried over for a new trial before a different jury—or dismissed if the state feels at this point that the possibility of obtaining a guilty verdict before another jury is remote. The case also may be disposed of by the defendant deciding not to risk another trial before a different jury, but instead to enter a guilty plea—usually to a lesser offense or in return for a recommendation by the prosecution to a sentence less than the defendant feels might be imposed following another trial.

Following a verdict of guilty or a plea of guilty, sentence normally is pronounced. However, if the defendant is granted probation, sentence is not pronounced. Similarly, if in Texas in a case where the death penalty was received, sentence is not pronounced until the appellate court for criminal matters has had an opportunity to review the matter and issue its mandate. At this point, proceedings are possible to prevent sentence; such proceedings to prevent sentence may be based upon a pardon, upon allegations of insanity, upon defendant's statement that he has good grounds for filing a motion for new trial or a motion in arrest of judgment, or upon a showing that the defendant escaped subsequent to conviction, which showing is accompanied by a denial by the person upon whom sentence is to be pronounced that he is the same person as the escaped defendant.

If the defendant has been convicted of more than one crime, the judge has discretion to determine if the sentences are to run "concurrently" or "cumulatively." If the sentences are concurrent, the time actually served by the defendant on either sentence applies to both sentences simultaneously. An "indeterminate sentence" may be pronounced in a situation where the jury has set the punishment at a term of years beyond the minimum prescribed in the statute under which the defendant was convicted; the practical effect of an indeterminate sentence is that the defendant must serve at least the minimum amount of time specified in the statute under which convicted, but not more time than that set by the jury. Under Texas procedure, the trial judge has discretion to allow the convicted defendant to serve the time on nights and consecutive weekends.[55]

During trial, counsel for the defendant typically will have been diligent in getting matters into the record of the proceeding which might constitute reversible error on appeal. After sentence, notice of appeal is routinely given by the defendant. If the defendant has not received a sentence of more than 15 years, he is entitled to bail while his appeal is being taken. If the appeal is taken, a record must be developed for review by the appellate court.[56] The record must be supplemented by a "brief"—a written explanation of why the defendant believes that the trial court was in error and an examination of the law applicable to the case. The brief argues questions of law only; the questions of fact, if the evidence reflected in the record is such that reasonable minds could have come to different conclusions on the questions of fact, are deemed to have been finally resolved in the trial court. If the defendant is unable to pay for the court reporter's transcription of the proceedings necessary for perfection of the appeal, the transcription must be provided to him without cost.[57] After all of this is completed, additional hearings are held in the trial court, and the trial court decides if the defendant is to be granted a new trial. When the trial court does not grant a new hearing, the record and briefs are transmitted to the appellate court.

The entire appellate process is regulated by a rather rigid timetable.

The record and briefs are then considered by the appellate court. Supplemental briefs may be filed by the state or by the defendant. A hearing is scheduled in the appellate court, and oral arguments are made on the legal issues raised in the briefs filed by the parties. After an opinion is handed down by the appellate court, motions for rehearing may be made and additional oral arguments offered in support of the motion for rehearing. If prosecution has been in the state courts and if the conviction in trial court has been upheld in the state's appellate court, the defendant may than appeal to the federal courts if his case involves questions under the U. S. Constitution. Different types of writs, new motions, and different briefs are required during the appeal into the federal court system, but, broadly and generally speaking, the appellate process in the federal court system has many similarities to the appellate process within a state.

If, at some point in the appellate process, the defendant is successful in getting a reversal of his conviction, his difficulties are by no means terminated; the usual remedy upon reversal is for a new trial to be ordered—and in the new trial it is possible that the defendant will again be convicted and possibly given a sentence greater than that assessed in the original trial.[58] Unless released on bail during the appeal process, the defendant in most states remains in a local jail while the appeal process—which may take years—is conducted. The local jail usually has few facilities, no rehabilitation services, and limited recreational possibilities; a general physical and mental deterioration of the incarcerated defendant is not uncommon during this time. Upon final conviction by the state courts, the defendant usually will be transmitted to the state penitentiary, from where the federal appeals may be conducted. In the event of reversal and conviction at a subsequent trial, the time spent in the county jail may be credited to the second sentence, but "extra credit" for good behavior is not, at least in Texas, allowed for time served in local custody.[59]

Parole laws differ among the states, but there appears to be increased innovation in this area. The Texas parole laws allow an individual to be regarded as eligible after one-third of his sentence or 15 years, whichever is less, have been served. Thus, an individual given a life sentence is eligible for parole after credit is earned for 15 years of time—a process which may require considerably less than a full 15 years of confinement.

The process from arrest to final conviction or acquittal, then, can be extended, emotionally exhausting, physically demanding, and financially ruinous—particularly if the defendant allows himself to be put to full trial and if appeals are taken. An individual who has been through this process has had his lumps indeed.

OBSERVATIONS AND SUGGESTIONS

To this point, focus has been placed upon the formal structure and legalistic bases of the criminal justice system. The presumption has been that the rehabilitation counselor assigned to a program of correctional rehabilitation will find it useful to have been provided with an overview of the constitutional foundation of the system, its statutory framework, and the procedures by which the system is supposed to function mechanically. For purposes of a broad but accurate overview, however, it also is necessary that the rehabilitation counselor have some insight into how the system is perceived by those upon whom the system most greatly impinges—the public offenders who will make up the rehabilitation caseload.

The principles of constitutional law, criminal law, and criminal procedure discussed in this chapter essentially represent a manifestation of theories being accepted at different times and points by persons in positions where decisions could be made; that which has been discussed here represents noble theories and fine concepts which commended themselves to those persons who write constitutions, to jurists, and to legislators. In any undertaking, however, there can be a wide discrepancy between the high principle implicit in a noble theory or a fine concept and the manner in which the lofty ideals are actually administered. This discrepancy can and does exist within the criminal justice system, and the rehabilitation counselor who is to serve a public offender caseload successfully needs to be aware of the discrepancy.

On paper, the system appears well balanced and frequently is made to appear to favor defendants too greatly.[60] To those who have been subjected to the system as defendants, however, as well as to many attorneys who have worked within the system either for the defense or for the prosecution, the process seems unduly oppressive. It is most appropriate that the typical criminal case be styled something like "The State vs. Jones," for that is an accurate description of the situation: the vast resources of government are pitted against the limited resources of an individual in any criminal case. The district attorney who is determined to obtain a conviction may be able to spend tens of thousands of dollars on the investigation, preparation, and prosecution of a defendant who, because of poverty, is represented by a court-appointed attorney who has little or no interest in the practice of criminal law.[61]

Similarly, in many cases the prosecution will have no significant evidence with which to support an indictment other than the testimony of police officers; such testimony, nevertheless, is sufficient to assure conviction in most cases. A large responsibility and enormous power, therefore, are vested in the police, but there are few practical restraints or checks upon that power. In fairness, one can stipulate that the public gets more than it pays for from its police—but it must be remembered that not very much is paid. The fact of the matter is that the police within a governmental subdivision can probably bring about the conviction of anyone police officials might want convicted—particularly if the individual is without position or if he is not affluent or if his previous record is not good or if he is not well educated or if he is a member of an ethnic minority and even more particularly if, as is the case with the average person sent to a correctional institution, he has a number of these characteristics. A police officer who is convinced of the guilt of a suspect under surveillance but who is unable to make out a case in accordance with the formal requirements of official procedures can plant evidence in the suspect's car or home or on his person—and it would be naive to suggest that this has never been done. With the highest of motives, the best of intentions, and the clearest of consciences, a rookie policeman who has gone out on a limb by initiating charges against an individual generally regarded as shady by veterans on the force can take the witness stand in court and, with impunity, shade and color his testimony—or refuse frankly to admit "I can't remember"—so as to skirt, if not surpass, the requirements for perjury; this probably happens several times a day in the courts of any large state.[62]

Under the system of law in the United States, defendants are supposed to be entitled to a presumption of innocence and judges are supposed to be impartial, but there are situations in which this is a myth.

It is entirely possible, in fact virtually inevitable, that the rehabilitation counselor who works with public offenders will have clients who are entirely innocent of the charges for which they are serving time or for which they have received probation. On the other hand, it is most unlikely that the rehabilitation counselor will ever assist a public offender who, from the standpoint of criminal law, is entirely without sin. A typical situation which the rehabilitation counselor may encounter is one in which the client is not guilty of the specific offense with which charged, but entirely guilty of some other offense—quite possibly a more serious offense. A majority of the criminal cases brought in this country are disposed of prior to trial, either through dismissal or through negotiated pleas. In negotiating a plea, it is common—especially where first offenders are concerned or where there are extenuating circumstances or where the prosecution and the defense are not confident about the probable outcome of a trial—for the prosecutor to agree to a guilty plea on a lesser charge or at least to go along with a recommendation for a minimum penalty.[63] Should every criminal case go to trial, the entire court system of the country would be bogged down with a hopeless backlog of cases overnight.

Prescribed procedures may be twisted and bent to obtain convictions, but, after all, it has not been suggested that the police have yet reached the point where citizens are capriciously singled out for conviction at random.

A majority of the inmates of correctional institutions probably do not belong in such institutions, but until new programs and approaches are developed, this will not be corrected.[64]

The basic requirement for effective rehabilitation of public offenders may well be the same as that for effectively rehabilitating other clients—adjusting attitudes. People end up in correctional institutions for various reasons: sudden crimes of passion; inability to cope successfully with the demands of living; unwillingness to conform to the requirements of a socioeconomic system which seems weighted in favor of others; disdain for structures which seem absurd and irrelevant. Unless crushed by enormous feelings of guilt, the public offender who has committed an isolated act of violence probably will represent a good prospect for successful rehabilitation. Other types of clients will require more skill and greater effort on the part of the rehabilitation counselor. Attorneys in general practice can predict with reasonable accuracy which clients from their unsuccessful cases will, upon release, return to society successfully and which clients will be returning to the courts to face new criminal charges. The clients who manage a successful and sustained reentry into society will be those who perceive the established socioeconomic system as something offering them potential personal benefits—and who have the marketable vocational skills which will lead them to the realization of those benefits. The clients who are headed for additional trouble, on the other hand, are those who cannot or will not allow themselves to be brought within the existing system. Unquestionably, there is much that the rehabilitation counselor can do with a caseload of this type, but there are limits which have nothing to do with the quality or intensity of the rehabilitation counselor's personal effort.[65] In attempting to modify the attitude of a client, it may be helpful if the counselor has some way of determining, at least in a rough manner, the reasonableness of an individual's resentment of the treatment accorded him under the criminal justice system; some legal advice may from time to time prove helpful and indeed essential if the rehabilitation counselor is to have an idea what his client is talking about. It is not, however, recommended that the rehabilitation counselor undertake the study of law; to perform his job effectively, the counselor will have more than enough to do staying abreast of current rehabilitation literature. A more efficient and expedient way to obtain legal information might be to develop and maintain social relationships with a few attorneys through churches, civic groups, or related mechanisms. Then, confronted in a counseling situation with a client's apparent bitterness about and hostility to the criminal justice system, the counselor will more readily be able to avoid the pitfalls of *not* being able to say, "Well, since neither of us is a lawyer, why don't we leave those things to people who are and get on with the things that we *can* do something about . . ."

NOTES AND REFERENCES

1. "The powers not delegated to the United States by the Constitution, nor prohibited by it to the States, are reserved to the States respectively, or to the people." Tenth Amendment to U. S. Constitution.

2. *American Federation of Labor v. Watson*, D.C. Fla. 1945, 60 F. Supp. 1010, reversed on other grounds 66 S.Ct. 761, 327 U.S. 582, 90 L.Ed. 873.
3. *Ibid.*
4. "This Constitution, and the Laws of the United States which shall be made in Pursuance thereof; and all Treaties made, or which shall be made, under the Authority of the United States, shall be the supreme Law of the Land; and the Judges in every State shall be bound thereby, any Thing in the Constitution or Laws of any State to the Contrary notwithstanding."
5. *U.S. v. Robinson*, D.C.N.D. 1952, 106 F. Supp. 212.
6. A city or county, of course, is a part of the government of the state in which such subdivision is located, with the power of the subdivision to enact local ordinances, therefore, a matter determined by the constitution or statutes of the state. Just as state law must give way when inconsistent with a properly enacted federal statute, local ordinances may not be inconsistent with existing state statutes. Nevertheless, local communities typically will be given express authority to regulate certain activities within the borders of the local subdivision, e.g. power to regulate traffic, and cities or counties generally have considerable latitude to enact other related ordinances which, while not generally relating to major offenses, have immediate and daily impact upon the lives of citizens.
7. In Texas, for example, the minimum penalty for certain types of homocide is less than the minimum penalty for the theft of certain types of farm products.
8. The matter of discriminatory law enforcement, with different minority populations or unpopular groups being singled out by law enforcement officials, is a manifestation of deeper social problems, the discussion of which is beyond the scope of this chapter. The rehabilitation counselor serving a caseload drawn from a population of public offenders, however, will not be long in noting that the representation of the poor, the uneducated, minority groups, members of unpopular organizations, or individuals with unorthodox life styles is, within correctional institutions, disproportionate to the representation of such minorities within the general population.
9. 10 Clark & Finley 200, 1 C. & K. 130. The opinion by Lord Chief Justice Tindal involved a defendant who had been indicted for having murdered the secretary to Sir Robert Peel while allegedly trying to kill Peel himself. Apparently, the "M'Naghten Test" came into disrepute in some circles rather rapidly, it having been reported that Queen Victoria objected to the defendant being adjudged insane because she "did not believe that anyone could be insane who wanted to murder a Conservative Prime Minister."

An Overview of Criminal Law and Criminal Procedure

10. Notable departures from the "M'Naghten Test" have resulted in the substitution of the "right-wrong test" (or, as it is sometimes known, the "wild beast test") for inquiries based upon "irresistible impulse" or upon whether the unlawful act "was the product of mental disease or mental defect." The leading case in which a court rejects the "M'Naghten Test" probably is *Durham v. United States*, U. S. Court of Appeals, D.C., 1954, 214 F. 2d 862, 94 U. S. App. D.C. 228, 45 A.L.R. 2d 1430.
11. The first ten amendments to the U. S. Constitution.
12. The constitutional guarantees and requirements, it should be noted, are not found only in the U. S. Constitution; state constitutions typically contain analogous provisions, although state courts generally seem more restrained in their interpretation and application of such state constitutional provisions than is true of the federal courts in their interpretation of the protections afforded individuals under the provisions of the U. S. Constitution.
13. Defined as a legislative act which pronounces a particular person guilty of a crime without benefit of trial or conviction. Hoehne & Rackley, *Synopsis of Texas Legal Rules, Principles and Doctrines*, 7th rev. ed., p. 353.
14. *Ibid.*
15. "No person shall be held to answer for a capital, or otherwise infamous crime, unless on a presentment or indictment of a Grand Jury, except in cases arising in the land or naval forces, or in the Militia, when in actual service in time of War or public danger; nor shall any person be subject for the same offence to be twice put in jeopardy of life or limb; nor shall be compelled in any criminal case to be a witness against himself, nor be deprived of life, liberty, or property, *without due process of law;* nor shall private property be taken for public use, without just compensation." Fifth Amendment to U. S. Constitution.
". . . No State shall make or enforce any law which shall abridge the privileges or immunities of citizens of the United States; nor shall any State deprive any person of life, liberty, or property, *without due process of law* . . ." Section 1, Fourteenth Amendment to U. S. Constitution.
16. Hoehne & Rackley, *Synopsis of Texas Legal Rules, Principles and Doctrines*, 7th rev. ed., p. 354.
17. *Ibid.*
18. Technically, it is the due process requirement of the Fourteenth Amendment that makes the Bill of Rights applicable to state action, while the due process clause of the Fifth Amendment accomplishes this with respect to federal action. For more detailed discussion, refer to Hoehne & Rackley, *Fundamental Concepts of American Jurisprudence*, pp. 343-351.

19. "Congress shall make no law respecting an establishment of religion, or prohibiting the free exercise thereof; or abridging the freedom of speech, or of the press; or the right of the people peaceably to assemble, and to petition the Government for a redress of grievances." First Amendment to U. S. Constitution.
20. "A well regulated Militia, being necessary to the security of a free State, the right of the people to keep and bear Arms, shall not be infringed." Second Amendment to U. S. Constitution.
21. See, for example, *U. S. v. Cruikshank*, 92 U. S. 553, 2 Otto 553, 23 L.Ed. 588.
22. "No Soldier shall, in time of peace be quartered in any house, without the consent of the Owner, nor in time of war, but in a manner to be prescribed by law." Third Amendment to U. S. Constitution.
23. "The right of the people to be secure in their persons, houses, papers, and effects, against unreasonable searches and seizures, shall not be violated, and no Warrants shall issue, but upon probable cause, supported by Oath or affirmation, and particularly describing the place to be searched, and the persons or things to be seized." Fourth Amendment to U. S. Constitution.
24. *Grau v. U. S.*, 53 S.Ct. 38, 287 U. S. 124, 77 L.Ed. 212.
25. A principle stated in *Carrol v. U. S.*, 45 S.Ct. 280, 267 U. S. 132, 69 L.Ed. 543 and subsequently reaffirmed in a number of cases. The principle, however, has been somewhat difficult to apply to wiretapping and other types of intrusion made possible by new technology. While the courts appear to have gone rather far with this amendment in recent years, many observers anticipate some retrenchment from the recent predilection of the courts to protect individual rights scrupulously.
26. Footnote 15, supra.
27. Particularly if the individual is represented by counsel who has had occasion to learn of an apparent indiscretion in grand jury proceedings. The use of grand juries, of course, represents a practice of questionable merit at this time, but that is another topic and quite beyond the scope of this chapter.
28. Footnote 18, supra.
29. "In all criminal prosecutions, the accused shall enjoy the right to a speedy and public trial, by an impartial jury of the State and district wherein the crime shall have been committed, which district shall have been previously ascertained by law, and to be informed of the nature and cause of the accusation; to be confronted with the witnesses against him; to have compulsory process for obtaining Witnesses in his favor, and to have the Assistance of Counsel for his defense." Sixth Amendment to U. S. Constitution.

An Overview of Criminal Law and Criminal Procedure 57

30. "Excessive bail shall not be required, nor excessive fines imposed, nor cruel and unusual punishments inflicted." Eighth Amendment to U. S. Constitution.
31. The courts say that the fixing of penalties for crime is a legislative function, and the courts will not interfere unless a penalty is clearly and manifestly cruel and unusual. Thus, the courts have refused to interfere in cases where prisoners have been confined in rather outrageous quarters, the infliction of the death penalty through various means has been upheld, deportation of aliens has been allowed, and the imposition of additional penalties in cases involving offenders with prior criminal convictions has been determined not to violate the Eighth Amendment. In a case involving a New Mexico territorial statute providing for 30 to 60 lashes on the bare back of one who stole a farm animal, plus confinement until costs of prosecution were paid by the offender, the court did not feel that this constituted cruel and unusual punishment. There has been some speculation that the U. S. Supreme Court might eventually categorize the death penalty as "cruel and unusual punishment" proscribed by this amendment, but most legal observers do not feel that this will happen any time in the near future.
32. "The enumeration in the Constitution, of certain rights, shall not be construed to deny or disparage others retained by the people." Ninth Amendment to U. S. Constitution.
33. Footnote 1, supra.
34. A principle implicit in the oft-quoted statement of a famous American capitalist who once boasted, "I never did break any laws in any of my operations—but I did cause quite a few laws to be written."
35. Knowledge by an individual that his act was wrongful or, to use the legal term, *"mens rea."*
36. For example, illegal sales of intoxicating liquor, criminal nuisances, volations of traffic law or motor vehicle regulations, violation of certain narcotics acts, etc.
37. For obvious reasons, a plea of intoxication is not always the best trial strategy, even though intoxication may be material to issues of ability to commit the alleged act or to mitigation of the seriousness of an act, as in homocide cases where intoxication might be proved up to establish the improbability of premeditation on the part of a defendant. Intoxication, of course, may have direct bearing upon a claim of mental disease and might enter into a case in that manner. Certain common crimes, e.g. driving while intoxicated or drunkenness in a public place, require intoxication as an essential element of the offense.
38. A simple way to distinguish between parties to a crime is as follows: "accomplices" help *before* the crime is committed (and usually receive the same punishment as the principal); an "accessory" helps *after* the crime has been committed; and a "principal" helps *during* the crime.

Hoehne & Rackley, *Synopsis of Texas Legal Rules, Principles & Doctrines*, 6th rev. ed., p. 219.

39. The kinds of acts described in Footnote 36, supra.
40. Such crimes being broken down into narrower offenses in many penal codes so as to cover a variety of possible situations, as under the Texas Penal Code, which distinguishes between "petty theft" and "felony theft," and which sets up as separate offenses "theft from the person," "theft by bailee," "theft by false pretext," etc.
41. This may consist of a number of things, such as two or more persons consulting and agreeing falsely to charge another with a crime; or agreeing to commit some specific offense punishable by law; or to do some act for the purpose of thwarting the processes of justice; or to effect some legal purpose with a corrupt intent or by improper means. The crime of conspiracy is one of the more difficult criminal offenses to prosecute successfully.
42. The "attempt" crimes require four specific elements: (1) intent to commit the act; (2) an overt act; (3) conduct beyond mere preparation; and (4) failure to complete the act. Hoehne & Rackley, *Fundamental Concepts of American Jurisprudence*, pp. 196-197.
43. There is increasing criticism of the practice of categorizing as "crimes" certain acts which, while offensive to socially acceptable moral standards, are essentially victimless because of the act occurring between consenting parties or because of only the accused being involved in the act. The rehabilitation counselor may find himself personally sympathetic to such criticism, but care must be exercised not to let his personal attitude influence the effectiveness of his work; for example, the rehabilitation counselor who spends time commiserating with the young man who has been convicted of possession of marijuana runs the risk of having the individual back on his caseload again.
44. Meaning the place in which the case is to be heard, this normally being the county in which the crime allegedly took place.
45. Meaning the court empowered to try the case. In Texas, felonies (crimes punishable by confinement in the penitentiary or by death) are tried in the state's court of general jurisdiction, the district court; misdemeanor offenses punishable by a term in the county jail are tried in county court; and offenses punishable by fine only are tried in justice of peace courts or in the corporation courts of a municipality.
46. The practice is for the accused to be advised of his rights following arrest. If an arresting officer did not personally advise the accused of his rights and if the accused was immediately taken before a magistrate without saying anything prejudicial to his case, a subsequent conviction presumably would be constitutionally permissible. The normal police practice, however, is to carry an apprehended person to jail for booking, with a magistrate then coming down to an office near the jail some-

An Overview of Criminal Law and Criminal Procedure 59

time during regular working hours. All newly arrested persons are then brought individually before the magistrate. (The most publicized case regarding these preliminary warnings probably is *Miranda v. Arizona,* 384 U. S. 436, 86 S.Ct. 1602, 16 L.Ed. 2d 694.)

47. The magistrate advises the accused of the charges against him; advises him of his right to counsel; and informs him of his right to remain silent, to have an attorney with him during interrogation, to terminate an interrogation at any time, to have an attorney appointed by the court if the accused is indigent, to have an examining trial (if no indictment has been returned and the case is of felony grade), and to refuse to make any self-incriminating statements.
48. In practice, an extremely rare occurrence.
49. Because of constitutional requirements, bail may be denied only in a limited number of situations. These include capital offenses where there is evident proof that a jury probably would assess the death penalty and cases where the accused may be convicted as a "habitual criminal." Although the defendant is in most other situations entitled to be released on bail, it is not an uncommon practice in more serious cases for the magistrate to require a cash bond higher than what the defendant can pay. Where the bail is set at an unreasonably high level, the defendant has no alternative other than to remain in custody while his attorney conducts habeas corpus proceedings in higher courts to get the bond reduced.
50. Which, loosely translated, means "I do not wish to contest the charges against me." The plea of *nolo contendere* is sometimes referred to as the "gentleman's plea of guilty," in that this plea has the same legal effect as a plea of guilty.
51. The defendant, however, must have a fairly clean record to use this procedure. If eligible to use the procedure and if probation is granted by the jury, the court must grant probation. The court, nevertheless, retains the power to grant probation even if not recommended by the jury and even though the defendant may not have been eligible to have the question of probation determined by a jury.
52. A motion for continuance is a request to have the trial delayed for some good cause, such as the absence of a material witness.
53. This amounts to a request for separate trials of the codefendants.
54. In most jurisdictions, it is possible for the defendant voluntarily to waive the right to a trial before a jury and to allow the case to be heard and decided solely by the presiding judge. The process of trial involves many technical details and complexities, the discussion of which is beyond the scope of this chapter.
55. This is subject to conditions which the trial judge may establish, including a requirement that bail be posted, payment of costs of prosecution, etc.

60 Fundamentals of Criminal Behavior and Correctional Systems

56. The "record" consists of copies of the pleadings, docket entries, the court's instructions to the jury, the verdict, the judgment, the sentence, the notice of appeal, appeal bond if one was made, written motions and court orders, and "bills of exception" (items objected to or excepted to by the defendant's attorney during the proceeding).
57. And by this time it is not uncommon for a defendant to have exhausted his financial resources.
58. If a longer sentence is set following the second conviction, though, the greater sentence cannot be based upon vindictiveness on the part of the trial judge who was reversed on appeal.
59. Procedures for allowing convicts extra credit toward the time served because of good behavior on their part represent a powerful tool in the administration of correctional institutions. Where authorized, the practice has the practical effect of allowing an inmate to be released by serving less time than the actual amount to which sentenced. For example, an individual sentenced to a minimum of 15 years might, assuming that the laws of his state allowed him to get an extra half day of credit for each day of exemplary conduct, be able to be released after ten years of incarceration.
60. Magazines with wide circulation have criticized the system as one in which "policemen are handcuffed."
61. The United States Supreme Court under Chief Justice Warren received much criticism for the protection afforded individuals in criminal cases. It seems significant to note that the court was not headed by an individual who had earned his professional reputation in the defense of criminal cases, but rather by a man of conscience who had spent much of his time working the other side of the street.
62. This writer once heard a defendant complain, "Everyone expects a hood like me to lie, but even I didn't expect a policeman to swear to tell the whole truth and then come on with a story like that . . ."
63. For example, a person who deals in narcotics has committed at least three separate offenses under federal law. If, however, the case is not strong or if it is the person's first offense, a plea of guilty to failure to pay the federal tax on narcotics, the least serious of the possible charges, usually will be sufficient to obtain dismissal of the remaining charges. In cases of this type, where both state and federal charges are involved, the state and federal prosecutors may work together to obtain the guilty plea; and if pending charges do not relate to the same offense, the prosecutors may even work out arrangements for the federal sentence and the state sentence to run concurrently.
64. A hard-nosed administrator of a correctional institution once flatly stated to this writer, "Eighty-five per cent of the people in here could be turned loose tomorrow without society being in any significant danger." What makes the statement significant is not that it was revealed

An Overview of Criminal Law and Criminal Procedure 61

to this writer but that the administrator has the courage and conviction to be willing to make the same statement in public, including in legislative hearings.

65. The disparity in the types of sentences handed down in different cases, for example. In talking to this writer about a youth, allegedly a Black Panther leader, who had been given the maximum sentence for possession of one marijuana cigarette, a prison official described comments made by the youth about another prisoner who arrived at the institution on the same day from another part of the state. The second prisoner was serving a two-year sentence for homicide. "The two of them got here on the same day, and the kid knows what the other guy did and what the jury gave him. He's been thinking it over," the prison official said. "Tell me this—how are we going to rehabilitate *that* kid?"

Chapter 4
The Judicial Role in Correctional Administration
GLENN R. WINTERS

> *Sed quis custodiet ipsos custodes?*
> (But who shall watch the keepers themselves?)
> Juvenal, *Satires*, VI, line 347

For the public offender the criminal process is an involved path across several different planes. As he is prodded along that path, the most prominent forces shaping his reformation are the correctional administration and the judicial system. While the administrative task is one of day-to-day regulation and care, the task of the courts is primarily that of overseer. This means that after sentencing the impact of the judiciary upon the individual offender is secondary. That is, its specific function is to define and review the discretion exercised by those to whom the offender is entrusted. The purpose of such scrutiny is to insure that the system of treatment is not only efficient but effective, fair and decent as well. This chapter will focus on the judicial function by delineating the manner, methods, scope, explanations for and effects of judicial involvement in corrections.

It is imperative, however, to emphasize first an important characteristic of this field. The number of court systems,[1] the variety of penal institutions and programs,[2] and the developing nature of correctional law[3] make accurate generalizations about the judicial response difficult, if not impossible. Nonetheless, it is possible to discern the general trend; it is that trend that will be described here.

The judicial system is involved with corrections from the time it passes sentence until that sentence is served. The operation

---
Note: This chapter was prepared with the assistance of Richard Matthews, a student at the University of Chicago School of Law and currently a research assistant for the American Judicature Society.

of parole, probation and penal institutions all fall within the scope of its review. The courts' sentencing power gives the judiciary the right to insure that its instructions are fairly implemented. To this end, the administrators who take the public offender after he is sentenced (whether they are administrators of penal institutions, members of the parole board or probation officers) are often characterized as officers of the court.

But, traditionally, these "officers of the court" have been allowed to make their way unsupervised. Thus, the historic role of courts in matters relating to the operation of corrections after sentencing has been minimal. The most common response was to defer to the administrative discretion of these professionals. The rationales for this position were numerous:[4] the management of criminals is an executive function and any judicial review would constitute an unwarranted, illegal intrusion; correctional authorities statutorily have unreviewable discretion; intervention would be useless because there is no relief available; the officials are professionals who know what is "best" in order to accomplish the objectives of the system entrusted to their care and management; intervention would undermine authority, ruin discipline and destroy the effect of already established practices; any intervention would open the door to a vast wave of petitions, thus making the courts constant referees in mundane matters; officials have sovereign immunity and cannot be brought into court; judicial meddling would discourage experimentation and implementation of novel penological theories; finally, the public offender forfeits his rights and cannot claim any as a "slave of the state."[5] State prisoners were denied relief in federal courts for several other reasons as well.[6] Up to this last decade, for whatever reason the particular court espoused, the constant policy was one of "hands-off"[7] or nonintervention.

Judicial reluctance to intervene is still evident, especially at the state court level, but to a much lesser extent.[8] Since 1963 there has been a growing recognition of the potential evils of unreviewed administrative power. As a result, concern about the validity of many correctional practices and policies has arisen. A number of pressures and attitudes explain the relaxation of judicial self-restraint in this field.[9] In the mid-1960's, a number of judges began to tour the penal institutions to which they sentenced offenders. This firsthand experience did much to change judicial policy. Judges began to perceive that their reluctance to intervene only strengthened the status quo and isolated the correctional system from the essence of democracy—public scrutiny. Numerous prison riots, such as the tragedy at Attica, also did much to increase judicial sensitivity. Such events made the courts aware of the legislative vacuum surrounding this field.[10] Judicial activism in other fields made it difficult to rationalize their abstention as well. Perhaps, too, the court system was moved by a perception of public offenders as another "minority" group whose lack of attractiveness curtailed their ability to be represented. At any rate, the policy of nonintervention began to be replaced by judicial inspection.

Aware that absolute power is apt to corrupt absolutely, the judicial system is taking steps to curtail the discretion of correctional administrators. Even though prisoners, parolees and probationers continue to lose a great majority of cases, they are at least being heard. The judicial system has changed its direction with regard to correctional law and that change can only benefit penology. A change of viewpoint of most correctional professionals is neither necessary nor the goal of judicial intervention. The goal is the formulation of what is, in effect, a code of correctional procedure. The hands-off doctrine is being replaced in order that correctional administrators recognize the necessity of working within the bounds of the Constitution.[11]

But how do courts in fact review corrections? American courts are restricted because they must wait for a case before they can actively intervene in any area. Because of this, the judicial role in corrections is essentially limited to responding to prisoners' petitions. That is, the confined, whether they are serving their sentence or whether their parole or probation has been revoked, are normally the only group that protests the discretion exercised by those in charge of them.

There are a number of ways prisoners may get into court to have correctional regulations and decisions scrutinized. It is important to note that most of the claims are heard in federal courts rather than state courts for two reasons. First, most claims have a constitutional or federal statutory basis. Second, many states deny certain claims or remedies (e.g., tort claims or *habeas corpus* petitions) to the incarcerated. Also, there is often a definite reluctance to proceed in the state courts because many of them are known to persist in supporting the hands-off doctrine.

The primary method of redress is the *writ of habeas corpus*.[12] Prisoners utilize it extensively because it is simple, flexible and can be utilized by a legally untrained person. It is used to challenge the legal authority for confinement or, recently, the manner of detention.[13] The court has the power to discharge the applicant from physical custody, enjoin the condition or treatment, or declare an action or decision invalid. The obstructions to such a petition, however, are great even in those states where it is available. The petitioner must have exhausted all alternate remedies before he may seek the writ, and he must be willing to endure an extremely lengthy process. Too, the writ may be refused if the prisoner is not entitled to immediate release from confinement.[14]

Next to *habeas corpus*, the most effective approach to redress is the *Civil Rights Act*.[15] Under it, the prisoner must show that a federal right (e.g., the right not to be subjected to cruel and unusual punishment, right to due process of law, etc.) has been violated by an official acting "under color of law." Unlike *habeas corpus*, the prisoner need not first exhaust his state remedies. Actions before the court under Section 1983 allow the greatest possible leeway to fashion "appropriate" relief. Thus the court may award monetary damages, issue an injunction against the correctional officials or let them know what is expected by making a declaratory judgment. From the viewpoint of judicial review, this action is the most appropriate. The one restriction is that it does not apply to federal officials; hence, only state-held prisoners may employ it.

The *writ of mandamus* is a third recourse available to the prisoner to compel prison officials to perform a duty owed to him. It is the appropriate procedure for controlling the ministerial, as opposed to the discretionary, acts of officials. Although it could provide an efficient means of judicial review, it is seldom used in prisoners' cases because of its intricacy. Too, the fine line between ministerial and discretionary acts is often indistinguishable and often proves to be the reason for denial of *mandamus*. Lastly, a federal court will not issue *mandamus* against a state official, thus severely limiting its application.[16]

Civil suits against officials or the government also serve as a method of obtaining judicial review of correctional discretion. Many states limit the right to sue in such cases or impose such burdens that it is practically impossible to prevail. Thus, in the main, tort suits have proven to be unsatisfactory instruments of review.[17]

Even more unsatisfactory has been the recourse of criminal prosecutions. Modern prosecutors have been understandably reluctant to invoke local statutes against correctional officials. At any rate, the criminal prosecution would serve a very limited purpose and would be applicable only in peculiar circumstances. Judicial review in such instances would amount to personal review rather than scrutiny of the whole institution.[18]

An excellent means of obtaining judicial review on something more than an individual basis is the *class action suit*.[19] It provides a means for resolving the common claims of a number of inmates, thus making it an effective vehicle for providing redress on a systematic, institution-wide basis. It avoids a multiplicity of suits, is applicable to the whole class and may be enforced by any member of that class. Although it has not been employed in this manner yet, it could be useful for prison administrators seeking to resolve a litigious issue. Unfortunately, it is rarely employed, especially in state courts.

Of all the various actions that may be brought, the most prevalent relief used by the courts in this area is the *injunction*. Monetary damages are inappropriate in most cases because no order to improve conditions results. Also it is important to remember that correctional institutions do not have a plethora of funds available; hence, a monetary claim may in fact defeat its purpose. A citation for contempt is possible but is exceedingly rare and probably creates more resentment than positive response.

In short, injunctive or declaratory relief, regardless of the action or problem, in most instances is most appropriate. It forces corrective action; it can be tailored to fit the circumstances; it has a more far-reaching effect; it brings the issue into public view on an institutional rather than a personal level; and it can be prohibitory or mandatory—either compelling action or restraining a practice. The function of judicial review of corrections is best accomplished when some type of prescription is made by the court. Injunctive or declaratory relief can provide the mechanism for making prescriptions that are at once helpful to the imprisoned and the imprisoner.

After being confronted with a claim by a prisoner and having decided to intervene, what are the categories of correctional programs the courts will be concerned with? Of course, the courts attempt to leave as much as possible to the correctional officials; however, two basic matters are particularly vulnerable to inspection. Regulations, practices or conditions that unnecessarily circumscribe the fundamental freedoms of the individual offender are singled out. The other special area of inspection is the group of judgments directly dealing with the offender's liberty. More specifically, the realm of judicial concern involves first amendment freedoms, disciplinary actions, conditions affecting the welfare of the inmates, procedural standards in decision-making, and attitudes of the officials and personnel.

Sol Rubin in *The Law of Criminal Corrections* noted that to some degree every institution has programs providing for discipline, custody, health and medical services, nutrition, classification, religious services, visiting, communication with the outside world, recreation and educational or vocational instruction.[20] The judiciary will review each of those programs to protect the dignity of the imprisoned, to insure that the standards of decency of a mature society are upheld, and to provide for procedural due process.[21]

As indicated above, the purely administrative aspects of corrections are left to the discretion of the appropriate agency while those of an adjudiciary character are reviewed. Since the line between the two is, at best, a gray one, the courts have attempted to establish a procedural format within which the administrative body should function if there is any doubt. If an administrative decision is challenged, the first point that the courts will review is likely to be the manner in which the decision was reached rather than the decision itself. It is also likely that unless the decision is clearly invidious, the reviewing court will defer to the administrative ruling if the decision-making process does not contravene "due process."

Major penologists recognize the value of an open, fair and not predetermined administrative process. Such a process can contribute to institutional harmony and make the rehabilitative task easier.[22] The President's Commission put it this way:

> The necessity of procedural safeguards should not be viewed as antithetical to the treatment concerns of corrections. The existence of procedures both fair in fact and perceived to be fair by offenders is surely consonant with the "collaborative regime" emphasized as desirable by modern corrections, in which staff and offenders are not cast as opponents but are united in a common effort aimed at rehabilitation. In prison no less than in society as a whole, respect for and cooperation with authority requires the guaranty of fairness.[23]

Since legislators have rarely assisted correctional administrators in formulating basic procedural standards, the standards have been constructed by the officials themselves. To their credit, many have adopted procedures that insure at least a minimal degree of fairness; as can be expected, however, few have achieved really objective or far-reaching self-imposed standards.

The school discipline, juvenile detention and welfare rights cases of the 1960's are symptomatic of the due process standards that are and will be applied to corrections.[24] In them the principle enunciated was that in any adjudicative proceeding that may result in the loss of liberty or rights or that may impose additional restraints, certain minimal safeguards are a necessity. This principle, as applied in recent corrections decisions,[25] means that the courts no longer presume that the interests of the state are superior to those of the individual. Instead they employ a "fundamental fairness" or "balancing" test to the conflicting interests.

The Judicial Role in Correctional Administration   69

The biggest concern is that of sacrificing some administrative efficiency to constitutional protections. Courts realize what a burden a trial-type hearing would impose on probation, parole or penal hearings and so they attempt to be flexible in their demands. If the hearing involves a serious matter which could lead to extensive punishment or a longer term of incarceration, they invariably demand more extensive safeguards. For example, in *Sostre v. Rockefeller*[26] the court held that a prisoner who may be sentenced to months in punitive segregation is entitled to such basic safeguards as the right to cross examine and call witnesses on his own behalf, the right to retain counsel and the right to a written record, among others. The offender is entitled to similar rights in a probation revocation hearing as well.[27] Thus, the procedures required obviously depend upon the gravity of the possible punishment.

The minimum safeguards to be required in the future undoubtedly will be similar to those employed in the federal system of corrections or those suggested in *The Manual of Correctional Standards*. They are notice of the rules (to insure that no *ad hoc* sentences are imposed); an impartial hearing; adequate notice of that hearing and the charges; advice as to the proper procedure; advice as to the charged person's rights; a summarized record of the proceedings and evidence; a statement of the basis for the decision; assistance from a member of the staff or an attorney (the latter only if the charge is extremely serious); the right to confront and cross examine witnesses (again only if extremely serious); and the right of appeal. The rules of evidence and trial procedure, however, are not deemed necessary. Thus, hearsay evidence would be allowed, provided the charged is given a chance to rebut it. While these safeguards will necessarily involve more time and expense, they will assure that degree of fairness which the President's Commission thought desirable (see note 23). In this regard, it is to be remembered that courts do not look for the efficient but the proper and just.

One area in which it is particularly necessary to have some check against arbitrary decision-making is classification. For instance, the parole and probation hearing processes are basically classification actions. Whatever is done in them so affects the offender that it warrants extra sensitivity. In penal institutions the classification process is just as vital to the offender. Decisions about where a prisoner works, how much privilege he has, in what quarters or institution he is placed, the degree of custody required for him, the amount of good time he has accrued, when he is ready for a parole hearing, his vocational aptitudes and other typical "classification" decisions have a significant impact upon the direction the imprisoned offender will take. Because of their tremendous impact, the courts are reluctant to let such decisions be entirely at the caprice of a small group of officials. In such cases there must be some check upon the possibility of arbitrariness. Officials making such classification decisions must have an expressed set of standards which they can follow and which can be reviewed if necessary. Another area of involvement is that of discipline and security. The Eighth Amendment guarantee against cruel and unusual punishment places the disciplinary actions of correctional officials under judicial supervision. While routine sanctions often are not questioned, those sanctions that involve the deprivation of a basic right must be clearly necessary. Where fundamental human liberties are affected, the administration must show that the incursion is in pursuit of protecting a compelling state interest. They also must demonstrate that there is no other method by which that interest (usually security) can be achieved that is less damaging to the prisoner's liberties.[29] The case of *Johnson v. Avery*[30] is a striking example. There the Tennessee authorities sought to obstruct the prisoner's right to petition for *habeas corpus* in the name of discipline and security. The Supreme Court held that the interests of discipline and efficiency must at times be subjugated by the greater interests of fair play and criminal justice. In short, the tool of discipline is not an all pervasive force that rationalizes every administrative order. When a fundamental right is obstructed, the administration must prove that it is necessary to do so to accomplish the primary goal of reformation. It is no longer possible to explain a regulation simply by saying that any other practice would be a menace to discipline. The onus of proof of legitimacy is being shifted to the administrators.

The group of formal sanctions available to correctional administrators is usually reviewable. Because such sanctions go onto the offender's original sentence, abdication by the court would amount to an abdication of its own sentencing responsibilities.[31] Thus, the decisions as well as the procedures invoking forfeiture of good time, transfer, an extensive term of "solitary," or an extensive term of segregation may be scrutinized by the courts. Decisions affecting "good time" are particularly reviewable when challenged because this is the most severe measure available. Revocation of it, like revocation of parole or probation, amounts to a resentencing of the offender. Courts are increasingly demanding that such measures be employed as a last resort rather than as a common penalty. The procedures, as noted earlier, for invoking such a measure are also likely to be stringent in their emphasis of safeguards.

Since 1968 corporal punishments of any kind cannot be justified regardless of the prisoner's offense.[32] In fact, if the punishment is such as would "shock the general conscience of a civilized people" it will be declared invalid.[33] Even if the punishment is relatively humane it may be found invalid if it goes beyond legitimate penal aims.[34] A similar test employed by the reviewing court is whether the punishment is "graduated and proportioned to the offense."[35] These doctrines (humane conscience, necessity and proportionality) establish an upper limit beyond which officials cannot go in meting out physical punishments. They allow the greatest possible freedom within bounds of common decency and fairness. The "civilized society" approach is vague and apt to be heavily subjective, but even so, it represents a significant strain of judicial thinking with regard to the Eighth Amendment and corrections. It has done much to alleviate the greatest cruelties carried on within prison walls.

One of the punishments frequently employed is solitary confinement. Although it has not yet been considered cruel and unusual, it has been restricted by the courts.[36] If the confinement is more than merely uncomfortable it is suspect. When the confinement is likely to destroy many or all of the offender's human qualities and dignities, it is tantamount to maiming—a punishment clearly banned by the Eighth Amendment. Courts have expressed grave concern over the psychological effect of punitive segregation and seem willing to limit it. Several have endorsed the prescription of *The Manual of Correctional Standards* which suggests that punitive segregation never be extended beyond 15 days.[37] It is interesting to note that in almost every case where solitary was combined with some other debasing condition (for instance, the denial of adequate food, health articles, ventilation or clothing) it has been found invalid. Here again the "civilized society" attitude has played an important role.

All this is not to suggest that courts will not countenance the punishment of a recalcitrant prisoner. It is merely a description of their attitude toward excessive disciplinary measures.

The judicial attitude toward prison conditions parallels its attitude toward punishment. If the environment in which prisoners are held bears no evident relation to any correctional aim (e.g., rehabilitation) then it is suspect. The Eighth Amendment is used by the courts to insure a basic degree of decency of confinement. Dilapidated unsafe buildings; unsanitary, unnutritious or inadequate food; overcrowded, filthy and unsanitary living quarters; insufficient lighting, ventilation or heating; insufficient medical facilities; improper guarding procedures; inadequate pest control; and inadequate separation of dangerous inmates are all conditions that courts have declared cruel and unusual.[38] Furthermore, some courts seem willing to require the release of the prisoners if such indecent surroundings are not remedied.[39] Recently in cases attacking conditions of imprisonment, the courts have not allowed prison officials to defend the conditions by arguing the need for discipline and security. The judicial response is that the decision to run a penal institution is a proper one for any state, but a decision to run a prison contrary to the provisions of the Constitution is not proper.[40] Indeed, the feeling is that the person incarcerated in such an institution receives more than the sentence the judge gives him. Since that added burden in no way depends upon the gravity of the offense committed, the offender is not receiving the individualized treatment necessary to rehabilitate him.[41]

Often some of the rights of prisoners are taken away or circumscribed for disciplinary reasons. For instance, a prisoner found guilty of assault might lose his recreational privileges or his access to the library. Such restrictions are purely a matter of administrative discretion according to the courts. However, certain privileges may not be completely forfeited (e.g., the right to medical assistance or personal mail). There are certain "preferred freedoms" that the courts feel should not be overly restricted. Those liberties that are necessary for continued welfare—mental, physical and spiritual—should be restricted as little as possible.

Other liberties are often restricted for security rather than disciplinary reasons. These restrictions, as was explained earlier, must be calculated to have a legitimate end. The maintenance of security, the prevention of violence and the maintenance of an orderly operation are all judicially recognized as legitimate ends. But even these are not always sufficient causes for incursion upon basic freedoms. Normally the need for the restriction is balanced against the probable consequences if it did not exist.

The standard as applied to the First Amendment freedoms of speech, religion, and petitioning for redress of grievances is more stringent. Limitations on the quantity of mail an offender may send out are considered valid. However, censorship of the contents is increasingly viewed with disfavor. Furthermore, the right to correspond cannot be totally abolished, absent a showing of absolute necessity. It is likely that the courts will move toward removing almost all restrictions on prisoner mail other than an inspection for contraband. The reasons for this trend are as follows: first, the tremendous significance of the right impaired; second, the fact that the removal would cause little detriment to security; third, having such restrictions bears little relation to rehabilitation; and fourth, restrictions on legal correspondence limit access to the courts, which is viewed with disfavor by the Constitution.[42]

74   Fundamentals of Criminal Behavior and Correctional Systems

The right to redress of grievances is not limited solely by restrictions on mail. It is often limited by denial of access to legal assistance. Such restrictions are no longer allowed by the courts. Even if the legal assistance the prisoner seeks is a "jail house lawyer," he should be allowed that right.[43] The courts now maintain a similar attitude toward deprivations of the free exercise of religion. Black Muslims have been the major catalyst in lifting most restrictions on freedom of religion. Restrictions are now allowed only if they are necessary to prevent inflammatory reactions.[44]

Another specific abuse which the judiciary seeks to change is that of racial discrimination.[45] Prison officials employing segregated facilities must demonstrate a need to overcome the assumption of invalidity. Discrimination in classification or discipline is almost certain to bring swift reversal by the courts.

Communication with the outside world is closely supervised. Restrictions on access to public media are questionable at best. Similarly, disruption of the flow of information to the prisoner is deleterious. Such restrictions are suspect because they can encourage a sense of isolation and alienation, thus making rehabilitation more difficult. Punishment of prisoners who exercise their right of communication with the outside world is also looked upon with disfavor. Even if the communication proves detrimental to the prison administration it should not be limited completely. The denial of visitors, except for compelling security reasons, is inappropriate. However, the courts do not view the prohibition of visitors to those on an inmate's mailing list as too repressive.

The lack of recreational, work, reading or educational facilities (or harsh restrictions on them) has not yet been challenged alone. The courts, however, are likely to look upon an institution restricting such facilities as improper when other aggravating conditions also frustrate the rehabilitative ideal. Recent cases reveal a judicial sentiment that desires the maximum desirable prison system rather than the minimally acceptable one.[46]

With regard to prisoners' rights, one court has said: "A prisoner retains all the rights of an ordinary citizen except those expressly, or by necessary implication, taken from him by law."[47] The courts will, in their increasing intervention into correctional decisions and regulations, attempt to protect those rights wherever possible. Any institution seeking to limit those rights to any significant extent will have a difficult time, absent a showing of an imperative legitimate end.

One area in which standards are still vague is that of the purpose of confinement. Officials may treat a prisoner in a manner detrimental to his welfare without contravening any constitutional or statute by standard. Some courts have intervened at that point on the basis that such treatment frustrates the primary reason for the confinement—rehabilitation. In the last few years there has been growing emphasis upon establishing rehabilitation as the essence of corrections. While rehabilitation is not the prime concern in every case, it is the clear purpose in the majority of them. In those cases where rehabilitation is the obvious objective of confinement (e.g., with juvenile, mental cases, first offenders, youthful adults, etc.), it is entirely proper for the judiciary to accept at least part of the responsibility for carrying out that purpose. Judicial reluctance to intervene in such cases only serves to frustrate the object of the court's own sentencing.

The chief attorney for the Bureau of Prisons has remarked that a court that will impose terms of imprisonment without being concerned with the kind of treatment that will be given is comparable to a physician who prescribes a drug without knowing its consequences.[48] The courts are assuming responsibility, along with the correctional administrators, for the rehabilitation and welfare of those who come before them.

Although there is no universal agreement about the purpose of prison, the generally recognized role of the courts is to insure that prisons are "to reform, not exterminate mankind."[49] To hold that the absence of a rehabilitation program constitutes a violation of the Constitution would be reading a particular theory of criminal punishment into the Constitution. However, present recidivism rates make it seem doubtful that any institution will be allowed to continue to offer a program that provides for no rehabilitation whatsoever. Indeed, imprisonment in such an environment practically postulates that the public offender can never be useful to society or himself. It is not altogether unlikely that courts will soon come to view such an attitude inhumane. A complete lack of care for the individual public offender and apathy about his personal improvement, when combined with "the precautions of right security," could constitute cruel and unusual punishment. In one recent case in Arkansas this was the holding.[50]

A shortage of funds to implement an adequate rehabilitative scheme is not uncommon in light of current meagre appropriations for corrections in general. When appropriations, personnel or facilities are inadequate, the concept of prison as a place of isolation and punishment prevails, and the rehabilitative ideal is subordinated or forgotten. To remedy such a situation, the courts may prod legislatures that are reluctant to bring the treatment of those confined in their states up to date. *Holt v. Sarver* seems to echo the Supreme Court's implicit pronunciation in *Griffin v. County School Board of Prince Edward County*[51] that when a constitutional right is violated, the federal courts have the power to require the appropriate state or local agency to raise funds to remedy that situation. The legislature that drags its feet may be forced by the federal courts to release the prisoners within its institutions or pay another state with constitutionally adequate facilities to hold them. This, however, is unlikely except in those instances where the state absolutely refuses to amend its correctional program.

A brief recapitulation of the courts' current role in corrections is in order at this point. First, the courts seek to alleviate the obvious and immediate systemic ills (attitudes, conditions, and practices) as well as the specific abuses. Second, they attempt to formulate standards of administration. Lastly, they provide impetus for the reform of penal systems.

It is important to note that the remedies the courts fashion can serve only to eliminate the surface problem; they rarely can prevent their causes. The courts can move to insure that the appearance is orderly, but it is the personnel involved in corrections, with the help of the legislatures, that must do the real work. It is really only they who can restructure the responsibilities and aims of penology. The enforcement of procedural standards by the courts is a good example. In itself, it is no panacea. What it does is satisfy the present objections to current arbitrary procedures. It works as a code of corrections until the correctional administration adopts a more satisfactory one. What courts are waiting for is what Rubin has described as a "positive response" by corrections.[52] The judicial system is not willing to submit to the sometimes selfish desires of corrections. The desire by correctional personnel to protect their administrative prerogatives and see to their own convenience has to change. Until it does, the court's role will continue to be as vital as it has been in the last four years.

The end of judicial abstention in the area of corrections has resulted in the end of such things as the imposition of physical abuse, the virtual isolation of inmates from outside society, the use of arbitrary procedures in decisions seriously affecting the confined, and restrictions on many basic freedoms. Those administrators who complain about intervention fail to remember that they could have prevented it. The power to change these aspects of corrections was theirs, and only a few perceived the necessity of change.

Two lessons can be learned from the history of judicial intervention in this and related areas. They are (1) the value of nonresistance, and (2) the value of anticipating the intervention. Administrators that anticipate the courts make their own jobs easier. A court rarely moves unannounced, and judicial response in corrections is no different in that regard. For instance, administrators who foresaw the abolition of racial segregation in prisons were able to take measures to initiate change and were not disturbed by waking up one morning with a new, complex and difficult task.[53]

One manner of anticipating the courts would be to approach the condition, regulation, order or whatever as if it were a legislatively or judicially imposed sentence.[54] If it is evident that no court could impose such terms in a sentence, then it would be best to seek an alternative path. For example, if, as in one prison in particular, there is a 50 percent chance that an inmate will be sexually assaulted each month, then an official could foresee that a decision to sentence any public offender to a 50 percent chance of sexual assault is clearly beyond the power of any court and consequently subject to chance. Such a practice of thinking and anticipating would do much to remedy most ills before they could be challenged.

From the standpoint of long-term reform, recent decisions demonstrate that review necessitates the application of progressive standards. The courts have found those standards in *The Manual of Correctional Standards*[55] and the directives of the U. S. Bureau of Prisons.[56] As has been noted:

> Deference to administrative authority does not require a Federal court to rubber stamp the actions of state prison officials. There are other sources of standards and knowledge . . . and the maintenance of Federalism does not prohibit recognition and acceptance of these other sources.[57]

The use of the guidelines drawn by experts in the field of penology combats the argument that the courts should not replace an expert's decision with one of their own. By following the policies formulated by the foremost correctional authorities, the courts thus lend an air of reasonableness and practicality to their decisions, and they are able to attach some degree of uniformity to the field of correctional law. Furthermore, the following of such standards allows others to anticipate what will be expected.

It is important to remember that the judicial system depends on professional correctional administrators. It is unlikely that the courts will ever intervene without their guidance and support. In this regard it has been said:

> The courts have not often overturned, on the ground of abuse, a correctional decision that professional correctional administrators would want to defend. No respectable administrator would countenance discriminatory treatment or senseless restrictions, and these are the courts' principal targets.[58]

The recent decisions relating to the rights of the convicted public offender constitute a minor revolution in the law. Judicial response to problems in corrections is of more than theoretical or academic interest. The response is important because of the impact it has had and will continue to have on the direction in which penology is headed. Most importantly, it is a reaffirmation of the intrinsic worth of every individual, no matter how degenerate and worthless some might perceive him to be. The recent growth of judicial concern with a number of fields, especially corrections, seems to be an enunciation of the principle that "the rights of the best of men are secure only as the rights of the vilest and most abhorrent are protected."[59]

NOTES AND REFERENCES

1. As of 1967 approximately 450,000 persons were confined and hundreds of thousands of others were under supervision through parole or probation programs in this country. The courts in each of the 50 states and Puerto Rico have the responsibility for those supervised offenders in their jurisdiction. The 92 federal district courts also exercise jurisdiction over those offenders claiming a constitutional or federal statutory right. Thus, at least 143 diverse judicial systems oversee correctional administrations.
2. The functions and practices of one state are almost always different from that of another. Uniformity of treatment or attitude is conspicuously absent. cf. Sol Rubin, The Law of Criminal Correction, 1963; and President's Commission on Law Enforcement and Administration of Justice, Task Force Report: Corrections, 1967.
3. The area of correctional law is relatively recent. For instance, more cases have been heard in the last four years in this field than the total of all the cases before that time. This means that the law is in part prospective, and unpronounced.
4. cf. note, Beyond the ken of the courts, 72 Yale L.J. 506 (1963).
5. Banning v. Looney, 213 F. 2d 771 (10th Cir.), cert. denied, 348 U. S. 859 (1954), Ruffin v. Commonwealth, 62 Va. 790 (1871).
6. Besides lack of jurisdiction, the federal doctrines of abstention, comity and exhaustion of state remedies obstructed review by federal courts.
7. This appropriate term originated in a document prepared for the Federal Bureau of Prisons. Fritch: Civil Rights of Prison Inmates, 1961, p. 31.
8. cf. Wright v. McMann, 387 F. 2d 519, 522 (2 Cir. 1967).
9. cf. Cohen, Sentencing, probation, and the rehabilitative ideal, 47 Texas L. Rev. 1 (1968).
10. cf. Rubin 13 Crime and Delinquency 206 (1967).
11. cf. Singer, Bringing the constitution to prison, 39 U.Cin. L. Rev. 650 (1970).

80 Fundamentals of Criminal Behavior and Correctional Systems

12. Statutory right for federal *habeas corpus* is found in 28 U. S. C. Sec. 2254 (Supp. IV, 1969) *cf.* Goldfarb and Singer, Redressing prisoners' grievances, 39 *Geo. Wash. L. Rev.* 175 at 267 (1970).
13. *cf. Coffin v. Reichard*, 143 F. 2d 443, 445 (6th Cir. 1944).
14. *Schack v. State*, 194 So. 2d 53 (Fla. Dist. Ct. Appeals), cert. denied, 386 U. S. 1027 (1967).
15. 42 U. S. C. Sec. 1983 (1964); *cf.* note, Prisoner's rights under section 1983, 57 *Geo. Wash. L. J.* 1270 (1969).
16. See Goldfarb and Singer, *supra* Footnote 12, p. 265.
17. *Ibid.*, p. 244.
18. *Ibid.*, p. 275.
19. Fed. Rules Civ. P. 23 (a); *cf. Holt v. Sarver*, 309 F. Supp. 362 (E. D. Ark. 1970).
20. *Supra* Footnote 2, p. 197.
21. *Trop v. Dulles*, 356 U. S. 86 (1958).
22. P. Hirschkop and M. Milleman, The unconstitutionality of prison life, 55 *Va. L. Rev.* 795 (1969); B. R. Jacobs, Prison discipline and inmate rights, 5 *Harv. Civ. Rights L. Rev.* 227, 224 (1970).
23. *Task Force Report: Corrections*, p. 13.
24. L. Kraft, Prison disciplinary practices and procedures: Is due process provided, 47 *No. Dak. L. Rev.* 9 at 53 (1970). The principal cases referred to are *Dixon v. Alabama State Bd. of Education*, 294 F. 2d 150 (5th Cir.), cert. denied, 368 U. S. 930 (1961); *Goldberg v. Kelly*, 397 U. S. 254 (1970); *In re Gault*, 387 U. S. 1 (1967).
25. *Sostre v. Rockefeller*, 312 F. Supp. 863 (S.D.N.Y. 1970); *Morris v. Travisno*, 310 F. Supp. 857 (D.R.I. 1970).
26. *Ibid.*
27. *Mempa v. Rhay*, 389 U. S. 128 (1967).
28. American Correctional Association, *Manual of Correctional Standards*, 3rd. ed. 1966, Chapters 15, 24. Hereinafter cited as *Manual*.
29. *cf.* Hirschkop and Milleman, *supra* Footnote 22.
30. 393 U. S. 483 (1969).
31. Jacobs, *supra* Footnote 22, p. 250.
32. *Jackson v. Bishop*, 404 F. 2d 571 (8th Cir. 1968).
33. *Hancock v. Avery*, 301 F. Supp. 786 (M.D. Tenn. 1969).
34. *Williams v. Field*, 416 F. 2d 493 (9th Cir. 1969).
35. *Weems v. U. S.*, 217 U. S. 349, 367 (1910).
36. *Wright v. McMann*, 321 F. Supp. 127 (N.D.N.Y. 1970); *Davis v. Lindsay* 321 F. Supp. 1134 (S.D.N.Y. 1970); *Covington v. Harris*, 419 F. 2d 617 (1969); *Jordan v. Fitzharris*, 257 F. Supp. 674 (N.D. Cal. 1966).
37. *Sostre v. Rockefeller, supra.*
38. Note, Prisoners are people, 10 *Nat. Res. J.* 867, 871 (1970).
39. *U. S. ex. rel. Curley v. Gonzales*, Misc. Nos. 8372-3 (D.N.M. 1970); *Holt v. Sarver*, 309 F. Supp. 362 (1970).

40. *Holt. v. Sarver, supra.*
41. Note, Judicial supervision of prisons, 24 *S.W.L.J.* 844 (1970).
42. David P. Flint: *Judicial Response to Problems of Prison Administration,* Report No. 33. Chicago, American Judicature Society, 1971.
43. *Johnson v. Avery, supra.*
44. *Pierce v. LaVallee,* 293 F. 2d 233 (2nd Cir. 1961); *Jackson v. Goodwin,* 400 F. 2d 529 (5th Cir. 1968).
45. *Washington v. Lee,* 263 F. Supp. 327 (M.D. Ala. 1966).
46. *Davis v. Lindsay, supra* Footnote 36.
47. *Coffin v. Reichard,* 143 F. 2d 443, 445 (6th Cir. 1944).
48. Jacobs, *supra* Footnote 22, p. 272.
49. Ill. Constitutional Art. 8, Sec. 14.
50. *Holt v. Sarver, supra.*
51. 377 U. S. 218 (1964).
52. Sol Rubin, Administrative response to court decisions, 15 *Crime and Delinquency* 377, 382 (1969): "A positive response by administration would show awareness that court decisions are minimal, that they do not purpose to solve administrative problems, and that they afford many hints to do more than the court has specifically demanded."
53. Rubin, 15 *Crime and Delinquency* 377 at 382; Kraft, *supra* Footnote 24, p. 11.
54. See Hirschkop and Milleman, *supra* Footnote 22, p. 834.
55. *Jordan v. Fitzharris, supra* Footnote 36.
56. *Wright v. McMann, supra* Footnote 8.
57. Hirschkop and Milleman, *supra* Footnote 22, p. 818.
58. Kimball and Newman, Judicial intervention in correctional decisions: threat and response, 14 *Crime and Delinquency* 1, 6 (1968).
59. *People v. Gitlow,* 234 N.Y. 132, 158 (1922)—dissenting opinion of Pound, J.

Chapter 5
Correctional Systems and Programs—An Overview
WILLIAM D. LEEKE AND HUBERT M. CLEMENTS

Introduction
The History of Corrections
Functional Objectives of Correctional Systems and Programs
Correctional Systems
Federal Administration of Corrections
Institutions
Correctional Programs
Legal Challenges of Corrections
Summary and Conclusions
Notes and References
Bibliography

INTRODUCTION

Corrections remains a world almost unknown to most law-abiding citizens, and there is a tendency to think that imprisonment is the total correctional process. However, this is a very simplistic view of an extremely complex system composed of a diverse amalgam of facilities, theories, techniques and people.

In a broad context, corrections together with the police and the courts constitute the criminal justice system, which is an apparatus society uses to enforce the standards of conduct necessary to protect individuals and the community. As such, corrections carries the immediate task of maintaining custody of offenders and the long-range goal of treatment, rehabilitation, and reintegration. For these purposes, the correctional process offers three alternatives—probation, institutionalization, and parole. Each of these three facets of corrections involves a system—the organizational and functional complex of administrative agencies, personnel, physical facilities, operational techniques as well as decision-making. In addition, on the dynamic side, either to fulfill specific ends or as an alternative to institutionalization, there are various programs dealing with the individual needs of the offenders.

The magnitude of the American correctional system is suggested by the fact that it "handles nearly 1.3 million offenders on an average day; it has 2.5 million admissions in the course of a year; and its annual operating budget is over a billion dollars."[1] In spite of its huge size, the correctional population is composed of individuals who share some common traits. They are primarily young, unmarried males who come from the lower social and economic strata of society. Most of them are unskilled, poorly educated, and have unstable work records. There are many who have a prior criminal record, low self-esteem, and are uncommitted to any major goals in life; a disproportionate share of them are mentally deficient, emotionally unstable, and prone to violent and other socially deviant behavior.

In spite of its remoteness from the law-abiding citizens, corrections recently has become a subject of national concern. As the rate of serious crime has increased, there is growing concern on the part of the President and national leaders. This growing concern has led to increased federal funding for correctional purposes. The United States Department of Health, Education, and Welfare and the Department of Labor have made appropriations to corrections, and individual state corrections also receive federal grants under the Omnibus Crime Control and Safe Street Act of 1968.

Though signifying moves in the right direction, this current concern also is an indication that corrections has not been adequate. The inadequacy is supported by some recent statistics on crime: the Federal Bureau of Investigation reported that serious crime rose by 148 percent in the 1960's while the population of the United States increased only 13 percent. Nevertheless, the share of government spending to fight crime in the 1971 budget is $1.3 billion—only about one-half of one percent of the gross national product.[2]

84 *Fundamentals of Criminal Behavior and Correctional Systems*

The current concern with crime and corrections is by no means accidental. The philosophy of corrections—and subsequently correctional practices—has undergone dramatic changes, which have important implications for contemporary as well as future developments. Moreover, the intricate organization of existing correctional systems and programs cannot be comprehended fully without a historical perspective.

THE HISTORY OF CORRECTIONS

Throughout history, man's approach to criminals can be conveniently summarized as a succession of four R's: Revenge, Restraint, Reformation, and Reintegration. With the addition of each "R," important changes were made in correctional procedures.

Until about the middle of the 18th century, *Revenge* was the primary response to crime. Corrections was motivated principally by punishment and retribution, the state taking upon itself the tasks of vengeance that earlier had fallen to a victim's neighbors or kinsmen. Banishment and corporal and capital punishment were techniques used. The offenders paid for their transgressions. Also it was believed that corporal punishment and execution could exorcise the evil spirits that were seen as the cause of a person's crimes, thereby preventing harm and contamination of the innocent.

In the late 18th and early 19th centuries, an important revolution in correctional philosophy was generated by the growth of Western democracy and the influence of contemporary rational philosophers and legalists. Criminals came to be seen not as possessed by evil, but as persons who had deliberately chosen to violate the law because it gave them pleasure or profit.

Legalists wished to establish a more rational and equitable legal system. Under such views, reactions to crime should be rationally based on a pleasure-pain principle—less punishment for less severe crimes, more punishment for more severe crimes. Imprisonment commensurate with the severity of the crime was developed as the major correctional tool. It also posed as a better substitute for corporal and capital punishment in the light of humanitarianism, which had become the prevalent factor of the time.

The correctional institutions, then, became places for "reflection in solitude leading to repentence and redemption." Simultaneously, institutionalization would be a lesson, teaching that crime does not pay. Thus, *Restraint* was the correctional philosophy during this period, and the architectural designs of correctional institutions were such that communications within and without were reduced to a minimum. The Pennsylvania and Auburn, New York systems, started in 1829, were illustrative of this approach. (As a point of interest, 61 correctional institutions opened before 1900 are still in use today.)

Reformation, the third R, was introduced in the late 19th century and early 20th century. The spirit of reformation was reflected as early as 1870, when the American Prison Association (now known as the American Correctional Association) established as its goal: "Reformation, not vindictive suffering, is the purpose of penal treatment." This second revolution came about as a direct response to the inadequacy of institutionalization, but it gained impetus through the growth of Freudian psychology and the social sciences. Institutionalization had not worked as an impartial and uniform reaction to crime. At the same time, the number of inmates confined continued to increase, resulting in increasingly overcrowded institutions.

Meanwhile, Freudian psychology suggested that crime might be an unconscious response to personal problems and the social sciences pointed to the influence of complex learning processes, to conflicting subcultural influences, and to conditions of class and ethnicity as sources of nonconformity. The result of these influences was a tendency to view the offender as a deprived or handicapped person whose major deficiencies were to be found in his mental or emotional makeup. Treatment, rather than punishment, was called for, professionalism and specialization rather than a generalized response. The *Reformation* movement thus introduced a complex approach to corrections extending far beyond just confinement and punishment. Many of today's correctional systems and programs are the product of the Reformation era, although there are varying degrees of sophistication in their practices.

However, reformation is still part of the present approach in corrections, although it does not constitute the ultimate goal. A fourth revolution apparently has come, bringing in the concept of *Reintegration.* The general feeling is that a focus only upon reforming the offender is inadequate and restrictive. Successful rehabilitation is a two-sided coin, including reformation on one side and reintegration on the other. Corrections must develop approaches which prepare the offender to deal with the compelling pressures that are exerted upon him by persons living in his community, by social, educational and economic pressures, and by our overall culture and subcultures. Only by such preparation will offenders successfully return to society as productive citizens. And only if it can be demonstrated that offenders can become productive, law-abiding citizens will community attitudes toward offenders be changed from rejection to acceptance.

The secession of the four R's suggests that we are in the period of Reintegration. This is reflected in work release, prerelease, and other graduated release programs. Nevertheless, by no means have vestiges of revenge completely disappeared, nor have restraint and reformation lost their significance in corrections. The modern approach in corrections is multi-purposed, although some objectives are to be given higher priority than others.

FUNCTIONAL OBJECTIVES OF CORRECTIONAL SYSTEMS AND PROGRAMS

The generalized goal of corrections today is to protect society by controlling offenders and preventing crime. Incarceration, custody, or institutionalization still has a role in the system, but it has come to be the least desired or the last resort. Of course, restraining the offender in custody protects society from crimes which he might otherwise commit; nevertheless, the constraint is merely temporary. In reality, offenders cannot be confined indefinitely, and this fact is obvious since the same laws which convict also provide for release. To be positive and truly "correctional," corrections must aim at returning offenders to society as law-abiding, tax-paying citizens. To achieve this end, the functions of correctional systems and programs should be rehabilitation and reintegration (i.e., building the offenders' physical, intellectual and vocational ability, restoring their mental and psychological health, and modifying their attitudes and outlook), thereby equipping them to return to society as productive, law-abiding citizens and, consequently, reestablishing the community's acceptance and faith. Even when incarceration is inevitable, treatment rather than custody should be the ultimate objective during confinement, in order to facilitate the return of the offender to society.

To summarize, *rehabilitation* is the primary objective in corrections; but in order to prevent recidivism which is a measure of failure in rehabilitation, a secondary, if not equally important, target is *reintegration*—community acceptance of the offender.

The above objectives are the basis upon which the existing correctional systems and programs are constructed, and they signify, too, the direction toward which correctional improvement must move. In an overview of correctional systems and programs, such a review of objectives is a prerequisite to the understanding of their background and trend of development.

CORRECTIONAL SYSTEMS

The administration of corrections in the United States is fragmented and lacks coordination. Not only is the responsibility for administration divided among levels of government, but also the various correctional services are disconnected and conflicting in many cases. The nationwide correctional system includes agencies at the federal, state and local level. The federal government, all the states, the District of Columbia, Puerto Rico, most of the country's 3,047 counties, and all except the smallest cities have one or more confinement facilities, even if it is only a primitive jail for temporary detention. Typically, each level of government acts independently of all the others. The federal government has no control over state corrections; the states usually have responsibility for correctional institutions and parole programs, but probation is often a county or municipal function; and counties do not have jurisdiction over the jails operated by cities and towns. The responsibility for corrections or confinement is thus divided among levels of government, each being independent of the other.

On the other hand, the administration of the various correctional services is even more disorganized in terms of functional efficiency. Probation, institutionalization, and parole are the three primary alternatives in the correctional process. Each of these services can be further classified according to the kind of offenders they deal with. Consequently, in a 1966 survey for the President's Commission on Law Enforcement and Administration of Justice, the National Council on Crime and Delinquency found that corrections was divided into nine functional services or segments: juvenile detention, juvenile probation, juvenile training schools, juvenile aftercare, misdemeanant probation, local adult correctional institutions and jails, adult probation, state correctional institutions for adults, and parole. Historically, each of these functional systems developed independently of the others, as autonomous systems and not as divisions of some existing service.

With few exceptions, these systems continue to operate as separate entities today. Each system, indeed, has become exclusive, especially when many of them are administered at different levels of government within states too. In most states, not more than two or three of the nine correctional services are consolidated under one correctional administration. Few states have any administrative arrangement or other mechanism to enable joint planning and evaluation of services in the interest of achieving a better balanced correctional program.

While Table 5-I gives a complete picture of this functional fragmentation of corrections at the state level, it is important to note in only three states, Alaska, Rhode Island, and Vermont are all nine correctional services organized in a single correctional agency. At the other extreme, five states have each juvenile institution and three states have each adult institution with a separate board. In a number of states, correctional services are administered by departments that also have other responsibilities, such as welfare, mental health, hospitals, public safety, etc. The result of this fragmentary administration of correctional services is the absence of any mechanism for planning and developing a comprehensive correctional program.

Furthermore, overall administrative inefficiency, division of responsibility, and functional independence of correctional services lead to some specific problems. The state of South Carolina, for example, finds that the dual—county and state—corrections system for adults presents inherent difficulties in collecting necessary statistical data, without which it is impossible to plan realistically for comprehensive correctional programs.

The primary problem resulting from the dual system is overcrowding. The counties have the authority to transfer to the South Carolina Department of Corrections, without regard to the latter's crowded conditions, escapees, the sick, the violent, troublemakers, and other problem inmates. Consequently, while the county prisons are utilizing only 53.8 percent of their available space, the Department of Corrections is operating at 133 percent of its maximum rated capacity.

On the other hand, since the Department of Corrections functions completely independently of the South Carolina Probation, Pardon and Parole Board, there are some communication problems. The personnel within the correctional institutions are faced with the responsibility of counseling inmates who have been rejected for parole. When neither the inmate nor the correctional officials have been told why the individual was rejected or what he must do in order to receive favorable consideration at his next parole hearing, it is impossible to counsel effectively. Also, if the inmate does not know why he has been rejected, there is no opportunity for him to profit from his past mistakes, and he is rarely able to use the additional time in incarceration constructively. Communication is but one facet of the many problems arising from functional independence of correctional services; nevertheless, it suffices in pointing to the need for a closer working relationship among the components of the correction system.

TABLE 5-I
PARENT AGENCY RESPONSIBILITY FOR ADMINISTERING CORRECTIONAL SERVICES, BY STATE JANUARY 1971

State	Juvenile Detention	Juvenile Probation	Juvenile Institutions	Juvenile Aftercare	Misdemeanant Probation	Adult Probation	Local Adult Institutions and Jails	Adult Institutions	Parole
Alabama	Local	Local	3 Separate & Independent Boards	Dept. of Pensions & Security & Local	Board of Pardons & Paroles	Board of Pardons & Paroles	Local	Board of Corrections	Board of Pardons & Paroles
Alaska	Dept. of Health & Welfare	Dept. of Health & Welfare	Dept. of Health & Welfare	Dept. of Health & Welfare	Dept. of Health & Welfare	Dept. of Health & Welfare	Dept. of Health & Welfare	Dept. of Health & Welfare	Dept. of Health & Welfare
Arizona	Local	Local	Dept. of Corrections	Dept. of Corrections	None	Local	Local	Dept. of Corrections	Dept. of Corrections
Arkansas	Local	Dept. of Welfare & Local	Juvenile Training School Dept.	Juvenile Training School Dept.	None	Local	Local	Dept. of Corrections	Board of Pardons & Parole
California	Local	Local	Dept. of Youth Authority	Dept. of Youth Authority	Local	Local	Local	Dept. of Corrections	Dept. of Corrections
Colorado	Local	Local & District	Dept. of Institutions	Dept. of Institutions	Local	Local	Local	Dept. of Institutions	Dept. of Institutions
Connecticut	Juvenile Court Districts	Juvenile Court Districts	Dept. of Youth Services	Dept. of Youth Services	Dept. of Adult Probation	Dept. of Adult Probation	Dept. of Corrections	Dept. of Corrections	Dept. of Corrections
Delaware	Dept. of Health & Soc. Servs.	Local	Dept. of Health & Soc. Servs.	Dept. of Health & Soc. Servs.	Dept. of Health & Soc. Servs.	Dept. of Health & Soc. Servs. & Local	Dept. of Health & Soc. Servs.	Dept. of Health & Soc. Servs.	Dept. of Health & Soc. Servs.
Florida	Local	Local	Dept. of Health & Rehabilitative Services	Dept. of Health & Rehabilitative Services	Local & Probation & Parole Commission	Local & Probation & Parole Commission	Local	Dept. of Health & Rehabilitative Services	Probation & Parole Commission
Georgia	Division of Children & Youth & Loc.	Division of Children & Youth & Loc.	Division of Children & Youth	Division of Children & Youth	Dept. of Probation & Local	Dept. of Probation & Local	Local	Dept. of Corrections	Board of Pardons & Parole
Hawaii	Local	Local	Dept. of Social Service	Dept. of Social Service	Local	Local	Local	Dept. of Social Service	Board of Parole & Pardons
Idaho	State Board of Health & Local	State Board of Health & Local	State Board of Health	State Board of Health	None	Board of Correction	Local	Board of Correction	Commission for Pardons & Parole

TABLE 5-1—(Continued)

State	Juvenile Detention	Juvenile Probation	Juvenile Institutions	Juvenile Aftercare	Misdemeanant Probation	Adult Probation	Local Adult Institutions and Jails	Adult Institutions	Parole
Illinois	Local	Local	Dept. of Corrections	Dept. of Corrections	Local	Local	Local	Dept. of Corrections	Dept. of Corrections
Indiana	Local	Dept. of Welfare & Local	Dept. of Corrections	Dept. of Corrections	Local	Local	Local	Dept. of Corrections	Dept. of Corrections
Iowa	Local	Local	Dept. of Social Services	Dept. of Social Services	None	Dept. of Social Services	Local	Dept. of Social Services	Dept. of Social Services
Kansas	Local	Local	Dept. of Social Welfare	Dept. of Social Welfare	Local	Loc. & Board of Probation & Parole	Local	Director of Penal Institutions	Board of Probation & Parole
Kentucky	Local	Dept. of Child Welfare & Loc.	Dept. of Child Welfare	Dept. of Child Welfare	Dept. of Corrections	Dept. of Corrections	Local	Dept. of Corrections	Dept. of Corrections
Louisiana	Local	Dept. of Public Welfare & Local	Dept. of Corrections	Dept. of Public Welfare & Local	None	Dept. of Corrections	Local	Dept. of Corrections	Dept. of Corrections
Maine	Local	Dept. of Mental Health & Corrections & Local	Dept. of Mental Health & Corrections	Dept. of Mental Health & Corrections	Dept. of Mental Health & Corrections	Dept. of Mental Health & Corrections	Local	Dept. of Mental Health & Corrections	Dept. of Mental Health & Corrections
Maryland	Dept. of Juvenile Services	Dept. of Juvenile Services	Dept. of Juvenile Services	Dept. of Juvenile Services	Dept. of Parole & Probation & Local	Dept. of Parole & Probation & Local	Local	Dept. of Correctional Services	Dept. of Parole & Probation
Massachusetts	Youth Service Board	Local	Youth Service Board	Dept. of Youth Services	Local	Local	Local	Dept. of Correction	Parole Board
Michigan	Local	Local	Dept. of Social Services	Dept. of Social Services	Dept. of Corrections & Local	Dept. of Corrections & Local	Local	Dept. of Corrections	Dept. of Corrections
Minnesota	Local	Dept. of Corrections & Local	Dept. of Corrections	Dept. of Corrections	Dept. of Corrections & Local	Dept. of Corrections & Local	Local	Dept. of Corrections	Dept. of Corrections
Mississippi	Local	Local	Board of Trustees	State DPW and Local	None	Board of Probation & Parole	Local	Dept. of Correction	Board of Probation & Parole
Missouri	Local	Local	Board of Training Schools	Board of Training Schools	Local	Board of Probation & Parole	Local	Dept. of Correction	Board of Probation & Parole

TABLE 5-I—(Continued)

State	Juvenile Detention	Juvenile Probation	Juvenile Institutions	Juvenile Aftercare	Misdemeanant Probation	Adult Probation	Local Adult Institutions and Jails	Adult Institutions	Parole
Montana	Local	Local	Dept. of Institutions	Dept. of Institutions	None	Board of Pardons	Local	Dept. of Institutions	Board of Pardons
Nebraska	Local	District Courts & Local	Dept. of Public Institutions	Dept. of Public Institutions	District Courts & Local	District Courts	Local	Dept. of Public Institutions	Board of Parole
Nevada	Local	Local	Dept. of Health & Welfare	Dept. of Health & Welfare	Dept. of Parole & Probation	Dept. of Parole & Probation	Local	Board Prison Commissioners	Dept. of Parole & Probation
New Hampshire	Board of Parole	Dept. of Probation & Local	Board of Parole	State Industrial School	Dept. of Probation & Local	Dept. of Probation & Local	Local	Board of Parole	Board of Parole
New Jersey	Local	Local	Dept. of Institutions & Agencies	Dept. of Institutions & Agencies	Local	Local	Local	Dept. of Institutions & Agencies	Dept. of Institutions & Agencies
New Mexico	Local	Local	Dept. of Corrections	Local	Dept. of Corrections	Dept. of Corrections	Local	Dept. of Corrections	Parole Board
New York	Local	Local	Dept. of Social Services	Dept. of Social Services	Division of Probation & Local	Division of Probation & Local	Local	Dept. of Correctional Services	Dept. of Correctional Services
North Carolina	Local	District & Local	Board of Juvenile Correction	Local	Probation Commission	Probation Commission	Dept. of Corrections	Dept. of Corrections	Board of Parole
North Dakota	Local	DPW & Local	Dept. of Institutions	Public Welfare Board	None	Board of Pardons	Local	Dept. of Institutions	Board of Pardons
Ohio	Local	Local	Youth Commission	Youth Commission	Local	Local	Local	Dept. Mental Hygiene & Correction	Dept. Mental Hygiene & Correction
Oklahoma	Local	Loc. & Dept. of Welfare & Institutions	Dept. of Welfare & Institutions	Dept. of Welfare & Institutions	None	Local & Dept. of Corrections	Local	Dept. of Corrections	Pardon & Parole Board
Oregon	Local	Corrections Division & Local	Corrections Division	Corrections Division	Corrections Division	Corrections Division	Local	Corrections Division	Parole Board
Pennsylvania	Local	Local	Board of Training Schools	Board of Training Schools & Local	Board of Probations & Parole & Local	Board of Probations & Parole & Local	Dept. of Justice & Local	Dept. of Justice	Board of Probations & Parole
Rhode Island	Dept. of Social Welfare	Dept. of Social Welfare	Dept. of Social Welfare	Dept. of Social Welfare	Dept. of Social Welfare	Dept. of Social Welfare	Dept. of Social Welfare	Dept. of Social Welfare	Dept. of Social Welfare

TABLE 5-I—(Continued)

State	Juvenile Detention	Juvenile Probation	Juvenile Institutions	Juvenile Aftercare	Misdemeanant Probation	Adult Probation	Local Adult Institutions and Jails	Adult Institutions	Parole
South Carolina	Local	Local	Dept. of Juvenile Corrections	Dept. of Juvenile Corrections	Probation, Parole & Pardon Board	Probation, Parole & Pardon Board	Local	Dept. of Corrections	Probation, Parole & Pardon Board
South Dakota	Local	Local	Board of Charities & Corrections	Board of Pardons & Parole	None	Board of Pardons & Parole	Local	Board of Charities & Corrections	Board of Pardons & Parole
Tennessee	Local	Dept. of Corrections & Local	Dept. of Corrections	Dept. of Corrections	Local	Dept. of Corrections	Local	Dept. of Corrections	Dept. of Corrections
Texas	Local	Local	Youth Council	Youth Council	Local	Local	Local	Dept. of Corrections	Board of Pardons & Paroles
Utah	Local	Juvenile Court Districts	Dept. of Social Services	Juvenile Court Districts	Division of Corrections	Division of Corrections	Local	Division of Corrections	Division of Corrections
Vermont	Dept. of Corrections	Dept. of Corrections	Dept. of Corrections	Dept. of Corrections	Dept. of Corrections	Dept. of Corrections	Dept. of Corrections	Dept. of Corrections	Dept. of Corrections
Virginia	Local	Dept. of Welfare & Institutions & Local	Dept. of Welfare & Institutions	Dept. of Welfare & Institutions & Local	Dept. of Welfare & Institutions	Dept. of Welfare & Institutions	Local	Dept. of Welfare & Institutions	Dept. of Welfare & Institutions
Washington	Local	Local	Dept. of Social & Health Services	Dept. of Social & Health Services	Local	Dept. of Social & Health Services	Local	Dept. of Institutions	Board of Prison Terms & Paroles
West Virginia	Local	Dept. of Welfare & Local	Commissioner of Public Institutions	Commissioner of Public Institutions	Local & Div. of Probation & Parole	Local & Div. of Probation & Parole	Local	Commissioner of Public Institutions	Div. of Probation & Parole
Wisconsin	Local	Dept. of Health & Soc. Services & Local	Dept. of Health & Social Services	Dept. of Health & Social Services	Dept. of Health & Soc. Services & Local	Dept. of Health & Soc. Services & Local	Local	Dept. of Health & Social Services	Dept. of Health & Social Services
Wyoming	Local	Dept. of Probation & Parole & Local	Board of Charities & Reform	Dept. of Probation & Parole	Dept. of Probation & Parole	Dept. of Probation & Parole	Local	Board of Charities & Reform	Dept. of Probation & Parole
Local	40	24	0	2	13	11	43	0	0
State-Local	2	20	0	5	11	13	1	0	1
State	8	6	50	43	26	26	6	50	50

Source: President's Crime Commission, *Task Force Report: Corrections*, pp. 200-201; Updated by ACIR and NCCD staff using 1970 State Comprehensive Law Enforcement Plans submitted to the Law Enforcement Assistance Administration, Department of Justice.

Some states also have some local services in addition to state services.

94 *Fundamentals of Criminal Behavior and Correctional Systems*

To summarize, the administrative agencies in the American correctional system involve federal, state and local authorities, and include organizations that devote a full or part-time work load to corrections. It is easy to identify these agencies when they are explicitly known as corrections departments or department of institutions, and department or board of probation and parole. But very often correctional administration is diversified under state agencies such as the Department of Social Welfare, Department of Justice, etc. and is not operated as a coherent, functional organization.

FEDERAL ADMINISTRATION OF CORRECTIONS

How the federal correctional system is administered is presented here for several reasons. President Nixon has called for massive reforms in the federal correctional system in order that it might serve as a prototype for the states. In fact, there already have been examples of programs initiated by the federal agencies and similarly practiced by state organizations. The federal system is basically similar to the state system in its functions, except that the former deals with federal law-breakers while the latter is concerned with offenders under state jurisdictions; thus, an elaboration of the federal system lends a better appreciation of the administration of corrections in general.

Three separate and distinct agencies can be identified in the federal administration of corrections: The *Federal Bureau of Prisons* which deals with the institutionalization aspect of corrections; the *Probation Division* of the United States Courts, which handles probation; and the *United States Board of Parole*, which is a division under the Department of Justice.

The Federal Bureau of Prisons was established on May 14, 1930, under an act which directed the Bureau to develop the federal prisons into an integrated system of classified institutions providing a program of custody and treatment based on the individual needs of the offender. At present the U. S. Bureau of Prisons operates 35 facilities covering eight correctional categories: youth and juvenile institutions, young adult institution, adult penitentiaries, adult correctional institutions, short-term camps, female institutions, community treatment centers, and a medical treatment center.

In 1925, probation was placed on a systematic basis in the federal courts under the provisions of the Federal Probation Act. Until 1940, when the Administrative Office of the United States Courts was created, administrative control of the probation service had been lodged with the Federal Bureau of Prisons as the authorized agent of the Attorney General. But by an act approved on August 7, 1939, the Administrative Office of the U. S. Courts assumed responsibility for the administration of probation. Today there is a Chief of Probation in Washington and 182 field probation offices in the nation responsible for the investigation and supervision of federal offenders.

The United States Board of Parole was created in the Department of Justice by 18 U. S. Code, 4201 as amended by Public Law 87-369, effective October 4, 1961. The law provides for an eight-member board, members being appointed for six-year, staggered terms by the President, by and with the advice and consent of the Senate. Although the board determines and reviews parole eligibility, the actual parole duties are performed by probation officers of the United States Courts.

The organization of administrative agencies varies from state to state, and from federal to state governments; however, the functions of institutionalization, probation and parole are fundamentally the same. These three aspects of corrections will be presented separately, each briefly in terms of its physical facilities, personnel, operational characteristics, problems, and directives for improvement.

INSTITUTIONS

Correctional institutions—commonly known as prisons and jails—are the most well-known aspect of corrections. The President's Task Force on Corrections estimated that by 1975 the state and federal institutional load would rise to a total of 237,000 inmates. At present, institutions account for 80 percent of the total correctional budget and 90 percent of the correctional employees. Despite the fact that other alternatives are considered more desirable than incarceration, treatment-oriented institutionalization is an indispensable part of the entire correctional system. Appropriately designed and constructed confinement facilities are the physical setting in which effective correctional programs can be launched for a substantial segment of the nation's offenders.

There are various kinds of institutions for correctional purposes—short- or long-term confinement, facilities for juveniles or adults, males or females, for maximum or minimum security; also, there is a variety of special facilities such as forest camps, local jails, work houses, reception and diagnostic centers, minimum-security prisons, and institutions with specialized functions such as trade training. Nevertheless, the traditional correctional institutions for adult offenders are often the main concern, because primarily the problems and potentials of correctional institutions are found in these institutions.

The architectural design and facilities of many of today's institutions manifest the vestiges of an age when custody and confinement were the only objectives of corrections. Too much of today's system is physically inadequate, antiquated or dilapidated, and above all, ill-suited to the modern functions of a correctional system. Most of the institutions are almost entirely custodial in a physical sense, and the constructions are such as to depersonalize and regiment the inmates. Traditionally these institutions are located far away from urban and population centers, and are built of stone, steel and concrete, for secure custody. Internally, the architectural structure consists of long corridors, repeated doorways, and desegregated cells or open dormitories. Water, lighting, and sanitation facilities are poor.

All these culminate in adverse living conditions for the inmate plus overcrowdedness, noise pollution, inadequate ventilation, and monotony of color and structure, which aggravate the feeling of loss of freedom and independence and help to nourish rackets, violence, corruption, coerced homosexuality, and other abuses. Moreover, the overcrowding and lack of privacy are unsuited to rehabilitation, since under such conditions it is difficult to conduct treatment programs, and almost impossible to promote self-discipline and responsible independence. Further, such an environment seriously impedes the conduction of educational, vocational training and other treatment-oriented activities. And remoteness from society and urban centers hinders the launching of community release programs or other reintegration programs, and the securing of adequate professional services and staff for those confined.

Indeed, the obsolescence of many existing institutional facilities is a major barrier to positive corrections today. There should be a fundamental change in institutional construction to keep in line with the current emphasis on rehabilitation, treatment and reintegration. New kinds of institutions, less forbidding in character and situated within reach of the community, are immediate and pressing. In addition, old institutions can be remodeled to create an environment conducive to positive responses. For example, living quarters can be improved by constructing private rooms with outside windows to restore individuality; wider corridors will relieve the sense of overcrowding; light and ventilation can be upgraded; and color and texture can be used to eliminate monotony.

In fact, a new kind of correctional institution has been proposed. Ideally for treatment, rehabilitation and reintegration, the model correctional institutions should be located close to population centers, so as to maintain close relations with schools, employees and industries. Such an institution might house as few as 50 inmates. Architecturally, it should resemble as much as possible a normal residential setting. The new role for institutions is to serve as a classification center, as the center for various kinds of community programs, and as a port of reentry to the community.

The changing functions of institutions also mean more dynamic management of facilities and a new kind of relationship between the inmates and correctional officers. Discipline and security are still fundamental in correctional institution operations, but it is also important for institution staff to provide educational and vocational programs, and to offer counseling, religious, psychological, social and recreational services. These institutional programs, together with other correctional programs, inject a dynamic spirit into the entire system.

On the other hand, treatment and rehabilitation leave a continuing problem—the inability to effectively limit and define the specific methods of treatment calculated to produce favorable results in a wide variety of individual criminal offenders. Close contact with the offenders certainly helps to solve this problem.

This calls for a new role for the correctional officer since he is in contact with the inmate at work, in quarters, at school, on the recreational field, and so forth. Training efforts need to develop this new kind of correctional officer, one who can combine the duties of custody and treatment, has a sound knowledge of administrative policy and goals, and is capable of observations and counseling. With this type of correctional officer the progress of rehabilitation in institutions can be accelerated considerably.

The above is far from a comprehensive sketch of the institutional aspect of corrections. The following summarizes the present standing of correctional institutions: they are antiquated, overcrowded, underfinanced; there is no real consensus as to their purpose; and the personnel are undertrained and overworked. To carry out the modern functions of correctional systems, there must be more dynamic programs because it is by these courses of action that institutionalization, when inevitable, is made more beneficial to the offenders. These institutional programs are to be examined together with other noninstitutional programs.

Probation and Parole

Although both probation and parole are correctional devices as alternatives to incarceration or institutionalization, they differ in that the former is an alternative to incarceration, while the latter is an alternative to *continued* incarceration. Very often probation is administered at the local level as a component of the judicial system, whereas parole is administered at the state level and by an administrative agency that is part of the executive branch of government. This administrative difference between probation and parole also is evident in the federal system. Despite these differences, probation and parole essentially pursue the same goal and use the same techniques; both aim at rehabilitation, surveillance, and economy; both assist agencies of law enforcement, prosecution, and institutional confinement; and under both, the community serves as the correctional arena and the individual or offender is under the supervision of someone who has access to coercive authority. Moreover, the operating principle emerges from the use of the benevolent purpose doctrine: namely, the goals of corrections best can be obtained by the preservation of maximum discretion on the part of judicial and correctional authorities. Since probation and parole utilize the same techniques, they present similar problems, and are in need of similar improvements, they will be dealt with simultaneously. Where differences exist they also will be noted.

The differentiation between probation as an alternative to institutionalization, and parole as an alternative to continued institutionalization is important in understanding the order of procedures in the entire correctional process. Technically, probation is a type of sentence which may be imposed on one convicted of a crime. The offender remains in the community, under the jurisdiction of the court. He is subject to conditions of good conduct and to the supervision of a probation officer. If he complies with the conditions for a specified period, his probationary status is terminated and he is discharged from the court's jurisdiction. If he does not comply, the court may revoke his probation and impose another type of sentence, including commitment to an institution. But, probation as a correctional technique implies a system of services and functions—investigation and supervision in the community subject to the authority of the court.

On the other hand, parole is the release of an offender from a penal institution after he has served part of his sentence, under supervision by the state and under prescribed conditions which, if violated, permit his re-imprisonment. Parole, then, is one way to try to continue in the community the correctional program begun in the institution and to help offenders make the difficult adjustment to release without jeopardizing the community. Supervision of the offender in the community by probation or parole without institutionalization poses advantages of alleviating the burden on institutions, and being more community- and treatment-oriented. Consequently, on the one hand there is the tendency that probation will be used increasingly in the future; on the other hand, indeterminate sentencing is becoming popular so that offenders can be placed under parole as early as possible.

The emphasis on rehabilitation and reintegration also has brought in new approaches in the supervisory—i.e. control and assistance—role of probation and parole. Instead of being limited to a "casework-plus-surveillance" approach, the role is now supplemented by other correctional devices; i.e. group methods, intensive counseling, more realistic concrete services such as employment, and other types of involvement in the community for improved social living.

The same correctional techniques of supervision—control and assistance—employed by probation and parole officers necessarily bring in similar problems in the two fields. One such problem is caseload standards for probation and parole officers. An arbitrary ceiling for a caseload has serious defects as a standard for individual performance. It is desirable to have an effective classification system through which to describe the various types of offenders who require different styles of supervision and the types of officers who can supervise them. Another problem is the extent to which unqualified persons have been employed in decision-making and as probation and parole officers.

The main barrier to probation and parole operation, however, is related to funding—shortage of funds explains the lack of staff and facilities, the scarcity or absence of psychiatric or psychological service, the absence of community services and resources, and the deficiency in research and training programs.

Another barrier to efficient probation and parole systems is related to their organization and administration. Both systems demonstrate a serious lack of organizational coherence, particularly in probation. As already mentioned, there are diverse administrative patterns in probation and parole. In some states juvenile probation is administered by the juvenile courts while for others, either correctional agencies are in charge or juvenile probation is placed under the state welfare department. Adult probation is combined with parole services although in many cases there are examples of probation being administered by a separate state board or agency or under local jurisdiction. This diversity is largely the result of historical accident, but the lack of coordination often forces probation and parole agencies and institutional agencies into a competitive position. Presently, when all attempts are being made to reduce institution-to-community disorientation, parole and institutional authorities have to cooperate closely if community programs such as furloughs, pre-release, and halfway houses are to achieve their objectives in reducing excessive strains during immediate release.

Controversy also is focused on the organization of parole administration, especially that of the parole board. It is desirable that there should be a centralized board exclusively responsible for decisions on parole release. The prime need at this time is to improve the efficiency of parole administration by appointing full-time board members and establishing meaningful professional qualifications.[3] Moreover, it is desirable to promulgate a national model for board hearings and refine methods for measuring the effectiveness of parole board decisions and parole supervision and services.

Institutions, probation, and parole—each a system on its own—together constitute the complex totality of corrections. The organization and administration of these three correctional processes constitute the network within which correctional programs are to be initiated to meet individual needs of offenders.

CORRECTIONAL PROGRAMS

Programs are projects developed for special individual needs. They represent innovations and experimentations in the correctional systems to more efficiently and effectively reinforce rehabilitation and reintegration. Each kind of program has its particular history, theory, objectives, techniques, problems, and future needs; in fact, by their significance in corrections each deserves special detailed coverage which is beyond the scope of an overview. The following brief summary merely represents an introductory account.

102 Fundamentals of Criminal Behavior and Correctional Systems

Today, all over the nation, there is a diversity of correctional programs being launched and those in operation are showing progress. Some programs, in some states, have a longer history than others, but a general trend is that innovative programs are increasingly indispensable in an effective correctional system. Broadly speaking, the many correctional programs today can be classified into three categories: traditional programs within institutions, community-based programs, and research and development programs. This classification is by no means definitive; all correctional programs are so closely interrelated that in fact, their practicability, operation, and success depend on one another.

Correctional Programs Within Institutions

Included in this category are programs designed to turn incarceration into treatment and to deal with individual deficiencies of the inmates. It is by these programs that institutionalization becomes fruitful and progressive rather than meaningless and regressive.

Work Programs for Inmates

Work programs in institutions serve several purposes: An occupation during incarceration prevents idleness, a depersonalizing factor often leading to riots and disturbances. Besides overcoming idleness, motivating inmates to work promotes self-respect, which is vital in rehabilitation. Work programs, appropriately designed, would offer all inmates an opportunity to earn money, thus promoting their self-sufficiency. Work programs allowing some cash for inmates also enable them to spend for personal purposes, such as gifts for wives and children. This is important in restoring personal dignity. Moreover, any work for the inmates, not necessarily training in vocational skills, can have the effect of habituating inmates to regularity in constructive and rewarding employment which they are to pursue after release. The anticriminal personal influences of work supervisors also are a major contribution of work during incarceration to inmate rehabilitation. Work programs for inmates also have their economic justification. Institutional industries can relieve the community of much of the costs in institutional maintenance, and help to develop institutions as self-sufficient units.

Work programs have been a dominant feature of American reformatories and penitentiaries from the outset. However, penal work programs have typically been repetitious and boring, and provided little incentive for diligent or enthusiastic performance. More attention should be paid to reward and incentive factors. Also, today there are several constraints upon the development of industrial work programs within correctional institutions. There are suspicion and resistance on the part of organized labor and business interests. The performance of institutional industries often has been unsatisfactory as a result of inferiority in product design and workmanship, unreliable delivery, and lack of imaginative and aggressive sales promotion.[4]

Traditionally, work programs have been more successful in federal institutions because they have a bigger market in the various federal departments, whereas the sales of institution-made products for non-governmental consumption have been restricted by state and federal laws. Nevertheless, in view of the desirability of productive work for inmates in terms of rehabilitation, it is worthwhile to expand paid employment and restitution during incarceration. The public also should be made to recognize that gross idleness in penal institutions works a serious detriment to the larger society, and that it is wasteful to support offenders without returns. Efforts also should be made on the part of the institutional administration to increase the market and adopt practices of private industry.

Programs Providing for Psychological and Social Services

Since present corrections is treatment-oriented, it is essential to have programs designed to meet the psychological needs of inmates, who are now considered as "patients." In the past, institutions often fostered idleness, corruption, brutality, and moral deterioration. For rehabilitation and reintegration purposes, there should be religious and recreational facilities. In addition, special attention to social education is noteworthy. Chaplains and psychologists can help inmates to modify and improve their morale or attitude. Courses in social education—dealing exclusively with questions of values and with adjustment in interpersonal relationships, marriage, alcoholism, and other personal behavior matters—are vital to the inmates when they reenter society, thereby helping to prevent recidivism. Social education courses are frequently conducted in conjunction with group and individual counseling programs.

Education, Vocational and Technical Training Programs

Education is an important means of rehabilitation. Lack of proper education and vocational skills are factors that contribute to crime. A federal test showed that the intelligence level of federal offenders follows the same distribution curve as the national population; however, their educational achievement lags five years behind the national average. Further, this deficiency in education and skills will be a detriment to employment after release, and possibly will lead to recidivism. Education, vocational or otherwise, keeps inmates occupied, drives away idleness, and injects motivation.

But frequently, the inmates' deficiencies are related to poor adjustment to the traditional educational process, and it is necessary to shift away from conventional classroom methods and toward instruction specially tailored to the inmates' needs. Innovative approaches are used, including learning laboratories, team teaching, and other up-to-date educational tools and techniques. The use of programmed material needs to be expanded.

Model Corrections Program

To develop a model corrections system will require massive funds; nevertheless, a program similar to the Model Cities Program would help to develop a truly effective corrections system. The model institution, relatively small, located close to urban and population centers, and highly diversified in programs, can provide excellent settings for research and experimentation and can serve as proving grounds of needed innovation. The exis-

Correctional Systems and Programs—An Overview 105

tence of a prototype is desirable for overall improvement in correctional efficiency and effectiveness.

Community Based Programs

One of the most promising developments in corrections has been the advent of community programs in the postwar decades and their recent growth in numbers and prominence. Community programs vary substantially in content and structure, but essentially all offer greater supervision and guidance than the traditional probation and parole programs, yet are a better alternative to institutionalization, being far less costly and more effective in reducing recidivism. A few types of community programs form the basic approach, although there are various modifications in their widespread application. Among the important programs are guided group interaction programs; foster homes and group homes; pre-release programs; intensive treatment programs; and reception center parole. Briefly these operate as follows.

Guided Group Interaction Programs

This is a kind of group-treatment program. The general strategy is to involve the offenders in frequent, prolonged, and intensive discussions of the behavior of individuals in the group and the motivations underlying it. The approach attempts to develop a group "culture" that encourages those involved to assume responsibility for helping and controlling each other. Well-known examples are the Highfields project in New Jersey, initiated in 1950, and the modified programs at Pinehills in Provo, Utah, and Essexfields, also in New Jersey.

Foster Homes and Group Homes

Foster-homes placement has long been one of the most commonly used alternatives to institutionalization of juvenile probationers. A number of states also have begun to develop group homes as a variant to traditional foster-home care for youths who need a somewhat more institutional setting or cannot adjust to family life. The utilization of these alternatives to institutional confinement has advantages of keeping the offender in the community where he must eventually work out his future. Besides, they carry less stigma and less sense of criminal identity, and they are far less expensive than incarceration.

Pre-Release Program

These are by far the most significant programs in terms of inmate rehabilitation and reintegration and call for more community efforts than anywhere else. There are a great variety of pre-release programs—work release, educational release, partial release, furlough and passes, etc. The actual design is dependent on individual needs and available resources in the hands of the correctional authority, but the rationale for all remains that of assisting inmates in the transition from institutions to free society. It is generally recognized that an inmate's reentry into society is a very critical period in his rehabilitation; however, even the finest of institutional treatment programs cannot always prepare inmates adequately for the transitional strife. Certain stabilizing influence is required for successful transition, and this can be gained by inmates working or studying, for some period of time before their release or parole, within the community where they ultimately reenter. Realization that the community is willing to help those who are desirous of helping themselves reinstates the inmate's self-assurance and confidence, and in turn restores his dignity and self-respect—a prerequisite for success. On a more immediate level, inmates are able to establish themselves in employment situations which may be retained after their release; they can support their dependents in the community while serving the final portion of their sentences; they can deposit money in trust for use after their release; and they can assume much of the financial burden of their subsistence while incarcerated, providing relief for the tax-paying public. A better understanding of the mechanism of pre-release programs and their effectiveness in preventing recidivism can be appreciated through examples of actual practice.

Programs of community work in operation today have their origin in the 1913 Huber Law of Wisconsin, which authorized

Correctional Systems and Programs—An Overview 107

judges and magistrates, in cooperation with the sheriffs, to impose conditional sentences in certain misdemeanant cases which would enable selected offenders to retain their jobs and, at the same time, fulfill the obligation of a jail sentence. The first prerelease guidance centers of the Federal Bureau of Prisons were opened in 1961 in New York, Chicago and Los Angeles. Each center accommodates about 20 federal inmates, who are transferred to it several months before their expected parole date. Thus they complete their terms in the community, but under careful control.

In the state of South Carolina, the Department of Corrections began a 30-day pre-release program in 1964. A Work-Release Program was launched in 1966, and in 1968 an Accelerated Pre-Release Program was initiated. A network of community based correctional facilities called community pre-release centers has been developed in the industrial and population centers of the state. The effectiveness of these programs is evident from the recidivism data in Table 5-II. The recidivism rate increased as the length of the transition period decreased, thus showing a negative correlation between recidivism rates and pre-release duration. Moreover, these data are more encouraging when compared with the recidivism rate for the nation, which is reported to be 60 percent or higher.[5] On the other hand, Table 5-III

TABLE 5-II
SOUTH CAROLINA DEPARTMENT OF CORRECTIONS'
RECIDIVISM DATA

30-Day Pre-Release Programs			90-Day Accelerated Pre-Release Program			6-Month to 1-Year Work Release Program		
No. Released	Returned to SCDC		No. Released	Returned to SCDC		No. Released	Returned to SCDC	
	No.	%		No.	%		No.	%
4,627	708	15.3	562	54	9.6	252	23	9.1
11-1-64 to 6-30-71			1-1-68 to 6-30-71			1-1-68 to 6-30-71		

Note: The above data and rates include only persons who were released from and reurned to the South Carolina Department of Corrections. The number, if any, who returned to prison at the county level or in another state is not known.

108 Fundamentals of Criminal Behavior and Correctional Systems

TABLE 5-III

CUMULATIVE EARNINGS, TAXES PAID, AND OTHER DISBURSEMENTS
FOR COMMUNITY PRE-RELEASE CENTERS OPERATED BY SCDC

	Totals for Month	Totals Since Inception
Total Men in Program—6-1-71:	169	
Gained:	50	1,214
Dismissed:	5	233
Released:	47	631
Paroled:	9	191
Loss:	61	1,053
Men in Programs—6-30-71:	158	

Fiscal Report		
Total Salaries Paid:	$53,872.87	$1,950,096.34
Average Weekly Salary:	98.31	
Amount Disbursed to Dependents:	8,292.35	301,065.32
Amount Disbursed to Inmates:	26,657.81	464,119.32
Amount on Hand:	40,176.40	
State & Federal Income		
Department of Corrections:	15,767.50	490,959.89
S. C. State Tax:	938.00	26,538.99
Federal Income Tax:	5,541.66	186,050.39
Social Security:	2,355.38	71,777.90

above, showing salaries earned and taxes paid by participants, is adequate evidence to establish the economic justification of pre-release programs.

Community pre-release programs also involve the offer of furloughs and the granting of passes. By allowing furloughs of two or three days duration, inmates are brought more circumspect in their action and conduct so as to insure their pass eligibility.

Pre-release programs are strongly community-based, since a necessary ingredient to success is extensive community involvement in their planning and operation. The business and industrial leaders must be willing to offer employment for pre-released inmates, while local civic, social and religious organizations and private citizens must be willing to accept the inmates and provide an amiable environment for their reentry. Community support, therefore, is what correctional administrators must secure.

Intensive Community Treatment

This type of community treatment program is some sort of controlled experimentation. One of the best-known efforts is the California Youth Authority's Community Treatment Project, which is now in its tenth year. This kind of operation has a vigorous evaluation design and serves research purposes, aiming at developing a treatment plan which is tailored to the needs of each type of offenders. The ratio of inmates to staff is lower and most of the techniques of treatment and control which are in use in corrections today are offered: individual counseling, group counseling, group therapy, family therapy, involvement in various group activities, and school tutoring services. Although this kind of treatment has been applied to delinquents, there are possibilities of extending to adult inmates, and it is desirable to do so in view of their implications in research and experimentation.

Reception Center Parole

Diagnostic parole is a program whereby all commitments from the juvenile court are referred to a reception center where they can be screened for eligibility for parole, either immediately or after a short period of treatment. These programs were conceived in part as a response to acute population pressures in overcrowded institutions, and they have proved to be successful in New York, Washington and California. At present, parole from reception centers has been confined to the juvenile field, but there is no inherent reason why this approach could not be taken with adults.

Research and Development Programs

While private industries annually invest substantial portions of revenue into research and development programs to improve efficiency, there has been little or no research done in the correctional field. Consequently, the correctional people's knowledge of effectiveness is very limited. If corrections in the United States is to improve its effectiveness, there must be substantial and continuous expenditures for research and development programs.

Included in the category of research and development programs are those programs not directly correctional with regard to inmates, but indirectly related to the efficiency and effectiveness of correctional systems. In the sense that these programs either upgrade their performance or facilitate better administration, they are an integral part of corrections.

Federal Programs

As an illustration of the nature of the federal program, the South Carolina Department of Corrections entered into a contract with the Federal Bureau of Prisons whereby inmates committed to federal institutions who are legal residents of South Carolina might be transferred to the community center nearest their homes for their final few months of incarceration. In this manner, federal inmates could derive the same benefits from work-release in their home communities as their state counterparts. This is an example of how state and federal cooperation can result in better correctional facilities for offenders.

Research and Evaluation Projects

Without sound research, correctional agencies find themselves unable to document objectively their success or failure. Consequently, research and development projects have been developed by correctional agencies. The South Carolina Department of Corrections, for example, established a Research and Development Division in 1969. In-depth studies of specific problems in corrections lead to fruitful solutions which can be applied by all agencies. A study of the causes of riots and disturbances, as an illustration, has come up with the preventive measures and methods of controlling riots and disturbances in correctional institutions. Another kind of research involves the application of statistical techniques. Data collection and analysis of the inmate population and programs aid evaluation of correctional programs and guide planning.

Manpower and Personnel Development Program

Manpower shortage is a common problem confronting many correctional agencies. This problem is becoming more imminent, especially when the current trend in corrections calls for innovative programs, intensive treatment, and community involvement. Consequently, there must be manpower and personnel development programs to cope with the gap in quantity and quality of available manpower. Some efforts already have been made by various agencies in this direction; nevertheless, the problem has not been eliminated. One such program attempts to train the correctional officer to share some counseling functions resulting in a more efficient utilization of manpower. Other programs include in-service training of staff, and tapping new sources of manpower. The Corrections Division of the Wisconsin State Welfare Department, for example, has provided a program for employees to further advance studies after a period of on-the-job training. Another possibility is the effective use of volunteers in corrections. Volunteers can be particularly effective in dealing with certain kinds of offenders. As an example, the students at the University of Colorado have been used very successfully as assistant counselors in wards of the local juvenile court and to youngsters in the two state training schools. At Royal Oak, Michigan, volunteers are a major element in an extensive program for misdemeanants which offers individual and group counseling, job placement assistance, and aid with family problems.

The various programs briefly portrayed so far are by no means exhaustive, although they represent the mainstream of positive actions that have injected progress and vitality into the field of corrections. By these increasingly diverse alternatives of treatment, the correctional authorities now are challenged by the need for decision-making. The emphasis on the individual offender and his potential for rehabilitation means that there are numerous important decisions which must be made after the imposition of sentence, such as the kind of treatment during imprisonment, the date and conditions of release from imprisonment, the revocation of parole, etc. In this respect, correctional authorities are thought to be more qualified than the sentencing judge to make judgments, because of their training and experience and because they are in a position to observe offenders following conviction. This need for discretion on the part of correctional authorities inevitably calls for considerations of the legal provisions and challenges.

LEGAL CHALLENGES OF CORRECTIONS

As an integral part of the criminal justice system, corrections must operate closely in conjunction with the legislature and the judiciary. The attitude and practices of the two branches of government have significant bearings on the flexibility of correctional administration.

Effective penal codes are essential to expedite correctional decisions. However, statutory provisions have been piecemeal, with a lot of anomalies and inconsistencies. There are certain offenses which carry mandatory minimum sentences of great severity and forbid the granting of probation or parole. Yet, there also exist some extremely high maximums which impose great strains on the correctional system where the gap between the date of granting parole and the maximum sentence often leads to possibilities of unfairness. Moreover, few sentencing codes set forth criteria for distinguishing between the occasional and the aggravated or repeated offender. These practices are certainly conflicting with, and also limiting the effectiveness of, the modern approach in corrections: individual treatment and motivation. Fortunately, the need for wide latitude and flexibility has been recognized; the Model Penal Code designed by the American Law Institute is a step towards the right direction. The Model Penal Code simplifies and standardizes the grading of offenses for sentencing purposes. It reduces all crimes to three grades of felony and two grades of misdemeanor. Each grade carries a maximum penalty, most of which are shorter than those now prevalent in the various states. The maximum can be extended by the judge

Correctional Systems and Programs—An Overview 113

if the offense is especially atrocious. The judge also sets a minimum term of imprisonment. Beyond these limits, correctional authorities have discretion to grant parole. Under the code, judges are granted flexibility to impose a sentence that fits the circumstances of a specific case, while parole boards are allowed to review reasonably soon after the correctional process has begun. At present, about 30 states and the federal government are taking a fresh look at their substantive criminal codes to look for a better coordination in the entire criminal justice system.

Recently, the courts have developed a growing interest in the field of corrections. The view has developed that the correctional administrators, who are most knowledgeable about the problems involved, should develop policies and procedures which will accommodate the needs of the system as well as the interests of convicted offenders; and that there should be increased legal controls in the correctional area. Some legal trends, such as providing access to the courts, religious freedom, and freedom from cruel or unusual punishment are discernible. It is now generally acknowledged that prisoners must be guaranteed reasonable access to the courts. In *Ex Parte Hull*, the U. S. Supreme Court confirmed the principle by announcing that "The State and its officers may not abridge or impair petitioner's right to apply to a federal court for a writ of *habeas corpus*."[6] The U. S. Court of Appeals for the Seventh District has decided that blanket discrimination against all Black Muslims would violate the First Amendment; but there are so many problems arising from this issue that they have placed serious strain on institutional authorities. The Eighth Amendment prohibits cruel and unusual punishment, and there have been quite a number of cases which define this right and deal with special problems. For example, the entire Arkansas prison system was found in violation of the Eighth Amendment in the *Holt v. Sarver* case, 1970.[7]

The legal challenges to corrections such as the above are certainly justified, especially since there have been examples of unfair treatment of prisoners in the past, supported by prevailing notions which question if it is humanitarian or benevolent and necessary to cede such a vast discretion to those who are in authority.

Desirable though these challenges may be, they also pose problems in the correctional arena. Increased legal controls can unduly limit flexibility and experimentation. Refuting some traditional discretionary powers of correctional administrators threatens correctional decision-making and displaces the professional correctional workers' expertise. In some circumstances, legal controls may make it difficult to maintain security within institutions and to protect the community against dangerous offenders. Indeed a balance must be struck in the correctional area between protection of the community and fairness towards the individuals accused. The extent of legal rights of offenders and control by correctional administrations needs to be meaningfully delineated. As a step in this direction, the South Carolina Department of Corrections has conducted a research project concerning all state supreme court, federal district court, and U. S. Supreme Court decisions related to corrections, in an effort to delineate the rights of persons confined in correctional institutions. Hopefully, these research findings will be used by correctional administrators to evaluate the practices in their respective institutions and take any reformative action necessary. This should reduce the growing burden placed on the courts by inmate grievances, as well as upgrade the standard of correctional practices.

SUMMARY AND CONCLUSIONS

Corrections is a complex totality, even in as sketchy review as the above. As an apparatus to protect society by preventing and controlling crime, corrections bears the important responsibility of rehabilitating offenders and reintegrating them into the community. The correctional process of the offenders often passes through one, two, or all three stages of probation, institutionalization and parole. Each of these constitutes a correctional service or strategy. Traditionally, probation and parole essentially involve supervision of offenders in community, whereas institutionalization keeps them under custody.

Correctional Systems and Programs—An Overview 115

To carry out these correctional functions, the entire system embodies a complicated structure of administrative agencies, a network of physical facilities and equipments, and an heirachy of diverse personnel who transform theory into practice. As contemporary corrections has evolved new concepts and theories of "individual treatment rather than massive custody," and community assimilation instead of isolation, there have been and should still be modifications in the actual practice of probation, institutionalization, and parole. However, the more striking aspect of this evolution is the new emphasis on devising dynamic programs to meet individual needs of the offenders, especially community programs to substitute incarceration and better equip offenders in their reentry into society. These new approaches call for more involvement and discretion on the part of the correctional authorities. To be flexible, they must be aided by some legislative and judiciary reforms, although they must simultaneously cope with some legal challenges to their autonomy.

For all these changes and movements, what, then, is the present standing of American corrections? Unfortunately, there have been too many inquisitions and too few constructive efforts, so that the present situation still falls far behind the optimum; correctional facilities are antiquated, overcrowded, and not conducive to the rehabilitation of inmates; there are not enough correctional personnel, and those who are employed are frequently poorly qualified and ineffectively trained; treatment and training programs are inadequate in the best correctional systems and nonexistent in other systems; there are inadequate funds for innovations even if they are conceived; and existing organizations of, and relationship among, agencies are by no means conducive to effective coordination of efforts.

Evidently, the direction of change in the present correctional system will still be toward the community, toward differential handling of offenders, and toward a coherent organization of services. This means upgrading corrections, introducing new divisions of labor, and establishing a better balance between institutional and community programs. To be more concrete, some imperative moves can be specified. The federal government

116 Fundamentals of Criminal Behavior and Correctional Systems

should have a definite role in corrections, just as it has in other major problems of national concern—investing tax dollars in programs and facilities, clarifying and simplifying the sources and procedures for obtaining federal funds which are currently available; ensuring that the guidelines for distribution of federal funds within states provide a fair share to corrections; inaugurating correctional systems comparable to Model Cities Program; and establishing regional research and resource centers. Corrections at the state and local level should aim at the following: increasing the use of indeterminate sentencing, to provide greater incentive on the part of offenders to improve themselves; decreasing the disparity between state and local institutions, for a more effective pooling and utilization of regional resources; providing comprehensive evaluation and diagnostic services for all inmates; providing a better coordination between probation, institution and parole; strengthening law reinforcement with regard to minimum standards of safety and sanitation in correctional institutions; developing comprehensive criminal justice data system for research and evaluation purposes; expanding the educational opportunities for correctional workers; providing full-time and professional parole boards; and others.

Above all, the most urgent need of the time is to make citizens realize the tragic truth in Chief Justice Berger's recent statement:

> In part, the terrible price we are paying in crime is because we have tended—once the drama of trial is over—to regard all criminals as human rubbish.

NOTES AND REFERENCES

1. Task Force on Corrections, *Task Force Report: Corrections.* U. S. Government Printing Office, Washington, 1967, p. 1.
2. The figures are reported in *U. S. News and World Report,* LXX (no. 1): Jan., 1971.
3. This recommendation is contained in National Council on Crime and Delinquency: *Correction in the United States, A survey for the President's Commission on Law Enforcement and Administration of Justice.* New York, N. Y., 1966.
4. A discussion on these problems is contained in Daniel Glaser: *The Effectiveness of a Prison and Parole System.* Indianapolis, The Bobbs-Merrill Company, 1964, Chapter II.

5. Criminal justice. *Newsletter*, 2 (no. 17): p. 131.
6. 312 U. S. 546, 549 91941. Other discussions of this point of access to courts are found in *Bailleaux v. Holmes*, 177 F. Supp. 361 (D. Ore. 1959); *Hatfield v. Bailleaux*, 290 F. 2d 632 (9th Cir.); *Kirby v. Thomas*, 336 F. 2d 462 (6th F. 2d 462) (6th Cir. 1964); *Bolden v. Pegelow*, 329 F. 2d 95 (4th Cir. 1964).
7. *Holt v. Sarver*, 309 F. Supp. 362 (E.D. Ark.) was a case involving the Arkansas prison farm system where the court held that the totality of confinement in the Arkansas institutions constituted cruel and unusual punishment.

BIBLIOGRAPHY

The American Correctional Association: *Causes, Preventive Measures, and Methods of Controlling Riots and Disturbances in Correctional Institutions.* Washington, The American Correctional Association, 1970.

Beto, George: A philosophy of corrections. *Collection of Papers Prepared for 1970 National Seminars Adult Basic Education in Corrections.* Honolulu, University of Hawaii, 1970.

Clements, Hubert M. and Leeke, William D.: The correctional officer as a counselor: A promising development in manpower utilization. Accepted by the *American Journal of Corrections*, unpublished.

Cohen, Fred: *The Legal Challenge to Corrections: Implications for Manpower and Training.* A Consultant's paper prepared for the Joint Commission on Correctional Manpower and Training, Washington, 1969.

Correctional Research Associates: *Community Work—An Alternative to Imprisonment.* Washington, Correctional Research Associates, 1967.

Czajkoski, Eugene H.: The new wave of therapy in corrections. *American Journal of Corrections*, 30:17-18, January-February 1968.

Empey, LaMar T.: *Studies in Delinquency: Alternatives to Incarceration.* Washington, U. S. Department of Health, Education and Welfare, 1967.

Gibbons, Don C.: Violence in American society: The challenge to corrections. *American Journal of Corrections*, 31:6-11, March-April 1969.

Glaser, Daniel: *The Effectiveness of a Prison and Parole System.* Indianapolis, The Bobbs-Merrill Company, 1964.

Heyns, Garrett: The road ahead in corrections. *American Journal of Corrections*, 30:6-10, November-December 1968.

Joint Commission on Correctional Manpower and Training, Inc.: *A Time to Act.* Washington, Joint Commission on Correctional Manpower and Training, 1969.

Leeke, William: A successful strategy in the war against crime. *FBI Law Enforcement Bulletin*, September 1970.

Leeke, William: Collective violence in correctional institutions. *American Journal of Corrections*, May-June 1971, pp. 12-16.

Leeke, William: *Testimony Before the Subcommittee on National Penitentiaries of the United States Senate Committee on the Judiciary.* Washington, D.C., May 18, 1971.

Leeke, William: *Testimony Before the House Select Committee on Crime, U. S. House of Representatives.* Columbia, S. C., November 20, 1969.

Leeke, William: *Testimony to Committee on Corrections and Penology of the South Carolina State Legislature,* July 28, 1971. (2 testimonies)

National Council on Crime and Delinquency: *Correction in the United States, A Survey for the President's Commission on Law Enforcement and Administration of Justice.* New York, N. Y., National Council on Crime and Delinquency, 1966.

Piven, Herman and Alcabes, Abraham: *Correctional Institutions, Pilot Study of Correctional Training and Manpower, Volume 2 of The Crisis of Qualified Manpower for Criminal Justice: An Analytic Assessment with Guidelines for New Policy.* Washington, U. S. Department of Health, Education and Welfare, Social and Rehabilitative Service, Office of Juvenile Delinquency and Youth Development, 1969.

President Nixon: *The White House, Statement by the President.* Office of the White House Press Secretary, November 13, 1969.

The President's Commission on Law Enforcement and Administration of Justice: *The Challenge of Crime in A Free Society.* Washington, United States Government Printing Office, 1967.

Richmond, M. S.: The practicalities of community based corrections. *American Journal of Corrections,* 30:12-18, November-December 1968.

South Carolina Department of Corrections: *1970-71 Annual Report, Community Pre-Release Programs.* Columbia, S. C., 1971.

Studt, Elliot: *Studies in Delinquency: The Reentry of the Offender into the Community.* Washington, U. S. Department of Health, Education, and Welfare, Office of Juvenile Delinquency and Youth Development, 1967.

Task Force on Corrections, The President's Commission on Law Enforcement and Administration of Justice: *Task Force Report: Corrections.* Washington, U. S. Govt. Printing Office, 1967.

U. S. Bureau of Prisons: *Annual Report 1969,* Washington, D.C., 1969.

Vining, Joseph E.: Prison industry: curse or blessing? *American Journal of Corrections,* 31:22-24, January-February 1969.

Waldo, Gordon P.: The dilemma of correctional research. *American Journal of Corrections,* 31:6-10, November-December 1969.

Wilson, John M.: The Presidential commission's crime report: An evaluation. *American Journal of Corrections,* 29:27-29, July-August 1967.

Chapter 6
Military Corrections
JOHN MORRIS GRAY

Installation Confinement Facilities
Disciplinary Barracks
Correctional Training Facility
Clemency for Military Prisoners
Correction—Not Punishment

In July of 1968, the President signed House of Representatives Bill 5782, to provide for confinement and treatment of offenders against the Uniform Code of Military Justice. This act currently identified as Public Law 90-377 provides for uniformity among the services in the administration of military correctional facilities and the treatment of persons convicted under the Uniform Code of Military Justice. The enactment of this measure eliminates disparity among the services with respect to statutory authority for the administration of military correctional facilities and the treatment of offenders in the same manner as the Uniform Code of Military Justice has placed all the armed forces on the same statutory basis in the administration of military justice.

The principal changes from legislation existing at the time of its enactment are: (1) it authorizes the Navy to establish a parole system for persons under its jurisdiction who are confined in a military correctional facility; (2) it authorizes each secretary to establish military correctional facilities as he considers necessary; (3) it equalizes the legal authorization for health and comfort items for indigent military prisoners; and (4) it provides the same legal basis to each secretary for remission and suspension of sentences, restoration to duty, and reenlistment of offenders.

To implement this law, the Department of Defense published in October of 1968, "Treatment of Military Prisoners and Administration of Military Correction Facilities" in order to establish uniform Department of Defense policies and procedures governing the treatment of military prisoners and the administration of places of correction. The basic policy contained in this directive is that discipline should be administered on a corrective basis rather than a punitive one, and military correction facilities should be administered uniformly.

Definitive instructions prescribing uniform procedures for the administration, treatment, and disposition of military personnel in confinement as prisoners are published in Department of the Army regulations.

The Army has three types of correctional institutions to carry out its program of correction. Installation confinement facilities, generally called *Stockades*, are located on major military installations throughout the world, and are intended to confine short-term prisoners who, for the most part, are to be returned to military duty and persons confined prior to trial. This type of facility might be compared to the civilian jail. *Disciplinary Barracks* are intended for military prisoners whose sentences include a punitive discharge or who are sentenced to confinement for a year or more. The Army's third and newest type of correctional facility is called a *Correctional Training Facility*. It was established to provide a broad problem-solving and correctional treatment capability and intensive military training for selected soldiers from Army stockades programmed for return to military duty.

INSTALLATION CONFINEMENT FACILITIES

At the stockade, the main correctional effort is toward solving immediate problems, improving attitudes, and motivation for honorable service coupled with an intensive program of military training and discipline. The stockade mission is to return promptly to duty the maximum possible number of servicemen and to identify promptly and expeditiously release from confinement, through separation from the service or transfer to a major military confinement facility, military prisoners who will not respond or are incapable of responding to correctional treatment of military discipline. Stockades are under the immediate supervision of an officer trained in correctional operations. Normally, they are under the command of the installation commander who has available to him qualified professionals, such as doctors, lawyers, chaplains, psychiatrists, social workers, and others who are made available to assist in solving problems of prisoners in stockades. Stockades are inspected at least annually by qualified officers and/or civilians trained in modern correctional procedures from the Office of the Provost Marshal General at the Department of the Army level to insure that stockades are operated in accordance with published regulations.

Installation confinement facilities, commonly referred to as stockades, are located on major military installations throughout the world and are generally under the command control of the installation commander. They are under the immediate supervision of an officer trained in modern methods of correctional treatment, called a correctional officer. Under our new concept of correctional holding detachments, all prisoners in the stockade with approved court-martial sentences of over 30 days are under immediate command of the correctional officer. Those in a pretrial status and those with sentences of 30 days or less remain assigned to their parent unit.

To accomplish the aims of the Army Correction Program, the stockade develops a program of correctional treatment based on the individual's needs. This correctional treatment effort includes evaluation, prisoner counseling, training, employment, clemency, and welfare activities.

The evaluation and counseling portions of the correctional treatment program are the areas in which the mental hygiene consultation service is of great assistance to the correctional officer.

The evaluation program is a continuous effort that begins with the initial in-processing and extends through clemency, transfer or separation actions. Our purpose is to determine if the prisoner has the potential for restoration to military duty and to determine what counseling, training, and employment would be most suited to the prisoner's individual needs. The evaluation process includes the following:

1. Studying the record of the admission interviews conducted by social work assistants and/or counselors from the correctional staff

2. Reviewing information provided by the man's unit commander as to his past performance and behavior

3. Studying recorded observations of correctional personnel who deal with the prisoner

4. Studying reports from the mental hygiene consultation service, surgeon, chaplain, and judge advocate which concern the prisoner

5. Studying relevant correspondence from individuals or agencies

6. Studying the record of previous criminal history, military and civilian

7. Studying pertinent military records

8. Studying reports of incidents and administrative disciplinary measures occurring during his period of confinement.

Adjustment to an individual's correctional treatment program are made whenever the need is identified during this evaluation effort.

Prisoner counseling also has an important role in correctional treatment efforts. Each prisoner is assigned to a military police noncommissioned officer counselor whose primary goal is to develop a relationship with the prisoner aimed at strengthening the inmate's ability to define and solve his problem.

Installation confinement facilities have a rather transient population and we must be realistic in what we expect to accomplish.

Military prisoners sentence to confinement for a longer period of time are sent to other Army confinement facilities. Civil-type offenders generally go to the United States Disciplinary Barracks; and military-type offenders—AWOL's—to the Correctional Training Facility, at Fort Riley, Kansas.

Because current crowded conditions in Army stockades preclude maximum effectiveness in prisoner motivation and retraining, the Department of the Army authorized the establishment of a new type of correctional institution called a Correctional Training Facility (CTF) at Fort Riley, Kansas, under the immediate supervision of the Provost Marshal General.

DISCIPLINARY BARRACKS

Our sole remaining disciplinary barracks is at Fort Leavenworth, Kansas. This facility is operated by the Army as a correctional institution for Army and Air Force prisoners whose sentences include a punitive discharge or confinement for one year or more, and who have six months remaining to be served upon arrival.

All of the facilities at the disciplinary barracks are directed toward the problems of the individual prisoner and administer treatment according to his individual needs. For the most part, the soldier is in confinement because he has a problem, and the immediate problem must be solved before an effective treatment program can be established. Prisoners with medical problems are given the benefit of the Army's medical services, including the professional skills of psychiatrists, clinical psychologists, and social workers, who are assigned to the disciplinary barracks staff. Those lacking in academic education are sent to school. The education program is supervised by civilian educators qualified in academic and vocational fields. All incoming prisoners are tested by means of standard achievement tests and those who test less than eighth grade level are required to attend day classes before they are assigned to a job.

A goal of the institution is that every prisoner complete General Educational Development (GED) tests and obtain a high school diploma before leaving the institution. College-level courses are available through a local college which gives resident credit for successful completion and awards an Associate of Arts degree to prisoners who fulfill the regular requirement for graduation. Prisoners who are morally substandard receive considerable attention from assigned chaplains. Those who are going back to

124 Fundamentals of Criminal Behavior and Correctional Systems

duty receive intensive military training, while those returning to civilian life are given vocational training to assist them in becoming productive members of society. On the vocational training side of the prisoner educational picture, courses and instruction are given in auto mechanics, barbering, greenhouse operations, landscape gardening, printing, screen process printing, sheet metal work, shoe repair and leathercraft, upholstering, woodworking, typewriter repair, and modern scientific farming methods. All vocational training instructors hold either a Military Occupational Specialty (MOS) or journeyman's union card, or both, and have had considerable experience in their respective fields.

CORRECTIONAL TRAINING FACILITY

One of the most significant major projects currently under way in the U. S. Army today is the establishment and organization of the United States Army Correctional Training Facility at Fort Riley, Kansas. This project, under development for over two years, is a bold and aggressive approach to the correction of military offenders. The correctional training concept makes a positive contribution to the Army mission and serves to conserve the valuable manpower resources of our nation. It is a project which is of vital concern to the Army Chief of Staff, military commanders, and military corrections personnel alike in dealing with the problems of divergent human behavior and moral responsibility.

The Army build-up during 1965 and 1966 resulted in a parallel increase in Army prisoner population. The number of military prisoners in confinement rapidly exceeded the effective operating capacities of installation confinement facilities within the continental United States. Concurrently, an analysis in depth of the mission and functions of installation confinement facilities indicated that they were not contributing effectively to the Army mission. Accordingly, the Army Provost Marshal General developed the intensive correctional training concept for military prisoners. Approval of the plan to carry out this concept was granted by the Army Chief of Staff in January, 1968; and the installation became operational in July, 1968.

The development of the plan for the Correctional Training Facility focused attention on the critical need not only for additional confinement facility space, but also for a meaningful method of correcting the behavior of military offenders. The concept for the U.S. Army Correctional Training Facility fulfills these needs; and at the same time, provides for the return of the prisoner to full duty status as a well-trained soldier with an improved sense of responsibility toward himself, the Army, and the nation.

The mission of the Correctional Training Facility is to provide the intensive training, close custodial supervision, and correctional treatment necessary to return military prisoners to duty with improved attitudes and motivation. The objective of the Correctional Training Facility is to return to duty the maximum number of well-trained soldiers in accordance with personnel assignment criteria and to minimize the loss of military manpower resulting from confinement.

The objectives of the correctional training concept are met through a ten-week program of intensive infantry training, motivational instruction, and correctional treatment. Prisoners assigned to the facility are kept fully occupied during all of their waking hours and afforded a high degree of close and continuing leadership, counseling and supervision. The facility is programmed to handle a maximum of 2,400 prisoners at any given time and will handle approximately 10,000 each year. Although the size of the facility may appear large, the correctional treatment effort is actually carried out at the correctional training unit level for groups of 200 prisoners each.

A staff and cadre of 518 military and 72 civilian personnel were gathered at Fort Riley to organize the facility and undergo training to equip them for effective operation under the correctional training concept. Prisoners convicted of military-type offenses, predominately AWOL and desertion who have 70 days or more remaining on sentences to confinement, are now being transferred from Army installations in the United States to the Correctional Training Facility. The initial group of 200 prisoners arrived on

July 1, 1968. Groups of 200 prisoners were scheduled to arrive weekly thereafter.

A ten-week correctional training cycle is prescribed with emphasis on intensive infantry training and correctional treatment. Professional services support is provided and a program of individual counseling and correctional treatment complements the training. The first half of the training cycle is designed to instill a sense of duty in the prisoners and an acceptance of their obligation to the service; during the second half, prisoners receive intensive infantry training under the guidance of specially selected leaders. The overall prisoner response to the correctional training program thus far has been highly favorable.

The cadre assigned to the battalions is comprised of an equal mixture of officers and enlisted personnel of the combat arms and the corrections specialty. It is these personnel who will provide the intensive leadership, supervision, counseling, and evaluation of assigned prisoners.

The planning and development of the Army correctional training concept placed primary emphasis on bringing experienced and proven leaders from the military community into the day-to-day operations of a correctional facility. This emphasis has contributed materially to the high degree of success in changing and motivating military prisoners toward honorable military service.

CLEMENCY FOR MILITARY PRISONERS

Our correctional system embodies every modern concept of penology which has been devised to further expedite the rehabilitation of prisoners. It has long been recognized that one of the best aids to rehabilitation of prisoners is to convince them that they are not hopelessly lost to society, that they will not necessarily spend their entire sentence in confinement, segregated from society. In other words, the prisoner must have some concrete hope for the future and a reasonable expectation that he will be released at a much sooner date if he behaves himself and proves that he deserves another chance in a free society.

Military prisoners confined in the United States Disciplinary Barracks are automatically considered for clemency within a short time after their arrival at the institution and on a regular and continuing basis thereafter. All prisoners are considered for restoration to honorable duty as a soldier, for reduction of sentence to confinement, or for parole as his individual case may warrant. Clemency considerations for military prisoners in stockades are the responsibility of the commander exercising control over the stockade.

Restoration to Duty

The prisoner must prove by his conduct, attitude, adjustment to confinement, work, and sincere attempt to better himself by taking advantage of the many opportunities to learn a trade or improve his education that he is worthy of favorable consideration. All prisoners are considered for restoration to honorable duty as a soldier, for clemency, or for parole as his individual case may warrant, and all prisoners who have good personal histories and who adjust themselves satisfactorily to confinement may reasonably expect to be released from confinement through one of these methods before the normal expiration of their terms of confinement.

No one single factor such as type of offense or length of sentence is used to determine whether a prisoner should be restored to duty. Rather, a combination of all known circumstances of the prisoner's case, plus personal observation, is used as the basis for determining whether he should be restored. Ordinarily, a prisoner will not be recommended for restoration to duty on his initial appearance before the classification board as the period of observation has not been of sufficient length to properly determine the prisoner's attitude; and the information gathered and studies made of the prisoner are not sufficiently complete to competently gauge his capabilities.

After a prisoner has been confined for a sufficient length of time to enable officers to observe and evaluate him, and if his record

128 Fundamentals of Criminal Behavior and Correctional Systems

is sufficiently good to warrant giving him another chance, the classification board may recommend that he be restored to duty. The recommendation then goes to the commandant for approval or disapproval.

Regardless of what recommendations are made by either the classification board or the commandant, the board proceedings will always be forwarded to the Department of the Army for final action. At this level, the case is considered by the Restoration Board in the Correction Division in the Office of the Provost Marshal General.

Restoration Board

The Restoration Board is composed of three experienced officers selected to provide a balance with respect to lay and professional attitudes, and familiar with combat conditions and the problems of enlisted personnel. The board considers each case on its own merits in order to render a just and fair recommendation to the Secretary of the Army, or to the official designated to act for them, in accordance with the policies outlined below.

The board must be guided by the restoration policy of the Department of the Army, which sets forth exactly what factors will qualify or disqualify a prisoner for restoration to duty.

Restoration Policy

The restoration policy of the Army is essentially as follows:

In the absence of exceptional circumstances, restoration to duty will ordinarily be precluded if the prisoner has been convicted of a crime generally recognized as a felony, or of desertion or absence without leave from units engaged in combat, or of desertion or absence without leave to avoid embarkation for overseas duty. A history of chronic alcoholism or psychoneurotic disorders will also ordinarily preclude restoration to duty. Exceptional circumstances to be considered include such factors as (1) a demonstrated behavioral change in the prisoner's demeanor from that evidenced by him at the time of commission of the offense for which convicted, supported by an established motivation to return to duty for honorable service; (2) a demonstrated ability to perform military duties in a creditable manner and a positive potential for honorable service; (3) a substantially clear civil and military record; (4) a reputation for honesty, integrity, and good behavior; and (5) age at time of offense for which convicted.

Prisoners convicted of purely military offenses whose records—both civil and military—are otherwise good may be restored to duty if their conduct in confinement and their attitude clearly indicate contrition and a desire to make amends.

A prisoner may be restored to duty if his case is not an exception to policy, at the direction of the Chief of the Correction Division in the Provost Marshal General's Office.

After completion of military training, prisoners will be restored to duty by enlistment in the Army.

On being restored to honorable duty, prisoners are considered to have completed punishment for their offense and effected rehabilitation and they will be assigned, trained, and employed as any other enlisted man. Commanders who have such enlisted men under their control will insure that such soldiers are afforded treatment identical to that of other enlisted personnel of their command.

Clemency

Clemency is a broad term and may be used in many different ways. It is generally defined, in the military sense, as meaning the reduction of a court-martial sentence. During active hostilities the primary purpose of military clemency is to restore a soldier to duty, with justice to the individual being given due consideration.

The need for clemency is ever present and must be given considerable thought by the authorities from the day a prisoner is confined until he again becomes a free man. It is a responsibility to be exercised according to the principles of justice, penology and modern knowledge of the inequalities of human personality, so as to follow the modern concept of insuring that punishment not only fits the offense but the offender as well.

Initial Clemency Consideration

Initial clemency consideration is usually given by the classification board at the displinary barracks when the prisoner appears before the classification board for his initial classification. The classification board makes such recommendations as it sees fit to the commandant. The commandant indicates his approval or disapproval of the classification board's recommendation and forwards it to the Department of the Army, where it is received by the Clemency Branch of the Correction Division in the Office of the Provost Marshal General.

Within this office there is a staff of case analysts trained in the social sciences, penology, and law. Each clemency and parole case is reviewed by one of these analysts who evaluate all reports and recommendations submitted by the disciplinary barracks. On the basis of all available information, the analyst reviews the case study, gives his own interpretation of the case, and obtains an opinion from other officials of the Correction Division as to whether the institutional recommendations are in harmony with policy, together with recommendations for or against clemency and parole. The analyst then appears before the Army-Air Force Clemency and Parole Board in the Office of the Secretary of the Army, and orally presents to the board a summary of the facts of the case, including all recommendations made in the field and in the Correction Division concerning both parole and clemency action.

Clemency and Parole Board

The Clemency and Parole Board consists of a civilian lawyer as chairman, a field grade officer of the Army, and a field grade officer of the Air Force. It considers all the material and recommendations submitted from the field, and any other written material submitted from other sources on behalf of the prisoner. Then each case is individually considered on its own merits, with due weight being given to such factors as nature and seriousness of offense; character, kind, and length of military service; civilian record; time served and conduct in confinement; age; mental and physical condition; and dependents.

After a case has been considered by the Army-Air Force Clemency and Parole Board, it is sent with recommendations to the Secretary of the Army, or in the case of Air Force prisoners, to the Secretary of the Air Force, for final action. After action by the Secretary of the Department concerned, the case is returned to the Office of the Provost Marshal General. If clemency has been disapproved, the commandant of the displinary barracks and the prisoner are notified by letter that the case was considered for clemency and as a result of such consideration, clemency was denied.

If the secretary grants clemency, the Clemency Branch then prepares and forwards to the commandant of the disciplinary barracks concerned, a letter notifying the commandant and the prisoner that the case was considered for clemency and as a result of such consideration a stated portion or all of the prisoner's sentence is remitted.

Parole may be granted to a carefully selected military prisoner who has served a portion of his sentence to confinement and whose release under supervision will be in the best interest of the prisoner, the Army, and society. It is based on the principle that a period of guidance and supervision in the community is a part of the entire rehabilitation program for prisoners. It is a means of helping the prisoner make the transition from controlled living in confinement to the normal life of a community. If the parolee fails to demonstrate his willingness and capacity to fulfill his parole obligations, he may be returned to confinement to serve the remainder of his sentence.

Parole Eligibility

A prisoner who is confined in the United States Disciplinary Barracks whose sentence includes discharge and confinement for from one to three years, who has served one-third of his sentence or aggregate sentence to confinement, but in no case less than six months, will be eligible for parole consideration at that time. A prisoner with a sentence of more than three years who has served not less than one year will become eligible for parole consideration at such time as the Army and Air Force Clemency and Parole Board may recommend, and the Secretary of the Department concerned may approve, but such time shall not be more than one-third of the sentence or aggregate sentences as lawfully adjudged and approved, or not more than ten years when the sentence is life or in excess of 30 years. The date of initial consideration establishes a review date and the prisoner will be considered annually thereafter until his release from confinement. A prisoner whose parole has been revoked previously will not be eligible for further parole consideration until he has completed one year in confinement subsequent to his return to military control, unless otherwise directed by the Secretary of the Army.

Prior to the time a prisoner becomes eligible for parole consideration at disciplinary barracks, the parole officer will interview him and offer parole advice to him, and at the classification board hearing he will present the results of such interview together with any other pertinent information obtained from relatives of the applicant and other interested individuals.

Each prisoner who desires parole completes an application for parole and submits it to the parole officer within 90 days prior to his date of eligibility for parole consideration. The parole officer will provide the prisoner with the necessary assistance to develop a satisfactory tentative parole plan prior to the submission of an application for parole.

An applicant for parole appears before the classification board for an interview at the time applications for parole are considered. The application of the prisoner will be processed by the classification board of the disciplinary barracks pursuant to classification procedures. Not less than 30 days before a prisoner's eligibility date for parole consideration, the report and recommendations of the commandant and classification board are submitted to the Office of the Provost Marshal General.

When the report and recommendations of the commandant and classification board are received in the Department of the Army, they are referred to the Clemency Branch of the Correction Division where they are processed in the same way as clemency recommendations outlined in the preceding section. After being presented by the Clemency Branch case analyst to the Army-Air Force Clemency and Parole Board, and the board's action has been taken thereon, the case is forwarded to the Secretary of the Army, or in the case of Air Force prisoners to the Secretary of the Air Force, for final action.

If parole has been approved, the parole officer assists the inmate in completing his parole plan, and after this has been done the prisoner is given a certificate of parole issued by the Department of the Army and signed by the commandant.

Conditions of Parole

The conditions and terms of parole must be reasonable and constructive, helpful rather than punitive, and flexible rather than rigid in their application. They are designed to promote the parolee's adjustment to his home, employment, and community and assist him to live as a law-abiding citizen.

Parolees remain under the legal custody and control of the commandant of the installation from which paroled, or to whom jurisdiction is transferred, until the expiration of the term or aggregate terms of confinement imposed. While on parole, a parolee is subject to the supervision of a parole advisor, who is an officer of the federal probation service. The parole advisor acts primarily as a guidance counselor to the parolee.

A paroled prisoner who complies with the conditions of his parole is released from the custody of the commandant at the termination of the term or aggregate terms of confinement imposed, as reduced by clemency action.

A parolee who successfully completes his term of parole is furnished a certificate of release from parole signed by the commandant.

CORRECTION—NOT PUNISHMENT

We operate to promote the reformation and rehabilitation of our men with a view to their honorable restoration to military duty, or return to civil life as useful citizens. Our physical plants have been developed over a period of 80 years. Our military police have been trained with proved methods, taken from the most advanced practices of modern penology. Of even greater importance is the fact that our officers and men are career personnel whose professional life takes them through the whole gamut of experience with the lawbreaker. We are in the position, unhampered by politics, to prove that society need not compound a criminal act with vengeance; that a savage act need not be repaid with savagery.

Chapter 7
Review of Relevant Research in Correctional Rehabilitation
DAVID M. PETERSEN AND CHARLES W. THOMAS

Introduction
Theoretical Perspectives on the Effects of Imprisonment
Conclusion
References

INTRODUCTION

The historical absence of a viable rapprochement between correctional practitioners and academic criminologists has substantially reduced both the quantity and quality of research which focuses on the effectiveness of alternative correctional strategies. Practitioners, on one hand, have traditionally viewed criminologists as unwelcome interlopers who seldom appreciate the "real problems" of correctional work, particularly because the criminologists generally lack acceptable practical experience. Indeed, many have come to view criminological research as either useless or as a direct threat to their programs, plans, and positions.[29] On the other hand, criminologists have often accepted similarly negative descriptions of their practitioner counterparts which depict the latter as rather poorly educated, dull, unimaginative creatures whose bureaucratic adherence to archaic rules and tradition have rendered them correctional eunuchs.

To the experienced observer, it is often tempting to write off this conflict as nothing more than another illustration of how egocentric adults become fond of playing juvenile games, each saying to the other, "If you *really* understood what's happening, you'd see things my way, but since you don't it's obvious that you just don't understand." We would certainly concede that a liberal dose of professional narcissism continues to block effective communication between the two groups in question. Unfortunately, each of us could quickly jot down illustrations in which one or both of these stereotypes become apt descriptions of people currently working in these related fields. Some criminologists do embark on research projects with the implicit, sometimes explicit, desire to demonstrate inequities in correctional programs. Many do not devote sufficient attention toward developing an adequate understanding of the daily workings and problems of the organizations within which their research is to be executed. The inability of most researchers to communicate effectively with those in applied fields is amply attested to by the minimal impact which criminological research has had on contemporary correctional practice. By the same token, rare indeed is the practitioner who is wise in the ways of research design, statistical analysis, causal theory, and the related bodies of knowledge which provide the tools of the trade for any criminologist. Far too frequently the criminologist is correct in asserting that both the implementation and evaluation of rehabilitation programs are based on little more than a peculiar potpourri of "gut-level" impressions, speculative observations, vague humanitarian ideals, and a unique sensitivity to that which is politically expedient at state, local, or federal levels.

Our purpose here is not to offer a critique of our fellow criminologists, nor is it to denigrate correctional practitioners. We do, however, suggest that the unusually poor quality of the literature on correctional rehabilitation is a major corollary of the fact that criminologists and practitioners have typically chosen to follow separate, frequently conflicting, routes toward the common goal of providing an explanation of attitudinal, motivational, and behavioral modification. Much of the research which has been done suffers from one or more fundamental defects which greatly detracts from its general utility. For example, only the most superficial attempts have been made at the development and verification of sound correctional theory which could, were it available, direct the focus of both basic research and program design.[9, 10, 14, 19] A direct legacy of this shortcoming has been that the preponderance of empirical research has had little cumulative effect because of its necessarily atheoretical orientation. Further, the level of technical sophistication which is characteristic of correctional research too often falls short of even marginal standards. In this regard, we have found sweeping generalizations founded upon little more than clinical observations of highly selective cases; affirmations of program effectiveness when the statistical data provided showed that the subject programs had little, if any, measurable influence; and the implementation of theoretically sound programs (work release programs are often a prime example) which stipulate such unreasonably stringent admission criteria that only the very best inmates, already prime targets for early parole, could be considered while those who would presumably profit most from the programs are precluded from entry.[2, 5] Moreover, a vast number of research reports provide nothing more than superficial, descriptive information on specific programs which have been implemented with no apparent attempt to outline the more abstract treatment principles which are involved in such a way as to allow consideration of the program or technique in somewhat different settings.

The question which obviously must be raised at this point is whether or not there is some common denominator which links the activities of both practitioner and criminologist. We feel there is, and the primary purpose of this essay is to provide an overview of what appear to be the major dimensions of an emerging tradition of theory and research which could reduce the gap between these two groups. Throughout our discussion the primary focus is on the often noted process of "prisonization" which Donald Clemmer described as the "taking on in greater or less degree of the folkways, mores, customs, and general culture of the penitentiary."[7] One reason for choosing this particular focus is simple. Since Clemmer's pioneering work, criminologists have shown an increasing interest in studying the effects of assimilation into the inmate subculture of the prison. Although this interest has in part been stimulated by a desire to assist in the development of treatment programs which can manipulate or counter the generally negative influences of the inmate subculture, the primary focus has been on the prisonization process as an ideal opportunity to pursue basic research on such central concerns as Edwin Sutherland's theory of differential association[33] and the more inclusive process of adult socialization and resocialization.[4] On the other hand, those working in the field of corrections have long been aware that the system of status and roles, attitudes, and social control maintained by the informal inmate community are more forceful determinants of behavior, attitudes, and self-concept of the individual inmates than are the formal patterns of influence maintained by treatment staff. Practitioners are well aware that any treatment program which they design must be able to overcome the negative influences of prisonization, particularly the negative attitudes toward both correctional staff and treatment programs which are frequently noted as immediate effects of prisonization. Indeed, criminological research has consistently confirmed the hypothesis that the effects of prisonization are so pervasive that the ability to control the direction of its influence may well provide the key to effective rehabilitation. Thus, explanations of prisonization have provided, and will continue to provide, a primary point of mutual interest and concern for both criminologists and practitioners.

THEORETICAL PERSPECTIVES ON THE EFFECTS OF IMPRISONMENT

Although we are all aware of the fact that any explanation of a phenomenon necessarily involves at least an implicit theoretical model, the emergence of clearly formulated correctional theory which might account for variations in the long- and short-term effects of confinement has been a slow and tedious undertaking. Even today, after more than a decade of considerable and sometimes unusually well-funded research, we would be overly generous to say that one or more sound theories are available which provide the basis for adequate explanations or predictions, let alone models which might guide the way to reliable programs of treatment and rehabilitation. Nevertheless, tenable theoretical positions are evolving which hold considerable promise. For convenience we have labeled the two most prominent perspectives the "deprivation model" and the "importation model."[8]

The Deprivation Model

The deprivation model, the first of the two perspectives to draw widespread support, is perhaps best articulated in the work of Gresham Sykes.[34, 35] The defining characteristic of this approach is that it attempts to account for the emergence and maintenance of the inmate subculture in terms of the responses of inmates to their common plight. Salient among what Sykes refers to as the "pains of imprisonment" are the loss of freedom, absence of heterosexual contacts, monotony of routine prison life, management of social stigmatization and the attack on one's self-concept which stigmatization represents, the omnipresent fear which is consequent to living amidst hostile and potentially violent men, and loss of a broad spectrum of goods and services. Proponents of this perspective argue that all inmates face a set of such problems, but further assert that the effective resolution of the problems is not to be found on an individual level. Instead, the recognition of their similar situation provides the cornerstone for an adaptive subcultural response. The greater the stress which is evoked by the common problems which are confronted, the greater the probability of an adaptive response. Given an adaptive response (i.e., the emergence of the inmate subculture), the degree of deprivation becomes mediated or reduced by the degree of integration into the inmate society (prisonization).

The seeming simplicity of this explanation has had much to commend it to both criminologists and correctional practitioners. Specifically, both groups acknowledge the fact that an effective program of rehabilitation presupposes a certain degree of interest, involvement, or commitment among those who become participants in the rehabilitative process. Were all other influences neutral, the requisite levels of what we might term "program legitimation" could presumably be generated within the context of the program. If, however, problems and pressures beyond the immediate context of the program were to foster the development of attitudes, values, and norms which prescribe a uniformly

140 *Fundamentals of Criminal Behavior and Correctional Systems*

negative or hostile stance toward *any* formally designed program, no mode of rehabilitation can be expected to become effective. Thus, if the advocates of the deprivation model are correct, if the commonality of the problems which confront large numbers of similarly situated inmates does provoke the emergence of an oppositional inmate subculture, the apparent failure of seemingly well-designed treatment programs to fulfill their intended function becomes considerably more interpretable. Rather than there being some unrecognized flaw in the design of the program under scrunity, the problem may well lie in the power of the inmate subculture to undermine whatever programs the formal organization of the institution seeks to implement. Ohlin's description of the oppositional orientation of the inmate society provides considerable support for the belief that this is indeed the case:[28]

> This [inmate] code represents an organization of criminal values in clear-cut opposition to the values of conventional society, and to prison officials as representatives of that society. The main tenet of this code forbids any type of supportive or nonexploitative liaison with prison officials. It seeks to confer status and prestige on those inmates who stand most clearly in opposition to the administration. . . . These criminal beliefs and attitudes place a high premium on physical violence and strength, on exploitative sex relations, and predatory attitudes toward money and property. They place a strong emphasis on in-group loyalty and solidarity and on aggressive and exploitative relations with conventionally oriented outgroups. . . . If the code is not actively promoted by the majority of inmates in the prison systems of the United States, it is at least respected and deferred to by them. Deviations from the code entail consequences in the form of the imposition of informal inmate sanctions.

Although limitations of space preclude a thorough review of the research in which operational tests of the deprivation model have been attempted, a brief review of the major findings is instructive. First, a small but very important series of studies have focused on the relationship between patterns of change and both the organizational structures of correctional institutions and the goals which these organizations seek to attain.[3, 15, 18, 23, 32] The logic in support of this type of analysis is straightforward. If it is true that the normative content of the inmate subculture is largely a function of the types of problems which must be resolved by similarly situated groups of inmates, and if a substantial number of these problems are associated with such organizational characteristics as the relative emphasis on custodial control, then variations in organizational structure should elicit different types of informal responses among the inmate population. General support has been found for such hypotheses. As the organizational emphasis shifts from the traditional goals of custody and control to one of treatment and rehabilitation, the negative influences of confinement are either reduced or reversed to positive changes. Obviously one could argue that the altered outcomes of confinement in treatment-oriented institutions is either a reflection of the greater allocation of organizational resources to various rehabilitative functions or that variations in outcome are really a corollary of the different types of individuals who are confined in treatment institutions. In short, it might be argued that the apparent variations in the outcome of imprisonment which are correlated with fluctuations in organizational structure are merely an illusion created by initial differences among the staff and inmates who are assigned to various types of institutions. When such alternative explanations are examined in carefully controlled analysis, however, differences in the effects of imprisonment by type of institution remain.[3] This suggests that variations in organizational structure and goals present quite different problems to the inmate population. Thus, the types of problem resolutions and the types of inmate leaders that might well be effective within a maximum security prison may be poorly suited for the situation of a minimum security institution.

Perhaps the primary significance of these organizational studies of the correctional system is that they represent an attempt to account for the emergence of an inmate society in terms of the basic adaptational problems which are created by the formal organization of the prison. Evidence in support of this perspective clearly demonstrates that a substantial proportion of the factors which either inhibit or promote prosocial changes does not lie, as many have previously argued, in the personality structure of the individual inmate or in the adequacy of a particular rehabilitative strategy. These studies do not, however, provide an explanation of the broad variations in the impact of imprisonment which are to be found within the context of a single institutional structure. Intrainstitutional patterns of attitudinal and behavioral change have nevertheless been the objects of study by proponents of the deprivation model.[7, 11, 34, 42] In these studies the general thesis is that as populations of inmates move in the direction of increased solidarity and cohesiveness, the deprivations associated with confinement decrease. Because the degree of solidarity and cohesiveness found within the inmate subculture is itself viewed as a function of the common problems which confront the inmates, the relative seriousness of various problems to different inmates or groups of inmates becomes a primary point of focus.

Interest in the explanation of intraprison variation in the degree of prisonization has been considerable, particularly during the last decade, and the number of published and unpublished studies is quite large.[13, 20, 38, 39, 40] Fortunately, the logic and basic findings of these analyses may be briefly summarized. Initially, it is important to note that although treatment-oriented correctional institutions may elicit a supportive informal response among the inmate population, the traditional custodial emphasis remains the dominant characteristic of most prisons in this country. Inmates, incumbents of positions at the very bottom of the organizational hierarchy in such institutions, enter a situation in which a high degree of polarization between staff and inmates has already been established. Members of the staff caution newcomers to "do your own time" and encourage conformity to formally prescribed rules, regulations, and routines. The expectations of the inmate hierarchy, however, typically oppose any supportive contacts with members of the staff or the acceptance of the organizational expectations which are articulated by the staff. Obviously the inmate is caught between two opposing worlds, and he is quickly called upon to ascribe his loyalty and allegiance to one or the other lest he elicit negative sanctions from both. The direction of his choice is in large part dependent upon (1) the presence of a viable alternative and (2) the relative importance of the supportive potential of the inmate subculture. In the typical custodial institution, affiliation with the formal organization is often not a potential alternative if for no other reason than the inability of the organization to provide adequate rewards for such affiliation. This implies that the degree of integration or prisonization will become a function of the importance of the inmate subculture to a particular inmate or to a group of inmates. A number of variables have been identified which appear to alter the relative importance of the subculture. First, the longer the sentence which an inmate receives, and therefore the greater the duration of his exposure to the influences of the subculture, the greater the degree of his prisonization.[6, 7, 42] Second, the greater the degree of the inmate's alienation from the formal organization of the prison, the greater the degree of his prisonization.[37] Third, the greater the level of interpersonal involvement with other inmates, the greater the degree of prisonization.[7] Finally, the greater the extent of involvement in illicit activities within the prison, the greater the degree of prisonization.[6]

The Importation Model

Relative to the many lay and pseudo-scientific misconceptions about the factors which affect the probability of prosocial changes occurring as a function of confinement, the deprivation model has much to commend it. Of particular importance, in our opinion, is the fact that it leads us away from the types of clinical perspectives which depict the personality structure of the individual offender as the appropriate locus for rehabilitative efforts, or, for that matter, from the extensions of this logic of individual responsibility which assume that modifications in the individual offender's capability (educational or vocational training, for example) are the panacea.[1, 16, 24, 25] Instead, attention is directed to the fact that the offender occupies a position within the structure of the formal organization of the correctional institution. The formal expectations, informal expectations, and problems which are associated with this position become major forces in shaping the consequences of imprisonment. In brief, one of the key contributions of the deprivation model is that its portrayal of the convict does not view him as being unlike the rest of us in some fundamental way, but instead as one of a group of like-situated individuals who are attempting to adjust in some functional fashion to the immediate contingencies and problems associated with their confinement. Still, a substantial number of flaws which seem inherent in this perspective have restricted its utility and have provided the foundation for an alternative perspective, the importation model.

The initial problem to which the importation model addresses itself is the exceedingly restrictive scope of the deprivation model. Specifically, in relating the emergence and maintenance of the inmate subculture solely to the conditions of imprisonment, the deprivation model implicitly adopts a closed-system paradigm of analysis. Certainly the available research has suggested that the operational goals of correctional institutions and the organizational structures which articulate these goals are of considerable importance. But it would be naive to assume that either the goals or the organizational structures are the product of nothing more than intraorganizational deliberation. Goffman noted this problem dimension some years ago in defining the prison as a "total institution [which] is organized to protect the community against what are felt to be intentional dangers to it, with the welfare of the persons thus sequestered not the immediate issue."[17] Although nominally established to punish the violator, deter potential violators, protect society against additional attacks, and treat or rehabilitate the inmate, prison officials are under the constant scrutiny of legislative bodies and, indirectly, the fad and fashion of public opinion. Because "cons" are stereotypically defined as uniformly aggressive, hostile, and violent, prison officials are under constant pressure to control such highly visible behavior as assaults, escapes, riots, and forced participation in homosexuality. In fact, while prison administrators show increasing support for the rehabilitative ideal, they are well aware that their efficiency is largely measured in terms of their ability to render their institutions "socially invisible."[31] Even in those institutions which emphasize rehabilitation, the notion that "you've gotta keep'm before you can treat'm" is often pervasive. In terms of the deprivation model, this does not mean that the closed-system perspective has no utility, only that it is a distortion of the reality of the situation which can result in the failure to consider a broad spectrum of extraprison variables.

A second point of criticism of the deprivation model is that the form of the response made by the inmate population to the conditions of their confinement does not provide a tenable foundation for explaining the form of the response which is made. In other words, although various problems associated with confinement may provide the stimulus for *some kind* of adaptive response, the *type* of response is not necessarily implied by the type of problem confronted. The typical case of the custodially oriented correctional institution provides an apt illustration. The normative content of the emergent inmate subculture in such settings has generally been described as negativistic and oppositional. Presumably this negativism is one dimension of the adaptive response which a custodial setting elicits. But why? It would be equally functional for the inmates to create a supportive subculture within which values and behavior supportive of the formal organization would be rewarded. Obviously this type of response would be functional in the sense that it would increase the probability of early release via parole, better job assignments, increased privileges, and so on. Once again, the restrictive scope of the deprivation model blocks an adequate explanation.

Finally, proponents of the deprivation model and importation model do not disagree on the assertion that factors within the immediate prison situation are significant determinants of intraprison variations in the impact of imprisonment. But, the advocates of the more general importation model argue, is it reasonable to assume that these are the only factors which affect the outcome of imprisonment?[8, 21, 22, 26, 36, 41]

It should become clear at this point that the importation model is not really an alternative to the deprivation model. Instead, each of these three major points of criticism is directed at facets of the deprivation model which are deficient due to the restrictions which are inherent in any closed-system model. The more inclusive model which is implied by the correction of the shortcomings characteristic of closed-system paradigms defines the scope of the importation model. Three factors become particularly important: preprison, extraprison, and postprison determinants of prisonization. Preprison variables are significant in that they reflect the preprison socialization and experiences which provide the foundation for the content of the inmate subculture. Because adult offenders are disproportionately drawn from the lower socioeconomic groupings and from disadvantaged racial and ethnic minorities, the common preprison experiences and values which the offender brings to the institution provide the foundation for the content of the inmate subculture.[22, 41] Further, once the subculture has emerged, those offenders who enter the prison whose preprison backgrounds are similar to those upon which the inmate subculture is founded are more likely to become readily assimilated or "prisonized" than those from unlike backgrounds. Extraprison influences are of similar importance because they, like variables directly related with the immediate conditions of imprisonment, are significantly associated with the problems which confront the inmate population.[7, 37] The quality of the contacts which inmates maintain with persons in the free society is not within the normal scope of the organization's control, but the isolation which the absence of contacts represents provides an apt illustration of how extraprison variables can create additional problems which in turn stimulate high levels of prisonization. Finally, postprison variables are necessary elements of an adequate explanation of the impact of imprisonment because the relative pressures of confinement are so strongly mediated by each inmate's expectations of his probable life-chances upon release. To the extent that his expectations are positive the priority of the immediate prison situation is lessened, but negative expectations provide still another problem which carries the potential of increased prisonization.[11, 15, 42]

Because the importation model may be viewed as a basic extension of the deprivation model, the entire body of empirical research which has examined hypotheses implied by the deprivation model also provide partial tests of the importation model. Unfortunately, research evidence on the hypothesized associations between factors beyond the context of the prison and patterns of adjustment and change within the prison is minimal. Several basic pieces of research are, however, encouraging. Of particular importance are the series of studies on social role adaptations within the prison[12, 30, 31] and those which have examined the U-curve hypothesis proposed by Stanton Wheeler.[11, 15, 42] The former studies, best developed by Schrag and his students, have shown that movement into the social roles which reflect the social structure of the informal inmate society is associated with a number of preprison variables including family background, socioeconomic status, occupational factors, prior criminal involvement and so on. Thus, while Schrag and others have viewed these interconnected inmate social roles as a reflection of the focal concerns and problems of the inmate society, the resolution of the problem posed by differentials in the type of social role assumed requires the consideration of preprison influences. The latter studies provide a similar stimulus for including noninstitutional variables. In Wheeler's work and other studies which have followed his approach, the general effect of postprison expectations has been explored. He found that those inmates who were farthest from release from confinement were the most prisonized. At first consideration this would appear to be a negation of Clemmer's finding that the longer an inmate was exposed to the influences of the inmate subculture the more extensive his prisonization became.[7] Wheeler, however, did not measure time in terms of the amount already served. Instead, he divided his sample into three groups: those who had served less than six months and who had more than six months remaining to be served; those who had served at least six months and who had more than six months remaining to be served; and those with less than six months remaining to be served. In effect, while Clemmer's measure reflects simply time of exposure, Wheeler's relative measure more closely approximates what Sutherland termed the priority dimension of interpersonal relationships.[33] In terms of our present discussion, the important point is that inmates began to disaffiliate from the inmate society as their point of return to the free society drew near. By invoking Merton's concept of anticipatory socialization,[27] Wheeler not only explained the curvilinear impact of prisonization, but also provided evidence that the postprison world provides a major determinant of prison adjustment.

CONCLUSION

Obviously our commentary has only scratched the surface of the criminological research which has focused on various aspects of the correctional process, and limitations of space have precluded any detailed examination of the relevant empirical research. Still, our purpose has been to examine what we feel to be two general traditions of criminological theory and research on what would appear to be a crucial concern of both criminologists and correctional practitioners. We believe the power of the deprivation perspective lies in its emphasis on the organizational structure of correctional institutions as a generator of deviance within inmate society via the problems which it presents to the inmate society. The strength of the importation approach, however, lies in its attempt to account for the normative content of the inmate subculture and for the differential acceptance of this content among categories of inmates. It should be carefully noted, however, that these two perspectives are not opposing explanations of the same phenomena. To the contrary, they are more appropriately viewed as complementary perspectives with variant points of primary emphasis.

The rationale for our interest in these two lines of inquiry is simple when evaluated in terms of its importance for programs which seek to initiate processes of adult resocialization, rehabilitation, or treatment. Briefly put, it is far too easy for those interested in the correctional process to operate within the necessarily narrow focus of their respective fields of specialization. But the therapeutic environment of a counselor's office, the sheltered context of group counseling sessions, and the practicality of solid vocational training programs are merely parts of the overall context within which the correctional process in its totality is to be found. None can be so powerful, perhaps so presumptuous, that they can hope to become effective in isolation from the broader context within which they exist. Fortunately or unfortunately, this broader context is in part the domain of the inmate society. Should the normative system of this society dictate opposition, hostility, and a manipulative orientation towards those who seek to initiate change, even the most elegant program is virtually predestined to abject failure.

REFERENCES

1. Abramsen, D.: *Crime and the Human Mind*. New York, Columbia University Press, 1944.
2. Ayer, W. A.: Work-release programs in the United States: Some difficulties encountered. *Federal Probation*, 34 (No. 1):53-56, 1970.
3. Berk, B.: Organizational goals and inmate organization. *American Journal of Sociology*, 71:522-534, 1966.
4. Brim, O. G., Jr., and Wheeler, S.: *Socialization After Childhood: Two Essays*. New York, John Wiley, 1966.
5. Case, J. D.: "Doing time" in the community. *Federal Probation*, 31 (No. 1):9-17, 1967.
6. Clemmer, D.: Observations on imprisonment as a source of criminality. *Journal of Criminal Law and Criminology*, 41:311-319, 1950.
7. Clemmer, D.: *The Prison Community*. New York, Holt, Rinehart and Winston, 1958. [Original issue, Boston, Christopher, 1940.]
8. Cline, H.: Determinants of normative patterns in correctional institutions. In N. Christie (Ed.): *Scandinavian Studies in Criminology*, Vol. 2. Oslo, Universitetsforlaget, 1968, pp. 173-184.
9. Cloward, R., et al.: *Theoretical Studies in Social Organization of the Prison*. Pamphlet No. 15. New York, Social Science Research Council, 1960.
10. Cressey, D. R. (Ed.): *The Prison: Studies in Institutional Organization and Change*. New York, Holt, Rinehart and Winston, 1961.
11. Garabedian, P. G.: Social roles and processes of socialization in the prison community. *Social Problems*, 11:139-152, 1963.
12. Garrity, D. L.: The prison as a rehabilitation agency. In D. R. Cressey (Ed.): *The Prison: Studies in Institutional Organization and Change*. New York, Holt, Rinehart and Winston, 1961, pp. 358-380.
13. Giallombardo, R.: *Society of Women: A Study of a Women's Prison*. New York, John Wiley, 1966.
14. Gibbons, D. C.: *Changing the Lawbreaker: The Treatment of Delinquents and Criminals*. Englewood Cliffs, N. J., Prentice-Hall, 1965.
15. Glaser, D.: *The Effectiveness of a Prison and Parole System*. Indianapolis, Bobbs-Merrill, 1964.
16. Glueck, S., and Glueck, E. T.: *Delinquents in the Making*. New York, Harper and Brothers, 1952.

17. Goffman, E.: On the characteristics of total institutions: The inmate world. In D. R. Cressey (Ed.): *The Prison: Studies in Institutional Organization and Change.* New York, Holt, Rinehart and Winston, 1961, pp. 15-67.
18. Grusky, O.: Role conflict in organization: A study of prison camp officials. *Administrative Science Quarterly,* 3:452-472, 1959.
19. Hazelrigg, L. (Ed.): *Prison Within Society.* Garden City, N. Y., Doubleday, 1968.
20. Hughes, P. H., Floyd, C. M., Norris, G., and Silva, G. E.: Organizing the therapeutic potential of an addict prisoner community. *The International Journal of the Addictions,* 5:205-223, 1970.
21. Irwin, J.: *The Felon.* Englewood Cliffs, N. J., Prentice-Hall, 1970.
22. Irwin, J., and Cressey, D. R.: Thieves, convicts and the inmate culture. *Social Problems,* 10:142-155, 1962.
23. Kassebaum, G., Ward, D. A., and Wilner, D. M.: *Prison Treatment and Parole Survival: An Empirical Assessment.* New York, John Wiley, 1971.
24. Levy, R. J.: *Reductions in Recidivism Through Therapy.* New York, Seltzer, 1941.
25. Lindner, R.: *Rebel Without a Cause.* New York, Grune and Stratton, 1944.
26. Mathiesen, T.: *Across the Boundaries of Organizations: An Exploratory Study of Communication Patterns in Two Penal Institutions.* Berkeley, Glendessary, 1971.
27. Merton, R. K.: *Social Theory and Social Structure.* (Revised and Enlarged Edition) Glencoe, Ill., Free Press, 1957.
28. Ohlin, L. E.: *Sociology and the Field of Corrections.* New York, Russell Sage, 1956.
29. Schnur, A. C.: Some reflections on the role of correctional research. *Law and Contemporary Problems,* 23:772-783, 1958.
30. Schrag, C. C.: Leadership among prison inmates. *American Sociological Review,* 19:37-42, 1954.
31. Schrag, C.: Some foundations for a theory of correction. In D. R. Cressey (Ed.): *The Prison: Studies in Institutional Organization and Change.* New York, Holt, Rinehart and Winston, 1961, pp. 309-357.
32. Street, D., Vinter, R. D., and Perrow, C.: *Organization for Treatment: A Comparative Study of Institutions for Delinquents.* New York, Free Press, 1966.
33. Sutherland, E. H., and Cressey, D. R.: *Criminology,* 8th Ed. Philadelphia, Lippincott, 1970.
34. Sykes, G. M.: *The Society of Captives: A Study of a Maximum Security Prison.* Princeton, Princeton University Press, 1958.
35. Sykes, G. M., and Messinger, S. L.: The inmate social system. In R. Cloward, *et al.: Theoretical Studies in Social Organization of the Prison.*

Pamphlet No. 15. New York, Social Science Research Council, 1960, pp. 5-19.
36. Thomas, C. W.: Toward a more inclusive model of the inmate contraculture. *Criminology*, 8:251-262, 1970.
37. Thomas, C. W., and Miller, M. J.: Adult resocialization in coercive organizations: A case study of self-defeating organizational structures. Paper presented at the meeting of the Eastern Sociological Society, New York, April 1971.
38. Tittle, C. R.: Inmate organization: Sex differentiation and the influence of criminal subcultures. *American Sociological Review*, 34:492-505, 1969.
39. Tittle, C. R., and Tittle, D. P.: Social organization of prisoners: An empirical test. *Social Forces*, 43:216-221, 1964.
40. Tittle, C. R., and Tittle, D. P.: Structural handicaps to therapeutic participation: A case study. *Social Problems*, 13:75-82, 1965.
41. Wellford, C. F.: Factors associated with the adoption of the inmate code: A study of normative socialization. *Journal of Criminal Law, Criminology and Police Science*, 58:197-203, 1967.
42. Wheeler, S.: Socialization in correctional communities. *American Sociological Review*, 26:697-712, 1961.

PART TWO

Criminal Typology

Typologies and Treatment

Characteristics of the Juvenile Delinquent

Characteristics of the Female Offender

Not Less than Two nor More than Six

Effects of Incarceration

Psychiatry in Corrections

The Role of Higher Education in the Correctional Program

Chapter 8

Criminal Typology

JULIAN ROEBUCK

Introduction
Suggested Typological Schema
Basic Assumptions
Methodology
Analysis of the Drug Pusher-Pimp Pattern on the Ten Dimensions of
    Study
Notes and References

INTRODUCTION

The elusive quest for an all-inclusive a priori typology by which criminal behavior can be predicted or explained has long intrigued laymen, literary men, lawyers, judges, penologists, and scholars in the physical and social sciences. Usually one's orientation foretells his classificatory schema and makes for etiological approaches to crime and delinquency that are varied, if not often contradictory and inadequate. With the development of the discipline of criminology and a plethora of research in the area of causation and treatment, many scholars have attempted to construct testable typologies of delinquents and criminals. These classification systems are of three types:[1] (1) empirical typologies, (2) ideal typologies, and (3) synthetic typologies; and they are geared toward the management, treatment, or etiological understanding of delinquents and criminals.

Systems of offender classification in the literature may be grouped in several ways depending upon the dimensions of study selected by the classifier for his typological system, namely, probability approaches, reference group typologies, behavior classifications, psychiatric-oriented approaches, social perception and interaction classifications, eclectic approaches, and cross-tabulation typologies.[2]

SUGGESTED TYPOLOGICAL SCHEMA

I propose that a behavior classification based on frequency of arrest pattern (translated into legal offense categories) be devised for a specific, incarcerated juvenile delinquent, or criminal offender population group. This suggestion is based on the hypothesis that specific patterns of criminality result from rather specific sets of social and psychological background variables, and that variables common to a particular pattern of criminality would be found to vary significantly from those common to other offender types. Past research indicates that this is the case.[3]

This initial step would designate offender types which then could be analyzed (and compared and contrasted) in terms of ten dimensions of study encompassing pertinent sociological and psychological variables:[4]

1. *Demographic variables:* (a) Age. (b) Marital status. (c) Educational level.

2. *Offense behavior and interactional setting:* (a) Time of onset; nature, number and types of official and unofficial delinquent and criminal acts (including adventitious, irresponsible, occasional, opportunistic, and planned acts). (b) Skills and levels of *modi operandi* utilized in delinquent and criminal acts. (c) Time periods between juvenile and criminal acts. (d) Versatility of offense pattern relating to criminal acts against property and persons. (e) Utilization of force or violence (with and without weapons) in the commitment of delinquent and criminal acts. (f) Solitary acts; group acts with juvenile gang, criminal gang, mob, or syndicate. (g) Role in delinquent and criminal groups; e.g. leader or follower. Specific criminal role; e.g. "rod man," "wheel man," "dealer," "pimp," etc. (h) Juvenile delinquent and criminal behavior techniques and skills; how, when, and under what circumstances these techniques and skills were developed.

3. *Group support of delinquent and/or criminal behavior:* (a) Frequency and duration of association with delinquent or criminal groups. (b) Similarity of subject's norms to those of the delinquent or criminal group norms. (c) Prescribed and proscribed behavior of delinquent or criminal groups to which sub-

ject belongs. (d) Subject's delinquent and criminal behavior supported by group norms of delinquent and criminal groups. (e) Status (and how gained) of subject within the delinquent or criminal group. (f) The relative integration of delinquent or criminal groups to which subject belongs. (g) The degree of integration of subject into delinquent or criminal group.

4. *Correctional processing:* (a) Police contacts. (b) Arrests. (c) Adjudications. (d) Dispositions and commitments. (e) Adjustment during commitment, probationary status, or parole status.

5. *Orientation and reference groups:* (a) Type of family background. (b) Social class. (c) Occupational group. (d) Ethnic groups. (e) Delinquent or criminal subculture.

6. *Self concept:* (a) Self image; i.e. what the actor believes about himself and how he describes himself to himself. (b) Self demands; i.e. what the subject aspires to be and what he expects of himself. (c) Self judgment; i.e. the result of comparisons between self image and self demands. It may involve pride or guilt, self-acceptance or rejection, self-satisfaction or hatred.

7. *Attitudes:* (a) Attitudes toward basic social institutions; e.g. the family, government, economic system, etc. (b) Attitudes toward the administration of criminal justice; i.e. law enforcement machinery, judicial processes, and correctional institutions. (c) Attitudes toward "squares" and "straight society." (d) Attitudes toward personal criminal pattern.

8. *Organic variables:* (a) General health. (b) Amputations, deformities, crippling diseases, head injuries. (c) Epilepsy, brain damage, encephalitis, abnormal brain waves (determined by EEG's), abnormal chromosomal structure (e.g. XYY chromosomes). (d) Somatotype (ascertained by William Sheldon's methodology).

9. *Personality structure:* (a) IQ. (b) Personality profile as determined by objective-type tests; e.g. MMPI (Minnesota Multiphasic Personality Inventory); personality profile designated by projective techniques; e.g. Rorschach Test. (c) Clinical personality profile resulting from clinical psychologist and/or psychiatrist's interview findings. (d) Conditionability determined by laboratory behavior conditioning tests (for explanation of condi-

tioning tests see H. J. Eysenck: *Crime and Personality*. Boston, Houghton Mifflin Company, 1964, pp. 40-43).

10. *Delinquent or criminal role career:* (a) Degree of criminal processing; criminal progression. (b) Criminal status level; e.g. occasional offender, ordinary criminal career, professional criminal, organized criminal. (c) Seriously mentally maladjusted criminal.

Obviously the variables listed within the ten dimensions represent an extended proliferation and some characteristics among them may be more precisely measured than others. Time and resources would probably preclude exact measurement of all these characteristics. The typologist of whatever persuasion could eliminate some of the variables dependent upon his needs and research resources.

The suggested typological schema endeavors (1) to provide a reliable set of general summary statements on several subcategories of offenders; and, (2) to enable researchers to compare and contrast several different types of offenders. Hopefully it would serve those who are interested in etiology, management, and treatment.

BASIC ASSUMPTIONS

Heretofore many criminologists have assumed that criminals may be differentiated from noncriminals without the necessity of first finding out how criminals differ from one another. This has led to a false dichotomy of criminals versus noncriminals as comprising two homogeneous groupings. No wonder some criminologists claim that their findings or the findings of others, reveal no significant differences in personality type between criminals and noncriminals.[5] Granted that some criminologists have demonstrated that offenders as a class share some psychological and sociological characteristics (as do noncriminals), this finding does not preclude significant differences among offenders. What are these differences, and on what behavior and personality dimensions may they be measured?

The cardinal assumption underlying the proposed typology in this paper is that patterned, arrest history labels (legal labels) may be used to classify both crimes and criminals; i.e. behavior categories as types may be constructed within the confines of legal categories (e.g. armed robbers, narcotic drug laws offenders, assaulters, etc.); and, that these legal categories vary significantly on social and psychological dimensions. The hypothetical classification schema is based on the following postulates:

1. The study of patterned behavior is the chief province of behavioral scientists and criminologists who are concerned with the explanation of human behavior.

2. Persons who are officially adjudicated criminals or delinquents are frequently ones who are involved in recidivistic and serious acts of law violation. Adjudicated offenders therefore offer an adequate base for criminal typologists' study samples.

3. There are variations among adjudicated offenders in the type and intensity of the criminal or delinquent role. These divergencies comprise variations in offense behavior as well as related social-psychological characteristics. Some offenders have a self-image as a criminal or delinquent. Others do not. Some offenders conceive of themselves as professional criminals. Others do not. Some offenders possess criminal skills and techniques and enjoy a status in the underworld. Others including occasional and amateur criminals are without these prerequisites and may "moonlight" at some-time criminal activities. On the other hand some persistent and professional criminals may moonlight at times at legitimate pursuits.[6]

4. Many offenders close on certain types of criminal activity during their career spans, albeit at one time or another they might commit several different types of crime. Stable patterns of criminal behavior may be accompanied by uniform social-psychological characteristics; i.e., certain social and psychological types close on certain patterns of criminal activity.

5. Behavioral and social-psychological changes may occur during the development of specific criminal career spans; however, these changes are limited and identifiable.

6. Criminal behavior has many causes. The sociological and psychological approaches (in combination) to criminal etiology are currently the most fruitful approaches. Recent genetic break-

throughs in the mechanism of heredity (e.g. abnormal chromosomal structure)[7] may enhance the etiological importance of the constitutional approach to crime causation. In fact, twin studies and EEG studies on psychopaths lend indirect support to the importance of constitutional factors in human behavior. Constitutional factors do not directly cause crime, but they limit behavior and they may propel some people into deviant behaviors. Certainly those suffering from genetic or constitutional disorders (abnormalities or subnormalities) are organically less well equipped to meet the demands of any normative structure than those not so encumbered. The constitutional dimension is provided for herein.

The sociological-psychological process that leads to one specific type of criminal career includes several causal variables and differs from that process which leads to another type of criminal career. The search for any overall cause or causes of crime is fruitless. The quest must be directed toward the causes of specific criminal patterns; e.g. the child molester shares no motivation with the armed robber.

7. Criminal typologies must include the explicit use of legal nomenclature and give special emphasis to criminal careers. The accessible official data concerned with official criminal histories exist in terms of legal nomenclature; i.e. arrests and convictions by criminal charges; and the criminal code contains more specific, hence more operational definitions of criminal behavior than any set of nonlegal categories.[8]

8. An interdisciplinary approach is necessary to any meaningful classificatory attempt.

METHODOLOGY

Preliminary Considerations

First, then, it is suggested that arrest patterns be ascertained from a longitudinal study of the known criminal offenses charged to a random sample of incarcerated offenders as revealed in their (individual) arrest histories. A type theory in which criminals are differentiated according to a single (usually most recent) offense has an extreme disadvantage because offenders show some variability in their offenses. Labeling a man as "armed robber type" on the basis of his most recent crime, even though he has had a long previous history as a con man, is unlikely to lead to any large amount of useful knowledge. By contrast, the proposed arrest history typology is based on the configuration of total known arrests for various criminal charges. The arrest history, a longitudinal measure of behavior, allows the investigator to observe the existence of a fixed pattern of criminal behavior, if any such pattern exists. An offender whose official arrest history shows nine robbery charges out of a total of twelve arrests may be taken as a hypothetical case. Classifying similar sequences of arrests on other charges, e.g. assault, drunkenness, housebreaking, etc. makes it possible to assign individual criminals to criminal pattern categories.

One of the basic assumptions underlying this typology is that arrest patterns will indicate a particular pattern of behavior or criminal career. If noncriminals manifest a pattern in their legal activities, then the logic of contemporary behavioral theory leads us to assume that the illegal activities of the criminal must also manifest an identifiable pattern. The typology is designed to classify criminals in terms of illegal careers as revealed in cumulative arrest histories. The most frequent charge or charges in the total arrest history of the subject is the basis for classification. The charges appearing in the later phases of the criminal's arrest history are given greater weight, since later entries would reflect more accurately the current state of his criminal development than would those entries occurring in his earlier arrest history.

It is certainly legitimate to question, as has been done by criminologists, the validity of differentiating between criminals on the basis of legal rather than behavioral categories. If legal criminal categories were only legal categories, any criticism would certainly be justified. However, studies by the author show that a considerable number of behavioral differences exist between groups of individuals with different arrest patterns, while the backgrounds of individuals within a specific category of arrest patterns have a good deal in common.[9] Thus, arrest patterns appear to be behavioral, as well as legal, categories of offenders. The fact that significant differences exist between arrest-pattern groups seems sufficient reason to follow this approach to criminal typology further. Of course similar motivations may provoke dissimilar behaviors at times; however, a consistent pattern of similar behaviors does indicate (in part) similar motivations.

Understandably, this index, because it is a product of official records, does not account for all the crimes committed by the subject in his criminal career. No offender is apprehended for every crime he commits; and, the offender may not be guilty of all the crimes he is charged with. However, the principal advantage in the use of arrest records stems from the fact, as Sutherland and Cressey (among others) have noted, that the further one gets away from a criminal's arrest history, the more obscure and distorted become the facts of his criminal activities.[10] Certainly, one would hesitate to use the offender's own story about his past offenses as a primary and exclusive typological criterion. Researchers have noted the reluctance of many offenders to divulge their unknown unofficial criminal activities. In any event, offenders' stories about their unreported criminal activities to the author during past research interviews, indicate an unofficial pattern of crime parallel to official arrest history pattern.

Several academic criminologists have made a limited use of the arrest histories of certain offender types for purposes of illustration and interpretation,[11] while institutional caseworkers and parole and probation officers have also made use of the arrest history in discussing criminal careers, and in developing the case histories of offenders. The police have recognized the importance of arrest history analysis. Some criminals often concentrate on one type of crime and, in fact, may specialize on a certain technique, or *modus operandi*, within this type. The technique may be significant in determining the direction of police investigation. In many instances, in fact, the police in large cities have combined or cross-filed their *modus operandi* files with their "rap sheets," in a rough attempt at classifying by criminal type those who have been arrested. Most large law enforcement agencies have appropriately titled spaces on the reverse side of their fingerprint blanks for noting the specific techniques used in the commission of each specific crime.[12] Given a filling station holdup by a lone-wolf bandit wearing a stocking over his face, the police investigator may well check his "m.o. file" and then begin to check up on the whereabouts of criminals who specialize in this form of activity.

The Arrest History Analysis Instrument

The instrument herein presented was developed empirically from an adult arrest history analysis of a sample of 400 inmates serving time at the District of Columbia Reformatory (actually a penitentiary) at Lorton, Virginia.[13] Thirteen arrest patterns were clearly and readily delineated with this device.[14] Therefore, it is reasoned that the following technique of analysis is applicable to other correctional population groups.

1. *Single Pattern.* This label is attached to an arrest history which shows a high frequency of one kind of criminal charge, e.g. robbery. In order for a history to be classified as a single pattern, it has to satisfy one of the following conditions: (a) It has to show three or more arrests, all of which are for the same charge, or (b) an arrest history which contains at least four arrests for a given charge and additional arrests for other charges is divided into three sections and qualifies for a single pattern if at least one of the four or more arrests for a given charge appears in the last section of the arrest history, and if the charge constitutes at least 33 percent of those charges which occur in the last two sections of the arrest history.

Obviously, not all numbers are divisible by three. When the number of arrests cannot be divided into three equal sections, the latter sections are given more weight. Following are four examples of how arrest patterns are ascertained.

Example 1. An arrest history with an incidence of four arrests is divided into three sections—1, 1 and 2. The first arrest (that arrest appearing first on an offender's rap sheet) constitutes the first section, the second arrest the second section and the last two arrests the third section. If all four arrests are for robbery, this arrest history would show a single pattern of robbery. If all four arrests in this instance were not for one criminal charge, the arrest history would show "mixed pattern."

Example 2. An arrest history containing five arrests is divided into three sections—1, 2 and 2. The first arrest constitutes the first section, the second and third arrests the second section and the fourth and fifths arrests the third section. Hypothetically, if the charge for the first arrest is robbery, the second arrest housebreaking, and the third, fourth and fifth arrests robbery, we would have a pattern of robbery.

Example 3. An arrest history containing seven arrests is divided into three sections—2, 2 and 3. The first two arrests constitute the first section, the next two arrests the second section and the last three arrests the third section. Hypothetically, if the charges for the first two arrests are for housebreaking, the third for robbery, the fourth for housebreaking and the last three for robbery, a pattern of robbery is demonstrated.

Example 4. An arrest history with ten arrests is divided into three sections—3, 3 and 4. The first three arrests comprise the first section, the fourth, fifth, and sixth arrests the second section and the seventh, eighth, ninth and tenth arrests the third section. Hypothetically, if the charge for the first arrest is assault, the second arrest disorderly conduct, the third arrest drunkenness, the fourth arrest drunkenness, the fifth arrest assault, the sixth arrest drunkenness, the seventh arrest assault, the eighth arrest petty theft, the ninth arrest drunkenness and the tenth arrest assault, this would constitute a double pattern of drunkenness and assault.

2. *Multiple Pattern.* An arrest history of two or more single patterns derived by the procedures set forth in Item 1 above.

3. *Mixed Pattern.* An arrest history of three or more arrests in which none of the charges forms a frequency pattern as defined above ("Jack-of-all-trades").

4. *No Pattern.* An arrest history of only one or two arrests. This is a residual category of those offenders with insufficient arrests to warrant analysis.

Despite the fact that the overwhelming number of incarcerated offenders are recidivists with fairly lengthy arrest histories, some successful professional criminals, and some successful organized criminals are occasionally found in correctional institutions without lengthy arrest histories—and these therefore could not be adequately classified by the proposed arrest history analysis. These residuals would have to be classified by other methods. Of course, in all probability, the dimensions of analysis listed under Typological Schema earlier in this chapter would help in this direction, especially dimensions 2, 3, 5, 6, 7, and 10.

For illustrative purposes, one criminal composite pattern found recently by the author on the basis of the preceding arrest history schema follows. This category comprises a group of 15 drug pusher-pimps incarcerated at an eastern penitentiary. The drug pusher-pimps arrest histories disclosed a clear-cut double pattern of narcotics drug law charges (sale), and arrests for procuring and/or "pimping." Scattered throughout these arrest histories were occasional charges for bad checks, short con games, and possession of stolen property. All offenders in this arrest group category had juvenile delinquency records; however, the official adult arrest records were used (exclusively) in determining arrest history pattern, drug pusher-pimp.

ANALYSIS OF THE DRUG PUSHER-PIMP PATTERN ON THE TEN DIMENSIONS OF STUDY

1. *Demographic variables:* Subjects consisted of a group of young adults (median age 30) without marital ties (eight single, and seven divorced or separated) operating at a SAT grade level of 10.5.

2. *Offense behavior and interactional setting:* These street peddlers systematically sold drugs (heroin, amphetamines, and barbiturates) via direct contacts to regular neighborhood users. Sales were made from the peddlers' apartments, back alleys, public men's rooms situated in poolrooms, hotels, restaurants, and bars. Customers were usually drug addicts and petty offenders (e.g. thieves, burglars, shoplifters, etc.). Prostitutes working within the drug pusher-pimp's stable peddled drugs for him to her customers (johns) and to other neighborhood users and street hustlers.

Subjects generally picked up small supplies of drugs at irregular intervals from an "unknown" seller whom they claimed to know only by a first-name telephone voice. Pickup spots (drops where the retail pushers picked up their drug supply) were frequently changed. They claimed no knowledge of the wholesaler's source. Moreover, all insisted that they did not belong to any organized ring of drug pushers; that they worked from an individual neighborhood base, though they admitted acquaintanceships with other neighborhood drug pushers and the occasional borrowing of drugs from one another to meet local neighborhood demands. The official records, correctional admission summary materials, and district attorney's reports confirmed (for the most part) these claims. Five offenders appeared to belong to well-organized retail drug rings. Whether these rings were syndicated remains a moot question—probably not.

All offenders on a part-time or full-time basis employed and supervised street prostitutes and small-time call girls ranging in number from three to ten. They directly and indirectly procured customers for their girls (via cab drivers, poolroom hustlers, poolroom managers, bartenders, bellhops, restaurant waiters, restaurant and bar managers, short con men, street hustlers). Arrangements, in terms of working conditions, rules of conduct (e.g. never get drunk or stoned on drugs with a trick), organization, and payoffs with the prostitutes varied from formal (in the sense of clearcut verbal agreements) to informal "understood" working agreements. The overwhelming number of these prostitutes were drug users (usually speed and downers) primarily dependent upon the drug pusher-pimp for drugs. Approximately one third were heroin users. Subjects obtained and paid for work site permissions (for the prostitutes) in bars, restaurants, and hotel lobbies; arranged fixes with the police; provided bail after arrests; hired and financed lawyers for court cases; furnished the girls money when they did time; acted as money lenders; occasionally escorted the prostitutes to bars and restaurants during nonwork hours; infrequently posed as surrogate boyfriends.

Though working arrangements, understandings, division of labor, mutual aid, and rational objectives (making money) characterized the liaison between drug pusher-pimps and prostitutes, the professional alliances were tenuous and there was a high degree of turnover among the prostitutes. Many girls drifted in and out of the work alliance without abiding by rigid rules relating to entrance requirements or termination agreements. In fact, informal understandings were frequently misunderstood or broken by parties of the first and second parts. Subjects rarely utilized consistent, formal methods of enforcement. When codes were broken by the prostitutes, they were "kissed off," i.e. refused any kind of future support, employment or association. When the prostitutes felt they were being treated unfairly, they simply moved on to other neighborhoods. Examples of working agreement violations by the prostitutes included failure to provide the drug pusher-pimp with his appropriate cut; "stiffing" on drug payments (welching on drug debts); "balling" for fun (having intercourse without charging for it); retaining an excess profit on drug sales; refusing or failing to fill dates with "tricks" arranged by the pimp; absenteeism from work; failing to keep in contact with the pimp; getting stoned with customers and therefore "giving the snatch without the cash." The subjects reported that girls who persisted in these violations acquired a "bad reputation" throughout the hustling world, and consequently "lost their license to practice" with pimps. They stated that the prostitute's fear of losing her license usually kept her in line.

In addition to selling drugs and "pimping," subjects occasionally acted as go-between-men between fences and shoplifters, i.e. they placed would-be sellers of stolen property in contact with criminal fences and consequently received a "finders fee" (from both parties).

These offenders, well versed in the argot of the hustling underworld, evinced verbal skills far beyond their educational level and prided themselves on their ability to con and manipulate people, i.e. prostitutes, johns, the police, competitors, drug purchasers, hotel, restaurant and bar owners, lawyers, etc. They formed a group of street-wise, non-violent hipsters who maintained that their native ability, sophistication, "cool cat" front and repertory of tricks, powers of deception, knowledge of feminine psychology, and dressing ability (wearing stylish clothing) enabled them to ply their trade. They disclaimed any consistent use of force, which they abhorred, or the utilization of weapons. Infrequently they (physically) pushed around recalcitrant and erring prostitutes, and occasionally hired "bully boys" to work them over lightly.

The juvenile records of these offenders disclosed an early entry (age 10 to 13) into delinquent careers: beginning with sneak thefts (from parents, neighbors, stores, school lockers), school truancy, use of marijuana (age 14 to 15), peddling marijuana, amphetamines, and barbiturates (age 16 to 18); and culminating (as young adults) with the buying and selling of stolen property, "pimping," and the sale of heroin. All at one time or another in their juvenile or criminal careers, "chipped" around with various types of drugs (exclusive for the most part of LSD and heroin). Only three were heroin addicts, and they claimed to have controlled their intake while hustling within bounds, i.e. they disavowed ever being "strung out" with a bad habit. Hashish, methedrine, and cocaine were their adult drugs of choice. None were problem drinkers, and they eschewed and avoided heavy drinkers whom they termed "rowdies," "fools," "heat bringers," "thugs."

The following quote illustrates their rationale in reference to drugs and working demeanor:

> An occasional drink is all right now and then. And of course a little hash, speed or cocaine if you are in bed with a broad. Never be a hog and get "strung out." To be a success in any hustle on the street you have to be careful, very careful with booze and drugs. Otherwise you turn into a sucker, a john, and all that love shit, and a customer not a dealer. You have to keep your cool and know what's happening at all times. When you get too tired without sleep, a little speed helps. Hustling is hard work. But never be a hog.

Most of them (12) as juveniles belonged loosely to near-group predatory (thieving) gangs. None were gang leaders and most of their juvenile delinquent offenses were committed as loners. They claim to have met and attached themselves to older hustlers (pool hustlers, prostitutes, fences, con men, pimps, and drug pushers) quite early in their careers (age 17 to 21) via poolroom, bowling alley, bar, pawn shop, and street contacts—and to have learned pimping and drug pushing techniques from them. Typical comments of one pusher indicate a tutorship:

> I found out early that you don't learn how to hustle from a bunch of gang thugs and young fools. Violence leads to small scores and to many busts. I always liked to run with older dudes who know what was happening . . . who could teach me a sweet hustle behind some bread.

Significantly enough most of these men (12) were pool hustlers at one time or another in their careers. These recorded comments designate this significance:

> Man if you know how to play pool you learn how to play all kinds of marks. You know, you have to learn how to make a game, you know, and never show your true speed. The same rules apply to other hustles. Of course you don't make big bread no matter how good a stick you are, but you learn a lot.

They were sexually precocious and promiscuous. Sexual interaction for the most part began and ended with casual relationships with juvenile promiscuous girls and prostitutes. Moreover, they insisted that they were born with a technique for handling women, and that sexual techniques and prowess were not the answer to their "success" with women. Their mental set toward women, their inability or unwillingness to feel emotion in a heterosexual relationship, and their con techniques and shrewdness in female selection probably explains their "success" with women. This point is confirmed by these statements frequently recorded in the interviews:

> Women are nothing but money holes. Keep your mind on the money not on the honey. Don't get strung out on any chick. Stay away from hard headed square broads. Stick to hustling chicks who can understand you. And forget forever all that love jazz. Stick with chicks who know where it's at between their legs, and what it's for . . . money. You don't have to be a great lover with a forked tongue or a big stud man. All you have to know is how to sweet talk them into making some bread. You get a woman really strung out on you and all you have to do is blow in her ear and she will come all over herself, and eventually make you some money too. Aways keep them guessing and play them cool.

3. *Group support of delinquent and/or criminal behavior:* These interviewees experienced an early and continuous association with juvenile delinquents and criminals. Their norms and behavior patterns were supported by and parallel to the norms and behavior patterns of drug pusher-pimps, con men, and other street hustlers who live by their wits. They had achieved and maintained a moderate level of status among a loose confederation of neighborhood street hustlers. They defined the human universe in two classes: hustlers or operators vs. suckers or marks; and subscribed to the dictum that only "slobs, fools and dumb squares work for a living." They expressed a sense of belonging to a category of successful cool hustlers—a category defined by them as a group of superior, knowledgeable, prestigious professionals who usually avoided hassles with lesser criminals and the police. Finally, they verbalized contempt for the heavy rackets and violent criminals.

At intermittent intervals they belonged to small working groups[15] of criminals including themselves and prostitutes; themselves and other drug pusher-pimps, prostitutes, criminal fences, shoplifters, poolroom hustlers, and gamblers. Though they were reluctant to discuss in a precise fashion the details of their criminal alliances beyond the pimp-prostitute nexus, their remarks and the official records indicated a loose confederation of mutual aiders and temporary criminal partnerships (on a piece basis) in this direction. They were thoroughly integrated into the lower echelons of the underworld; and they claimed high status among their confederation of peers.

4. *Correctional processing:* All of these men had frequent police contacts (a median of ten as juveniles) and arrests (a median of five as juveniles and 15 as adults). All had been placed on probation at least once as juveniles or as adults. Five had been commited to juvenile institutions. All had served misdemeanor sentences; five had served previous felony sentences. They managed to maintain "adequate adjustments" in probationary, incarceration, and parole statuses. Those incarcerated were "model prisoners," because of (a) their ability to manipulate other prisoners as well as prison officials, and (b) their eschewing of violence.

5. *Orientation and reference groups:* Subjects were for the most part products of unstable and broken, urban, lower middle class (working class) noncriminal families. Parental nationality was mixed. All had worked at one time or another at street trades (delivery boys, newspaper boys, golf course caddies, stable boys, etc.). Most could type and all were equipped with clerical skills. At brief intervals as young adults, most had irregularly worked as used car salesmen, clothing salesmen, street and house to house peddlers. All designated underworld hustlers as their chief reference groups. They described successful hustlers as intelligent, generous, well dressed (silk and mohair suits, expensive alligator shoes, flashy jewelry), property owners (poolrooms, apartment houses, hotels, bars), who enjoyed a leisurely, playboy existence.

6. *Self concept:* These subjects viewed themselves as clever, intelligent, generous, sophisticated hustlers, who for fortuitous reasons beyond their control (bad luck) had taken a few falls (busts). They aspire to be more successful hustlers with higher status in the underworld than they now enjoy. Though relatively satisfied with themselves as they are, they are keenly aware of their status as inmates. And though attributing this status to luck, their stories disclosed that they know about many professional mistakes, e.g. trusting unreliable confederates; unsuccessful attempts to bribe various officials; unsuccessful attempts to negotiate drug fixes, etc. They look forward to establishing themselves more securely in the underworld, i.e. becoming more financially affluent and prestigious. They aspire to make more money illegally, maintain a high standard of living (lavish apartments, good-looking broads, expensive cars, unlimited resources to gamble and throw parties with, etc.), and simultaneously remain out of jail. As a group they embodied a conceited, egocentric, outwardly self-contained, highly aspiring category of offenders.

7. *Attitudes:* Subjects verbalized negative attitudes toward the basic social institutions and their memberships, particularly the family, government and the economic system. They viewed these institutions as associations formed, organized, and controlled by a small elitist group of people with a license to steal. Racketeers at the top constrain, subjugate, and exploit a lower echelon mem-

bership of dumb, square sheep. Squares, "eight to five men" are robots who support lazy women and unnecessary children in the suburbs, encumbered by a fixed, stultifying, oppressive life style which is marked by double mortgages, car payments, drying and washing machine payments, doctors' bills, clothing bills, rancid home cooking, and monotonous sex. Women are ungrateful, devious receptacles. All members of the administration of the criminal justice system from the police to the prison hack are either corrupt or too dumb to take money.

In regard to their criminal pattern these subjects viewed themselves as performing a useful, lucrative role in the hustling underworld, i.e. by providing broads and drugs defined by them as necessary commodities.

8. *Organic variables:* Subjects were on the whole in general good health, without physical deformities and known organic or neural disorders. Adequate research data were not available on item *c* epilepsy, brain damage, encephalitis, abnormal brain waves, abnormal chomosomal structure, and *d* somatotype. Impressionistically, they appeared to be ectomorphic in body type.

9. *Personality structure:* All were at least of average intelligence with a median IQ of 115 on the Gurvitz Revised Beta. All had high elevations on the following MMPI (Minnesota Multiphasic Personality Inventory) scales: Pd, Ma, Sc. All Pd scales ranged between 65 and 70. Clinical findings by a Ph.D. in psychology (ascertained separately and blindly) paralleled the MMPI profile. In brief, these men were classical psychopathic personalities of the manipulative type.

10. *Delinquent or criminal role career:* These offenders represent a group of professional criminals (street hustlers) regularly and systematically engaged in illegal activities requiring a moderate degree of criminal skills (con techniques) thoroughly processed in the lower echelons of the underworld. They began their criminal careers as predatory near-group, gang delinquents. Through late adolescence and young adulthood they progressed from what Alan G. Sutter[16] would call "easy players" to would-be "ideal hustlers"; i.e. they mediated the flow of drugs and prostitutes from adult hustlers to adolescent consumers. Finally, they

closed on the provision of drugs and prostitutes (occasionally the processing of stolen property) to adult customers. Involvement and association with older professionals (street hustlers) from whom they learned hustling techniques as young adults, paved the way for their eventual possession of what Walter Reckless describes as "ordinary criminal careers."[17]

Thus, by what Donald Cressey[18] would call differential association and by virtue of a ready-made personality structure (psychopathic personality), they were marvelously equipped for their criminal role—drug pusher-pimp. The meshing of social-cultural and personality factors is easily discernible. Rehabilitation attempts with this type of offender are obviously difficult. Certainly when incarcerated they should be segregated from younger, less recidivistic and criminalistic offenders. As Donald Clemmer[19] would say, these offenders become quickly prisonized (institutionalized in a negative sense) in a correctional setting.

NOTES AND REFERENCES

1. Carl G. Hempel Symposium: Problems of concept and theory formation in the social sciences, *Science, Language, and Human Rights.* Philadelphia, University of Pennsylvania Press, 1952, pp. 65-80; Theodore N. Ferdinand: *Typologies of Delinquency, A Critical Analysis.* New York, Random House, 1966, pp. 41-77.
2. See Marguerity Q. Warren: Classification of offenders as an aid to efficient management and effective treatment. *The Journal of Criminal Law, Criminology, and Police Science,* 62:239-258, June 1971, for, among other things, an excellent review of juvenile delinquent and criminal typologies in the literature. She proposes a very interesting cross-tabulation of 16 typological systems on the basis of six cross-classification bands (offender subtypes).
3. Julian B. Roebuck: *Criminal Typology: The Legalistic, Physical-Constitutional-Hereditary, Psychological-Psychiatric and Sociological Approaches.* Springfield, Thomas, 1967, pp. 106-200.
4. The dimensions of study chosen by the typologist depend upon his theoretical point of view. In this direction I leaned upon my own past research and the typological schemas found in the following sources: Don C. Gibbons: *Changing the Lawbreaker.* Englewood Cliffs, New Jersey, Prentice-Hall, 1965, pp. 74-129; Marshall B. Clinard and Richard Quinney: *Criminal Behavior Systems: A Typology.* New York, Holt, Rinehart and Winston, 1967, pp. 12-19; Theodore N. Ferdinand: *Ty-*

pologies of Delinquency, A Critical Analysis. New York, Random House, 1966, pp. 80-232; Ruth Shonle Cavan: *Criminology,* 3rd ed. New York, Thomas Y. Crowell Company, 1962, pp. 96-242; Richard L. Jenkins and Lester Hewitt: Types of personality structures encountered in child guidance clinics. *American Journal of Orthopsychiatry, 14:*84-94, January 1944; Robert L. Jenkins and Sylvia Glickham: Patterns of personality organization among delinquents. *Nervous Child,* 8:329-339, July 1947; F. Redl: In Witmer and Kotinsky (Eds.): *New Perspectives for Research on Juvenile Delinquency,* Children's Bureau Publication No. 356, 1956; Walter C. Reckless: *The Crime Problem,* 3rd ed. New York, Appleton-Century-Crofts, 1961.

5. Karl F. Schuessler and Donald R. Cressey: Personality characteristics of criminals. *American Journal of Sociology,* 55:476-484, March 1950. One, of course, could justifiably question the uneven selection of personality tests made by these authors. The point is that this kind of invidious personality test comparisons, with an effort to preclude the value of personality variables in crime causation, is weak and virtually meaningless since neither homogeneous grouping of criminals nor noncriminals were utilized by the various personality testers.

6. See Ned Polsky: *Hustlers, Beats, and Others.* Chicago, Aldine, 1967, Chs. 1, 2, and 3.

7. Julian B. Roebuck and Bob Atlas: Chromosomes and the criminal. *Corrective Psychiatry and Journal of Social Therapy,* 15:103-117, Fall 1969.

8. Paul W. Tappan: Who is the criminal? *American Sociological Review, 12:*96-102, February 1947. See also Paul W. Tappan, *Crime, Justice, and Correction.* New York, McGraw-Hill Book Company, 1960, pp. 1-22.

9. Julian B. Roebuck: *Criminal Typology,* pp. 106-185. See also pages 42-96 which include the research findings of other sociologists, some psychologists and some psychiatrists who have made similar findings.

10. Edwin H. Sutherland and Donald R. Cressey: *Principles of Criminology,* 6th ed. Chicago, J. B. Lippincott Company, 1960, pp. 32-36.

11. Walter C. Reckless: *The Crime Problem,* pp. 87-95, 119-128, 154-177; Paul W. Tappan: *Crime, Justice, and Correction,* pp. 122-130, 138-140, 149-150, 153-154, 166-167, 204-205, 226-229.

12. Maurice J. Fitzgerald: *Handbook of Criminal Investigation.* New York, Greenberg, 1951, pp. 119-125.

13. Julian B. Roebuck: *Criminal Typology,* pp. 97-104.

14. *Ibid.,* p. 103.

15. See Donald R. Cressey: Delinquent and criminal structures. In Robert K. Merton and Robert Nisbet (Eds.): *Contemporary Social Problems,* 3rd ed. New York, Harcourt Brace Jovanovich, 1971, pp. 157-163, for a definition of small working groups of criminals rationally organized for the execution of particular types of crime.

16. Alan G. Sutter: Worlds of drug use on the street scene. In Donald R. Cressey and David A. Ward: *Delinquency, Crime, and Social Process.* New York, Harper and Row, 1969, pp. 802-829.
17. Data sources for findings included within the ten dimensions: Correctional admission summaries and recorded interviews. Data analysis within the ten dimensions is obviously designated in qualitative terms. This does not preclude the analysis of similar data quantitatively. Moreover, the age-old problem of the articulation and simultaneous measurement of variables from two levels of analysis (in this case sociological and psychological) is now possible (quantitatively), e.g. see Don Cahalan's (a social psychologist) *Problem Drinkers: A National Survey.* San Francisco, Jossey-Bass, 1970, pp. 96-113, for the simultaneous analysis, measurement, and prediction of several sociological and psychological variables relating to problem drinkers. He utilized a multivariate analysis.
18. See Edwin H. Sutherland and Donald R. Cressey: *Principles of Criminology,* pp. 74-95, for differential association theory.
19. Donald Clemmer: Leadership phenomena in a prison community. *The Journal of Criminal Law, Criminology, and Police Science,* 28:851-872, April 1938; Donald Clemmer: *The Prison Community.* Boston, Christopher, 1940, re-issued by Rinehart, 1958. See further for information concerning the manipulative techniques utilized by offenders of this type in a correctional setting: Clarence A. Schrag: Social Types in a Prison Community. Unpublished M.A. thesis, University of Washington, 1944; Leadership among prison inmates. *American Sociological Review,* 19:37-42, February 1954; Gresham M. Sykes: *The Society of Captives: A Study of a Maximum Security Prison.* Princeton, Princeton University Press, 1958; Norman A. Hayner and Ellis Ash: The prison as a community. *American Sociological Review,* pp. 577-583, August 1940; Gresham M. Sykes: Men, merchants and toughs: A study to reactions to imprisonment. *Social Problems,* 4:130-138, October 1956.

Chapter 9
Typologies and Treatment
WILLIAM E. AMOS AND CHARLES F. WELLFORD

Introduction
The Theory and Methodology of Typologies
Criminological Typologies: General
Treatment Typologies
Conclusions
Notes and References

INTRODUCTION

The issue of the characteristics of those we place in correctional institutions cannot be divorced from a discussion of what we propose to do in the name of rehabilitation. While it may be important to know the age distribution of those in prison, that can be established only if we have determined in what way age is related to effective treatment. The analysis of inmate characteristics must, we suggest, be related to the intervention strategies we have available and are willing to use.

In recent years, renewed and increased attention has been paid by criminologists to the development of offender typologies, with special reference to the relationship between offender type and treatment configuration. While any offense-specific or offender descriptive analysis could be conceived as an effort in type construction (i.e., the armed Negro robber, the murderer, etc.) the more recent efforts, on which this paper will focus, tend to be directed toward the development of an exhaustive and mutually exclusive classificatory schema that not only will be causally relevant but also treatment-predictive (and specific). Thus, we will

---

Note: The views expressed herein are personal, not as a Board Member of the United States Board of Parole, and are not necessarily the opinions of the Department of Justice.

consider only systemic typologies, or rather, those conceived to be interpreted as being systemic (i.e., closed, exhaustive and mutually exclusive).

The paper is organized into three major sections. First, a discussion of the methodology and theory of type constructions with emphasis on the contributions of Weber, McKinney and those few who have engaged in the meta-thoretical analysis of criminological typologies. Second, a survey of the most significant typologies that seem to meet some of the criteria outlined in Section I that are felt to have a potential relationship to the determination of treatment strategies but have not been fully developed in this regard. Finally, an analysis of those systemic typologies that have been most clearly related to treatment selection.

THE THEORY AND METHODOLOGY OF TYPOLOGIES

Discussions of typological approaches in sociology have been most explicit since the time of Max Weber who gave this approach its first systemic presentation.[1] It is now clear that Weber's concept of the "ideal type" is simply one method of typology construction (a point to be expanded in the following section) and that many of the polemical analyses of Weber are ill conceived since their attack is primarily a defense of another method of typology construction.[2] Of much more lasting significance is Weber's discussion of the necessity for typological procedures and, eventually, general typologies in the social sciences.[3]

As numerous authors have observed, Weber's methodological writings were an attempt to combine and change the two variants of Hegelian social theory that emerged, particularly in Germany, during the 19th century.[4] The first of these variants has been most frequently labeled *objectivism* and is associated with the work of H. Rickert. This position accepted the Kantian distinction between fact sciences and value sciences (as made explicit by A. Ritschl) and proposed that since the social sciences dealt with values, they could not attain the levels of understanding (i.e., "generalizability") of the natural sciences. Thus, Rickert and others emphasized the factual-historical aspect of the social sciences, the "case" approach, and the impossibility of abstract conceptualization. The second variant, *intuitionism*, is most frequently identified with the work of Dilthey and the concept of *verstehen*. Again, there was the acceptance of the Kantian dualism and the contention that there could be no general theory in the social sciences because of the peculiarity of the object of address. However, Dilthey argued that since values (or meanings) were the object of sociological address, the method of study must be subjective (i.e., by intuition or understanding—*verstehen*) and the results of such analysis must be considered particularistically (i.e., variable with each culture or social system) and thus below the level required for generalization. Both positions concluded, for different and conflicting reasons, that the social sciences (and in particular sociology) could not attain the level of explanation of the natural sciences because the "data" did not permit generalization.

Weber's response was that a characteristic of all sciences was that of abstraction—the selection of attributes to be considered as determinative and definitional. He contended that a science must select from the range of attributes observable within any designated field those that are most relevant to our understanding of the object of address. While this process of abstraction may not be as obvious in the natural sciences as in the social, Weber contended it was integral to each, and therefore concluded that general theory was possible in the social sciences.* Weber's proposal of the ideal type method was an attempt to identify the methodology that sociology should follow in developing the "building-blocks" of a general theory. While Weber was more explicit in describing what the ideal type was not (not an average, a hypothesis, the essential units, etc.) than in what it was (abstraction, fictional, etc.), it is clear that its reliance on *verstehen* would be significant (this will be developed in the following section).

---
*For Weber, general theory is best understood as systemically complete as opposed to multi-systemic.

It is true that Weber did not always organize the types he developed into exhaustive typologies (thus Parsons' charge that Weber was a "type atomist");[5] however, he did make explicit the necessity for the methodological and theoretical consequences of typology for the social sciences. It is the explicitness and persuasiveness of Weber's discussion that makes him relevant today. His analysis is not an historical footnote but rather the vital statement concerning the *necessity* of typological analysis in sociology.

Only recently has there been advancement beyond Weber's position, most notably in the work of John McKinney.[6] His concern has been with the analysis of what he calls the "constructive type," which is defined as a "purposive, planned selection, abstraction, combination, and (sometimes) accentuation of a set of criteria with empirical referents that serves as a basis for comparison of empirical cases."[7] The constructed type is seen as encompassing more specific forms of typification, such as the ideal type. The focus is, however, on the abstraction and organization, as developed by Weber—the variation from Weber is in the rendering of the ideal type, and other forms of typification, as special cases of the procedure general to all sciences.

In McKinney's analysis of the various modes of typification, six "major polar axes" around which types can be constructed are identified. These are the ideal-extracted, general-specific, scientific-historical, timeless-time-bound, universal-local and generalizing-individualizing. The most important of these axes is the ideal-extracted (or empirical), for it is most relevant to our later discussion of type construction in criminology.

As indicated earlier, Weber's analysis of the ideal type emphasized its "fictionality," that is, the fact that all empirical referents are deviations from the ideal and thus the ideal type is not found in reality though it is possible (primarily in a logical sense) that it may *really* exist. This position was prompted considerably by Weber's notion of *verstehen* and has seriously hindered the development of typologies in sociology because of its apparent (if not real) metaphysical implications. Thus, critics of Weber have moved toward another mode of typification associated with

Emile Durkheim—the average, statistical or extracted (from reality) types. Frequently, however, these latter types lack precisely what Weber maximized, explanation of the configurations (i.e. their meanings).

The constructed type (as defined above) attempts to integrate the purposeful-selective element (i.e., the type is theoretically determined) and the empirical probability (as opposed to possibility). This latter is best expressed by Howard Becker:[8]

> The accentuation or stressing of salient features of the constructed type, and its "closure," is fictional only in the sense of empirically "limited fiction." Examination of the empirical evidence must always enable the researcher to say, "The probability that this type will ever be matched in reality is— . . ., [and] not inherently nil."

Statements of probability are elements of the constructed type but do not solely determine its characteristics. There is no fictional character to the constructed type (there are empirical referents and ranges of variations) and it is derived from some more general theory (types are to be found in typologies that are organized by purposeful organization) and thus logically exhaustive of that which it addresses.

The proposition that will organize the critical analysis of this paper is to be found in the works of Weber and McKinney, the essential elements being that typologies must be complete, theoretically meaningful, empirically probable, observable, predictive and directive[9] (i.e., they are at such a level that they organize interventive efforts).

Criminology and the Analysis of Typologies

While many criminologists have utilized the method of typification, few have contributed to its analysis. Among those who have made significant contributions in this regard are Riemer,[10] Gibbons,[11] and Ferdinand.[12] (This is to imply that others have made less than significant contributions, in that their contributions are frequently lists of what types should "look like," how they should be derived, etc., without an analysis of the problems involved in or the detailed characteristics of typification.)[13]

Riemer contends that treatment typologies must be causal typologies. In his opinion, criminal typologies have been overwhelmingly descriptive and oriented toward prediction and thus offer little insight into the treatment needs of the offender. He states the following:[14]

> With the overemphasis upon research in crime risks and probabilities of recidivism in our discipline, the prison psychiatrist finds himself without the assistance of the sociologist in the most important field of modern prison reform: classification and treatment.

To counteract this tendency, Riemer suggests we direct our attention to the construction of ideal types based on sound sociological theory, then the operationalization of these types, and finally the measurement of the relevance of these types for control and treatment efforts. The specifics of his "guide to research" are similar to those developed by Sutherland as discussed in the section entitled Criminological Typologies: General. Riemer proposes that we look for "sociogenic constellations" that are active in the process of crime causation, as they are associated with offenses or sub-types of offenses. His own research has focused on one of these offense types and its sub-type, embezzlement. While this approach generates certain problems, to be discussed below and again in the section Criminological Typologies: General, the technique has remained prominent in modern criminology.

The importance of Riemer's analysis is to be found in his transmission to criminology of the basic element of the Weberian notion of ideal types (the purposive-abstractive element) and his insistence on the necessity for empirical referents of the type. Though not as completely developed, this clearly anticipates the work of McKinney discussed above. Though relatively ignored, this article is a concise and clear statement of *an* approach to typification that has much significance for our consideration of treatment typologies.

A more thorough discussion is to be found in the publications of Don C. Gibbons. In his discussion, Gibbons analyzes the possibility of criminal and delinquent typologies being based on legal categories, the relationship between types and causation and treatment, and the importance of specificity. Although he does not discuss some of the more basic issues as identified above (particularly the question of mode of construction), he does provide a coherent discussion of those problems that he does address.

The propositions made by Gibbons are interrelated and can be concisely stated in their final form. He suggests that typologies (especially those to be utilized in treatment) must be based on causal dimensions that are selected on the basis of existing theory and research. This condition can be met at various levels of generality, but Gibbons opts for the least general level; that is, the types must be empirically probable (as in McKinney's analysis) and their characteristics must be such that they are alterable (assuming that the goal of science is control as well as understanding). On the basis of these characteristics, Gibbons concludes that legal categories cannot provide the base for type construction, a point we must pursue further.

He suggests, first, that there are certain methodological impossibilities generated by the use of legal categories. For example, the problem of "plea copping" (the change in charges during the offender's movement through the system of justice), the fact that offenders do not consistently commit the same form of deviant acts and the fact that offenses frequently involve multiple acts. In addition, there is the "most serious difficulty" which arises from the strong supposition that "they do not identify theoretically significant types."[15] The essence of the argument is that there is no reason to assume that the causal explanation is not manifested in general categories of behavior but rather is to be located at other more behaviorally relevant levels. As Gibbons states, "There is little reason to suppose that persons who are characterized as 'burglars' or who are typed in terms of some other specific legal offense are the product of a uniform causal process."[16] Furthermore, such procedures would lead to an almost unmanageable number of types, the logical end of which would be empirical enumeration.

Thus, many of the types developed by criminologists are "defined" out of the boundaries of relevance, as was indicated earlier in this paper (though for different reasons).[17] This is, we feel, perfectly legitimate, particularly given the goal of a treatment typology. Even among that possibly most homogeneous offender category, criminal homicide, there are recognized causal variations (including, of course, victim precipitation).[18] Another set of criteria are therefore added to our analytic battery to be used in assessing the "goodness of fit" of competing treatment typologies in criminology.

Roebuck[19] has observed that an obvious omission in the Gibbons effort is the failure to include the question of multiple systems in the analysis of typology construction. Roebuck correctly observes that most attempts to develop typologies of crime and/or delinquency have separated rather than integrated sociological and psychological explanations (a point to be expanded later in this paper). Roebuck is for "multi-discipline" types but has not analyzed the problems in their construction—autonomous positions are much easier to handle as his own substantive efforts indicate.[20]

Theodore Ferdinand has provided us with an intermediary analysis of the problems of integrated (or what he calls "synthetic") typologies. He suggests that typologies must synthesize independent ideal types:

> Thus, assuming that delinquency is influenced both by psychological and social forces, a synthetic typology of delinquency would describe the behavior of individuals with typical personality styles in typical social situations. By examining systematically the personality types that psychological theory suggests in terms of certain common social situations, it should be possible to construct a synthetic typology that coordinates the insights of both points of view in the explanation of delinquency.[21]

Assuming that the integrative emphasis does not need explication or defense, there are two other elements in this approach that need further elaboration.

Ferdinand contends that the types must be "ideal," in the Weberian sense, and that the typologies to be synthesized are independent.* The above presentation of McKinney's work has already questioned the validity of ideal type analysis in its pure form on the grounds of the problems generated by the characteristic that there are no empirical referents for the type. This becomes even more grave when we begin to think of typologies for treatment, where the treatment would not be linked to the type but to deviations (of varying degree and quality) from it. Ferdinand utilizes the ideal type concept to emphasize the role of theory in typification but in so doing fails to critically analyze this mode of typification or to consider the work of others (like McKinney and Becker) who have.

The problem of independence presents us with a new and perplexing issue—the one that stymies most integrative efforts. The alternatives implied by Ferdinand are reductionism (using only sociological or psychological typologies), autonomy, and synthesis (as in a contingency table). Given such alternatives his choice seems most admirable. The problem is that there is at least one other position, that of internal and external relations.[23] In this approach to the system relations, the postulates of independence and dependence are themselves integrated. Thus, each system is said to have internal elements (those not to be explained by other systems), external relations (meaningful outputs) and boundary conditions (requiring meaningful inputs). Thus, independent synthesis is not the only means of integration; internal-external integration is an alternative means that in terms of its acceptance in philosophy and social theory is more powerful than the procedure proposed by Ferdinand. His approach is only one of at least two different methods of integration.

Criminological analyses have made their most important contribution to the methodology and theory of typologies in the areas of integration and specificity (i.e. emphasis on the utilization of

---

*The notion of independence is made more explicit in the following passage: ". . . sociology, cultural anthropology, psychology, and physiology are all independent disciplines in the sense that the implications contained in one cannot be inferred from the others."[22] This leads Ferdinand to the utilization of a field theory model to account for the interaction of independent forces.

Typologies and Treatment 185

the type). While the analyses are not themselves complete in the sense that major questions concerning the use, construction and organization are not answered (and frequently not even asked), the trend (if Gibbons and Ferdinand constitute a trend) is toward more systematic analysis of the full range of issues. Combined with our understanding of more purely theoretical efforts, we are now in a position to begin a survey of constructed typologies in criminology.

The major typologies can, as suggested earlier, be organized into those that have been developed or used explicitly for treatment orientation and those that seem to meet some of the requirements discussed above and have implications for the determination of treatment, but have not been as explicitly applied in this way. As we shall see, the latter have been more prevalent and have been overwhelmingly descriptive and minimally analytic (with a few exceptions to be noted below).

CRIMINOLOGICAL TYPOLOGIES: GENERAL

Since the emergence of criminology as a distinct discipline, there have been a variety of typologies that have been developed, primarily as categorizations of general causal elements. In this section we will briefly review and criticize the early, and in general ideal typologies, then proceed to a discussion of the more recent causal typologies of this mode[24] and then finally attend to the studies of inmate types. Our concern will be with the construction of the typologies and the degree of treatment specificity they contain or potentially contain.

The positivist school of criminology is most frequently identified with Lombroso and his contemporaries, particularly Ferri and Garofalo.[25] The typological efforts of Lombroso and Ferri remain relevant today. Lombroso, after moving beyond his earlier biologistic explorations of crime, maintained that there were three major types of criminals: the born criminal, the atavistic criminal accounting for about one third of the offenders; the insane criminal, including the mentally ill and deficient and accounting for less of the criminal offenses than the other types; and, the criminaloids, "a large general class of those without physical stigmata, who are not afflicted with recognizable mental disorders, but ... under certain circumstances indulge in vicious and criminal behavior ... (accounting for) well over half of all criminals."[26] The typology of Ferri[27] is similar in that he maintained criminals were either insane, born, occasional or criminals by passion.[28]

Though one might criticize the method of construction, in the sense that the "research" was methodologically inadequate (selectivity of sample, sample size, analysis) and that basically the types are solely derived from the theory, the fact that they arrived at a classification that has persisted in many forms in criminology attests to their continuing impact. The types can be rendered more modern by saying they refer to constitutional, psychological and sociological causal types. The tendency to separate these "types" of explanatory modes has persisted until quite recently in criminology and many of the more recent typologies are merely restatements of those developed by Lombroso and Ferri.[29] For our considerations we can thus see the major problem of the use of general typologies as treatment modes, namely they are not treatment specific. Rather, they combine varieties of specific causal elements and patterns and tend to create a simple treatment dichotomy reflected in the division between psychiatric services and "institutional treatment," a division that permeates much of our correctional apparatus today.

While this distinction permeates many of the more recent typological efforts, another form of typology construction (still of the ideal mode) has emerged in criminology, one alluded to earlier but to which we must now return for further consideration. This form stresses the legal category of "behavioral system" approach and is most notably present in the works of Sutherland,[30] Cavan,[31] and Bloch and Geis.[32] Since the basic statement is that of Sutherland's (as developed by Cressey), we will direct our attention primarily to his formulation.

Sutherland is careful to observe that the "behavior system" approach to "increasing the homogeneity" of those units to be explained is not likely to be able to handle all forms of criminal behavior, and therefore cannot be an exclusive and systemic typology—rather, it must be a series of types. Still, we can consider these as typologies, for others (in particular Bloch and Geis and Clinard[33]) have not been so careful in their use of Sutherland's formulation.

A behavior system has three main characteristics. First, it is not merely an aggregation of individual criminal acts but a "criminalistic philosophy" linked to those acts. Second, the behavior is not unique to an individual. Third, the members identify with each other. The intention is therefore to identify offense and/or offender types that involve high degrees of cohesion and similarity of role definitions. The most obvious of these forms would be, for Sutherland, the professional thief.[34] Here there is a range of illegal behaviors, but these are prescribed by the role definitions of "professionals" and there is felt to be a "common culture." Sutherland's assumption is that within other legal categories (such as kidnapping) other behavior systems may exist and between offenses behavior systems provide the descriptive causal link.

We must emphasize again that Sutherland saw limited scope for this approach stating:

> It is not understood that the entire area of crime can be covered in this manner. Rather it is understood that certain crimes cluster in systems, are organized, are combined with other behavior in such manner as to form systems, and that certain other crimes stand somewhat isolated and outside of systems . . . legal categories designating less systematic crimes . . . can be combined or refined in such a way that the behavior designated by them can be studied . . .[35]

It is clear that Sutherland was proposing the development of an explanatory typology that would relate behavior, norms and type of criminal act(s). This has been attempted by Gibbons in a direct concern with a treatment typology to be discussed later on in this paper.

Those who have attempted to follow Sutherland have, in general, failed to gain this insight into his effort and have rushed to the development of offense specific behavioral types. Bloch and Geis handle as separate types of crime professional criminality, organized crime, homicides, assaults, sex offenses, property crimes, petty offenses and white-collar crime. Their discussion of these types ranges from case studies to detailed descriptive research, and infrequent references to causal analogues for the types. While it is again clear that there has been no empirical testing of the usefulness of the typology, this is not its major weakness. The major weakness is that it is not complete, does not provide statements that are related to treatment, nor are the categories exclusive or finite. In short, while it may serve other, possibly heuristic purposes, typologies of this character are inadequate as treatment typologies. This same proposition applies to Cavan (casual offender, occasional criminal, episodic criminal, white-collar criminal, habitual criminal, professional criminal, organized crime, mentally abnormal criminal and the nonmalicious criminal) and Clinard (criminally insane; extreme sex deviates; occasional offenders; prostitutes and homosexuals; habitual, petty criminals; white-collar criminals; ordinary criminal careers; organized criminals; and professional criminals)—both of these are within the ideal mode of type construction, vary from description to explanation, and describe the types at levels of causal generality that offer little guide to explanation for further research, or treatment.

Again let me emphasize that, in our consideration, the approach taken by Sutherland is potentially useful if not transformed in the ways in which those typologies discussed have been transformed. The movement of Sutherland's successors has been toward categories that apparently have different bases of creation, are differentially related to causal statements, and are overwhelmingly involved in the (unnecessary) distinction between social and psychological characteristics of types and the attempt to distinguish, by offenses, degrees of commitment to criminal careers. While this latter technique may be useful, our feeling is that it is not adequate as the sole determinant of a causal and/or treatment typology. In sum, we find that the typologies developed by many criminologists in the past, and in the present, are based on what now seem to be unnecessary assumptions about the structure of types; have not been based upon or generated by research; are frequently not systemic, exclusive or causally relevant; are, in a few cases, suggestive of possible techniques of typology construction; and are not specific enough to aid in the development of treatments and/or the determination of maximally efficient treatment strategies.

Special Cases: Ferdinand, Rubenfeld

Some recent efforts at typology construction do not lend themselves to the historical-developmental discussion and critique of the preceding section. Again, these are overwhelmingly ideal modes, are (in some cases) not systemic, and have as their major difference an emphasis on causal types and integrative typification characteristics, and thus a greater potential for use in the treatment setting.[36]

Theodore Ferdinand[37] has developed three ideal typologies and has also made a preliminary attempt at integrating the elements of these typologies. The three typologies are based on social class position, delinquent behavior (especially as it occurs in groups), and personality characteristics, which result in the following types of acts and actors:

Class	*Behavior*	*Personality*
Upper-Upper Class	Mischievous Indulgent	Impulsive
Lower-Upper Class	Aggressive-Exploitative	Neurotic
Upper-Middle Class	Criminal	Symptomatic
Lower-Middle Class	Fighting	
Working Class	Theft	
Lower-Lower Class	Disorganized Acting-Out	

Ferdinand suggests there are certain determinative links between the types for individuals (e.g., LL, aggressive-exploitative, impulsive), and for groups (e.g., LL, Theft, Neurotic). Logically, all combinations of the three ideal types are possible; however, in the "synthesis" (recall earlier discussion), the movement would be toward the identification of the ideal combinations.

There are a number of other problems in this analysis (in addition to the mode of integration) to which we should direct our attention. First, because the separate types involve a nonintegrated theoretical structure, their integration does not become axiomatic; rather it becomes problematic, thus necessitating research prior to the integration. Second, this requires that the individual types be studied independently, and it is very questionable if this will be possible in many instances (e.g., upper-upper class delinquency, and the problems of operationalizing the psychoanalytic concepts that are used in describing the personality structure). Third, the individual typologies and the synthesis are primarily justified by reference to other theoretical efforts and only minimally to any adequate research. Fourth, the synthesis is incomplete and may not be possible because the types are not mutually exclusive in a causal sense as Ferdinand implies. Rather, they overlap in many cases that he considers problematic (e.g., class structure and personality type are highly correlated); thus, the synthesis may be built into the classification itself. Fifth, there are the general problems of the use of purely ideal types discussed earlier. Finally, the typology has few implications for treatment and control short of psychoanalysis for all delinquents (which indicates a further problem, that in the final analysis the typology is overwhelmingly psychological, with social class being a limiting element and behavior a direct by-product of the "real cause" and the limiting condition). Though we appreciate the effort and its goals, the general conclusion is that this approach to type construction has severely limited the desirability of the output. This, of course, does not detract from Ferdinand's analysis of the problems of type construction, nor the fruitfulness of following his emphasis on integration and age gradation.

Rubenfeld[38] also provides a typology of delinquency based on an extension of containment theory, with a greater emphasis on psychoanalytic internal elements. One aspect of this impressive theoretical effort is the construction of four psychocultural processes that account for different reasons for delinquency. The processes are described in terms of four class levels (LL, UL, ML, UM) and are used by Rubenfeld as examples of the psychocultural theory he has developed. He recognizes that the four processes do not represent a complete typology, that they are in need of empirical validation, and they are primarily suggestive of a procedure of type development. Our evaluation of their potential must be based on these limitations announced by the author.

Due to the self-imposed (but necessary) limitations of this paper, we cannot develop the basic theory utilized by Rubenfeld. Therefore, we will attempt to summarize the types of delinquency discussed by drawing heavily on summative quotes from Rubenfeld and then render them more relevant to our focus. Rubenfeld describes the four (types) processes in the following ways:

> Process I (LL)—depicts a boy who may be heir to the attitudes of a mother profoundly cut off from collaboration with effective men; and who is heir also to a male identity that lives as best it can with its own undependability, indigence, and impulsivity . . . his ego resources are too meager . . . he may slump back into the misshapen identity of his origins, a cultural discard.
>
> Process II (UL)—(are) babies of women who, because they were economically supported by their husbands, were able to bring a good deal more dependable support to the children's first years . . . they attach goodness to their mothers and others, and it is this capacity for romanticizing friendships and idealizing friends that helps create a gang solidarity . . . (which is) alienated from authority.
>
> Process III (LM)—no longer hopes for conforming achievement . . . only his wanderings and adventures with his companions, with their occasional delinquencies, (are an) escape from relentless pressures to aspire to goals which he believes (usually secretly) are beyond his powers . . . Accomplishments are barred (by) injuries to interpersonal functions of ego.
>
> Process IV (UM)—cannot let the adults be; he demands that they be other than what they are. (They) clutch tenaciously to being in and of the moment, while his nondelinquent peer is less afraid of having been and is interested as well in becoming.

While these quotes cannot adequately convey the organization of Rubenfeld's position, it is hoped they indicate his intent. The intention is the organization of class determinants, family structure, identity crises and ego formation into a series of analytic categories of delinquent behavior. The net impact on treatment is that the "outlook is gloomy," that is, the correctional setting can only minimally alter personality structure and finds it impossible to cope with social structures.

In Rubenfeld we have a preliminary effort in integrative type construction. The major problem, which is evident in the quotes, is that the explanations of Process I and Process II are primarily sociological and those of Processes III and IV (middle class) are primarily psychologically oriented. This indicates that the "integrated" elements are not really autonomous but rather their meanings are to be understood in terms of one system which in Rubenfeld is the psychological. The movement to integrative types has removed, by definition, the potential for those types that have preoccupied other criminologists (the "insane" and career offender). It does not seem necessary for such a condition to exist if system autonomy is integrated with notions of systems relations. Again, other criticisms can be generated (most of which Rubenfeld anticipated), but the one just discussed seems to be most crucial given his intentions. The general point is that his range of types seems to be unnecessarily limited to certain types and also to be characterized by psychological (i.e., internal) reductionism.

Ferdinand and Rubenfeld are significant in their attention to the problems of integration in typological construction and in their separation of delinquent types and adult types. This latter point, while frequently mentioned in the literature, has only recently been given systematic consideration. Both efforts lack treatment specificity and, in the case of Rubenfeld, deny the efficacy of treatment on the basis of the characterological significance of childhood.

Inmate Typologies

In the area of inmate typologies, we would anticipate a much greater relevance to intervention specification in correctional institutions. For reasons soon to become apparent, this would not seem to be the case. While the typologies themselves may be more empirical and generalized, they also tend to reflect very simple modes of construction and are of minimal aid in treatment selection (particularly within institutions).

Inmate types and typologies have also received considerable attention. Their major difference from the typologies of Sutherland, *et al* is the emphasis on the definition of the types by reference to their roles and behavior within the institution and then relating these to noninstitutional variables. The types typically are related to different degrees or modes of adaptation to the "prison community." The major figure in this area of study is Schrag.[39] Though others, such as Clemmer,[40] Hayner,[41] Sykes[42] and Korn and McKorkle,[43] have also dealt with the construction of inmate typologies, the prototype is to be found in Schrag's efforts. Other works are best interpreted as a demonstration of the perceived universality of the types Schrag originally formulated and has continued to modify.

In a study of a reformatory type institution, Schrag observed,[44] by the use of the basic sociometric method, that inmates could be classified by the role they played in the prison community, in particular the adjustment or degree of adoption of the inmate code.[45] The modes of adoption were first identified as the "right guy," "square john," "ding," and "politician." They have since become the antisocial, prosocial, asocial and pseudo-social types. The antisocial inmate type is highly prisonized; the prosocial is minimally prisonized; the asocial is rejected by both conventional and inmate societies; and, the pseudo-social operates between the two systems without internal commitment to either. Schrag places the determination of these "inmate social types" on career variables with heavy emphasis on the extent of previous participation in criminal activities prior to commitment to the institution. The antisocial inmate, for example, performs that role because the conduct norms he has acquired from participation in the criminalistic subculture are those that are central to the inmate code. Donald Garrity[46] has recently devised a means for determining inmate types in the Schrag model from social case history information, thus facilitating the use of these types.

Though there are methodological questions we can raise concerning Schrag's methodology (institution type, validity of sociometric data, the question of bias from forced responses, the problems of clique analysis of sociometric data, and the lack of statistical analysis in Schrag's research—i.e., he simply counted selections to determine leaders, outcasts, etc.), the fact that the analysis has been supported in other research settings (as noted earlier) and by more refined analyses (e.g., Wheeler,[47] Garabedian[48] and Garrity) would lead us to accept the classification as describing an aspect of the reality of prison life. Our concern then must be with the adequacy of this typology as a treatment typology.

As indicated earlier, the inmate typologies do not provide us with much insight into treatment determination. Again, the typology breaks down into sociological types (antisocial and prosocial) and psychological types (pseudo-social and asocial). While the typologies may be useful in prediction of parole success[49] and institutional adjustment[50] their characteristics are not treatment specific. This does not mean they cannot be so adapted; but the modifications required would seem, on the basis of the previous discussion, to be of such a magnitude that their current usefulness would be minimal. Their value may be in emphasizing the fact that treatment typologies must consider factors relating to the character of total institutions and other institutional situational factors that are not to be found in general (even causal) typologies. The work of Schrag and others has made us aware of the transformative effect that correctional institutions have on all types of offenders who are incarcerated, and thus the potential usefulness of considering these factors in constructing treatment (institutional) typologies.

TREATMENT TYPOLOGIES

Introduction

Prior to our analysis of specific treatment typologies, we must briefly describe the status of the treatment of offenders. There are two issues involved: (1) what is the extent of the use of treatment typologies; and (2) what are the forms of treatment to which offender types can be related in the manner described above.

In an obvious sense, the history of modern correctional reform has been the history of attempts to develop treatment typologies. From the separation of the young from the old to the most modern classification process, the intent has been the designation of those to whom certain programs and/or settings seem most appropriate. However, now as in the past this trend to classification and correction has been overwhelmed by the earlier function of incarceration, punishment (as well as considerations of institutional manpower requirements). Thus, classification has been primarily based on security requirements with the resulting typology of maximum, medium and minimum security prisoners.[51] On the basis of a recent survey of reception centers and classification processes at the state level, Loveland has concluded that with few exceptions the classification process involves little more than security determination and that the recommendations of classification summaries have no significant impact on subsequent treatment decisions.[52] The author's own experience in the analysis of the classification process at Eastern State Penitentiary has resulted in the conclusion that until treatment typologies are developed and operationalized we can expect nothing else from this vital element in the treatment process.[53] Thus, though the intent of classification involves the basic ideas of a treatment typology, that which has emerged from this process has been, with few exceptions, a security typology.

A problem related to our efforts and to the failure of classification has been the paucity of treatment procedures. In many correctional systems, the treatment alternatives are community, psychiatric or "social-environmental" (which refers to a variety of relatively unstructured and undefined treatment procedures that can frequently be described as humane detention). Though it is not appropriate in this paper to review the typologies of treatment that extend this simplistic model, we should at least have some rudiments of such a typology at our common disposal before analyzing specific treatment typologies. For this purpose, we can use the summary chart on the following page which is taken from Gibbons.[54] While there are obvious sub-types within each of these categories, the categories would appear to cover the full range of treatment alternatives in and out of institutions. We should not, however, develop treatment typologies on the basis of present treatment procedures, for the typology may lead us to the development (or renewal) of treatments and/or the

TABLE 9-I
SUMMARY OF PATTERNS OF TREATMENT

PSYCHOTHERAPY

Type	Treatment Goal	Nature of Therapist	Number of Clients or Patients	Length of Treatment Period	Frequency of Treatment	Appropriate Treatment Circumstances
1 Individual "Depth" Psychotherapy	Uncover individual problems, lead patient to insight, develop new patterns	Psychiatrist, clinical psychologist, psychiatric social worker	Only one patient in each therapy case load or experience	Depends upon severity of problems, but frequently extensive	Normally, treatment should be intensive, i.e., several times per week	Private, quiet surroundings such as private office of therapist
2 Group Psychotherapy	Same as individual therapy, but also, get person to see other's problems	Same as above, but patients are therapy agents, too, to some extent	Small group, fifteen persons or less	Depends upon severity of problems, but shorter than individual psychotherapy	Same as above	Private surroundings where patients not observed by outsiders
3 Client-Centered Therapy	Uncover individual problems, patient is led to analyze himself, change	Person trained in eclectic procedures of client-centered work	Only one patient in each therapy case load or experience	Shorter time than "depth" therapy, often a few weeks or so	Usually intensive, i.e., several times per week	Private, quiet surroundings such as private office of therapist

ENVIRONMENTAL THERAPY

Type	Treatment Goal	Nature of Therapist	Number of Clients or Patients	Length of Treatment Period	Frequency of Treatment	Appropriate Treatment Circumstances
4 Group Therapy	Discover group pressures to problem behavior, develop new norms	Initially, some person called "therapist," but ultimately, group members	Small group, fifteen persons or less in most cases	Depends upon problem to be solved, but usually fairly long, i.e., one year	Fairly intense, once per week or more frequently	Private surroundings where patients are not observed by outsiders
5 Milieu Management	Develop new behavioral norms in more general living group than therapy group	Initially, some person(s) named as therapist, but ultimately, entire group	Living group or associational group of larger size than group therapy	Fairly lengthy to extremely long-term, may extend over several years	Treatment tends to be continuous, rather than interwoven with nontreatment	Stable living group situation such as apartment or some similar arrangement
6 Environmental Change	Develop new behavioral norms in wider social environment than above	Usually, no specific person as therapist, in long run, environment	Usually, large group, often many members of large social environment	Fairly lengthy to extremely long-term, may extend over several years	Treatment tends to be continuous rather than interwoven with nontreatment	Social environment to be changed, such as community area

selection of appropriate combinations from those of the type indicated in Figure 9-1. At the present time, it would appear from a variety of indications (e.g., observation, recidivism, etc.) that we are not yet making maximum utilization of those treatment procedures now available.

In sum, the precedent for the use of treatment typologies is well established in correctional systems as in the recognition and use of a variety of treatment procedures. The minimal fruitfulness of these precedents has resulted, significantly, from the absence of a successful and practical treatment typology that would focus classification and indicate the deficiencies of treatment alternatives. We will now consider three attempts to fill this vacuum: the PICO distinction between amenables and nonamenables; the Gibbons' typology; and, the concept of interpersonal maturity levels as it has been adapted to a variety of treatment needs and conditions in the California correctional system.

PICO

The Pilot Intensive Counseling Organization[55] was organized to study the influence of "individual interview therapy" on older delinquents (age 17 to 23) who were designated as either amenable to treatment or nonamenable to treatment. The procedure of the study is summarized as follows: (1) identification of eligible wards (those with commitments of over six months and in-state parole and without juvenile court commitment or gross impairment of mental functioning); (2) classification of eligibles into amenables and nonamenables; (3) random assignment of eligibles into control and treatment statuses; (4) administration of therapy to treatment assignees; and (5) evaluation of post release behavior of all four categories of subjects. Our concern will be with steps two, four and five.

The therapy consisted of "once-or-twice-weekly individual counseling sessions . . . for an average of about nine months."[56] The therapists were graduate-level trained clinical psychologists or psychiatric social workers who operated with a caseload of

25. The nontreatment time of controls and experimentals was similar. To a degree, this study is a search for optimal use of this form of treatment. It is much more limited by the treatment intent than is desirable if exhaustive typologies are the goal.

Reports on this project are consistently vague with regard to the earlier means of type determination. The following passage is representative:[57]

> Amenability to treatment was ascertained through pooled clinical judgments by a team that studied wards at intake into the reception-guidance center. During the period covered by the intake of the subjects of the present report, the ratio of amenable to non-amenable judgments was approximately 50/50. Although the most salient ingredients of amenability *appeared* to be the *quality* of anxiety, the typical amenable ward might be more fully described as "bright, verbal and anxious" . . . also influenced by awareness of problems, insight, desire to change and acceptance of treatment" [emphasis added].

The classification was based on the pooled clinical judgments of the reception staff (similar in training to the therapists). At no time in the reporting of the basic data of this project are the criteria of typification made more explicit. While this in itself does not invalidate the types and their usefulness, it does raise many questions including the ability to generalize the procedure and the contamination of the follow-up results from uncontrolled sources of subject variation.

Later studies have been characterized by the attempt to develop better measures of amenability. In 1963 it was reported that an eight-item scale had been developed that successfully differentiated amenables and nonamenables.[58] The items were selected from the case histories of the subjects of the initial PICO study. The scale and the results of a constructed sample study were to be published in 1964 but as yet have not been made available.[59] We can, however, anticipate the major criticism the scale must face, namely that it accepts the original clinical determination as binding and relevant. Thus, if there were errors or biases systematically introduced originally, they will be reproduced (and possibly magnified given the elimination of potentially correc-

Typologies and Treatment

tive, subjective factors) in the scale. If our suspicions are correct that the amenables had other attributes differentiating from the nonamenables which influenced the efficacy and selection of treatment, then the scale becomes not a typology of offenders, in the sense described in earlier sections, but a typology of those who do or do not relate to a particular form of treatment. Again, the limitations of the treatment intent of the project are obvious. The development of "objective" measurements of these types will not alleviate this condition; it may in fact accentuate it.

In analyzing the results of this project, we must keep in mind the aforementioned criteria of eligibility. The population consisted of all the eligibles for the period 1955 to 1960. The various measures of "success" apply to this selected group (what they refer to as the "normals"). We do not know what portion of the total intake was defined as ineligibles, or their characteristics. Thus, the typology is not exhaustive, but we do not know the extent of its inexhaustiveness.

The staff of the PICO project have concluded that the dichotomy is useful based on the analysis of the success rates of the four groups. A combination of the measures of "success" (return to state custody, proportion of good discharges, proportions of parole revocation, and parole performance) results in the following ranking of the four categories (from high to low): treated amenables, control amenables, control nonamenables, and treated nonamenables. Though the use of return to only *state* custody raises the question of other "solution by migration," the degree of difference between the treated amenables and all others suggests the validity of that designation, regardless of what it designates (see above). Furthermore, there was the finding that the control groups were very similar in post-release measures, indicating the efficacy of the treatment associated with the type. The major interpretative difficulty involves the performance of the treated nonamenables, for their success rates increasingly diverged from the two control groups as the time of release increased.[60] This, of course, suggests that the treatment adversely affected their success. There are a variety of explanations we might generate to handle this finding; however, it would seem more appropriate to proceed to a more intensive study of the interaction between nonamenability and interview therapy.

In sum, the typology is poorly reported and described, lacks precision (to date), is not exhaustive, seems overly dependent on the preconceived treatment procedure, and is not generalizable. Finally, the data, though meagerly reported and analyzed, presents problems of type use (the case of the nonamenables), and the typology implies the existence of a large segment of the population that is not treatable. These latter results seem to be highly undesirable in a treatment typology. Therefore, we repeat our earlier contention that the typology is really a measure of which inmates are maximally benefitted by the treatment technique, and that all other inmates are left untyped (i.e. either not "normal" or unamenable).

Gibbons' Typologies

There are two typologies generated by Don Gibbons, one for juveniles and one for adults. Though he states that the types are based upon research, it is not described, reported or analyzed in any of his publications. For evaluative purposes, it is more appropriate for us to consider these as ideal typologies given the apparent inconsequential role of the "research." In this mode, the typologies are closely allied with the behavior systems model developed by Sutherland (as previously discussed).

The major assumptions underlying the typologies are clearly expressed by Gibbons as follows:[61]

1. Sociologically, "criminals" or "delinquents" are persons who play criminalistic roles heavily and/or who are identified by "society" as criminals or delinquents. (Persons who come to be tagged as offenders by the legal processes are frequently ones who are involved in repetitive and serious acts of law violation; but individuals who engage in petty and isolated acts of illegality are also sometimes reacted to as violators. Both of these groups are "criminals" or "delinquents" because they have been so labeled by the official machinery of social control.)

2. Criminal or delinquent behavior is one social role, but not the

Typologies and Treatment 201

only one, that persons play. Criminal or delinquent individuals also play roles as "citizen," "father," "employee," and so forth.

3. Among persons identified as criminals or delinquents, there are variations in the character and intensity of the deviant role. These include variations in both (a) actual deviant role behavior and (b) role-related social-psychological characteristics. The illegal acts carried on by offenders vary from one individual to another. Also, some persons have no self-image as a deviant, whereas others exhibit such self-definitions. In turn, among individuals with deviant or nondeviant self-conceptions, variations are exhibited in the particular kind of image held ("tough guy," "right guy," "smart hustler," and so on).

4. Stable patterns of criminal or delinquent roles, involving recurrent forms of deviant activity accompanied by uniform social-psychological role characteristics, can be observed in the population of offenders. In these terms, it can be said that types of criminalistic deviance exist.

5. Although behavioral and social-psychological changes occur in specific criminal or delinquent roles during the development of the role, these changes are limited, orderly, and identifiable. As a result, it is possible to define specific, stable criminal and delinquent role-careers. Offenders do not engage in random and unpredictable patterns of role-behavior, they do not "play the field" of offenses.

There are two clusters of variables expressed in these assumptions (though they may not be independent), namely role-careers and causal factors. The role element is composed of offense behavior (dominant current offenses), interactional setting (the relevant social interactional environment of the offense), self-concept, attitudes (using the Schrag typology), and role careers (the developmental pattern of criminal and delinquent activity). The causal (i.e. background) dimension includes social class position, family background (especially parent-child relationships), peer group associations (which overlap with the interactional setting), and contact with defining agencies (exposure to and attitudes toward police, court, welfare agencies, etc.).

The resulting typologies are analyzed in terms of the nine categories. In some cases, different types may be similar with regard to some of the categories, but in all cases there are at least three variations. The types generated by this analysis are as follows:

202 Fundamentals of Criminal Behavior and Correctional Systems

Juvenile
1. Predatory gang delinquent
2. Conflict gang delinquent
3. Casual gang delinquent
4. Casual delinquent, nongang member
5. Automobile thief—joyrider
6. Drug user—heroin
7. Overly aggressive delinquent
8. Female delinquent
9. Behavior problem delinquent

Adult
1. Professional thief
2. Professional "heavy" criminal
3. Semiprofessional property criminal
4. Property offender—"one time loser"
5. Automobile thief—joyrider
6. Naive check forger
7. White collar criminal
8. Professional "fringe" violator
9. Embezzler
10. Personal offender—"one time loser"
11. Psychopathic assaultist
12. Violent sex offender
13. Nonviolent sex offender — "rape"
14. Nonviolent sex offender — statutory rape
15. Narcotic addict—heroin

Following the discussion of all of these types there is a chapter in which each type is linked to a specific form of treatment. It would be impractical to reproduce Gibbons' analysis of each type;[62] therefore, we will discuss just one of these by way of illustration and then proceed to an analysis of the typologies with reference to the issues raised in the earlier segments of this paper.

Gibbons suggests that in the adult typology the "major therapy problem" is the semiprofessional property criminal. He is described in the following ways:

1. Offense behavior: direct assaults on personal property; employ simple crime skills; crime is an occupation.
2. Interactional setting: usually two-person criminal events.
3. Self concept: sees self as a criminal; defines society as corrupt.
4. Attitudes: diffuse, bitter and resentful towards all of society; right guys.
5. Role-career: previously predatory gang delinquents, large number of arrests and convictions.
6. Social class: lower-class.

7. Family background: parental neglect; unstable family of procreation.
8. Peer associations: with other criminals in all spheres of life.
9. Contact with defining agencies: extensive.
10. Treatment: intensive group therapy to break down "criminalistic philosophy."

It should now be clear what the major criticism of Gibbons' work must be—it is, at best, a series of unrelated hypotheses, at worst, a gross distortion of the typological effort initiated by Sutherland and an effort that will lead us nowhere in our search for a treatment typology. In addition, the typology lacks specificity despite the number of categories, does not include psychological variables, is probably not operational or usable in an actual correctional setting, is not based on any identified research or systematic theory, and does not specify treatment procedures or needs but rather designates treatment on the basis of further theoretical assumptions (e.g. the semiprofessional thief is to be "reoriented" from favorable definitions of law violation to unfavorable definitions despite the fact that this notion has yet to be demonstrated, nor has group therapy been proven to be effective in this change if the condition exists and is meaningful). By way of further elaboration we will discuss the theoretical basis of the typologies and their potential usefulness.

It has been a contention throughout this paper that a typology must be exhaustive and it must deal with social and personality system variables. Furthermore, we have indicated that the ideal type mode, to be exhaustive, requires a uniform theoretical scheme. It is our contention that the Gibbons' typologies are not so conceived and, in fact, do not even cohere. If we take, for example, the causal dimension, there is no apparent theoretical justification for selecting only those sub-dimensions with which he chooses to work. Thus, whole ranges of variables are excluded, most notably those involved in the subcultural theory of Cloward and Ohlin, and more purely psychological constructs. While these can be eliminated (i.e. they are themselves not necessary conditions of a typology), we suggest the Gibbons' effort does not present us with a justification for their exclusion. In fact,

204 Fundamentals of Criminal Behavior and Correctional Systems

there is no theory of inclusion, which is our major point; thus, any other categories (sub-dimensions) could be added, making the potential range of typological criteria equivalent to our range of *speculation*. We can only assume that these sub-dimensions were included because they were considered (how is not specified) most relevant. It is the vital question of relevance determination (the selective factor) that is not attended to by Gibbons.

Furthermore, there would appear to be very real problems involved in the use of the typology. Foremost is the problem in developing measures of such variables as hostile attitude, self-concept, and peer group associations that could practically be utilized in a correctional setting. Second, experience would suggest that variations from the types would be more frequent than the types themselves and the typology does not specify how to handle degrees of difference and deviant cases. Let us take the most obvious problem, the multiple offender. What do we do with the offender who is convicted of charges of rape, aggravated assault and rape; or the offender who is involved in "plea copping" (the criticism made by Gibbons of typologies based on legal categories)? In these cases how would we score the offense behavior dimension and the dimensions of role-career and interactional setting? Also with regard to offense behavior, on what basis do we categorize the various degrees of offense seriousness? In the case of the semiprofessional thief we have a range including breaking into warehouses and all forms of robbery—offense behaviors that in terms of the components of seriousness may vary significantly. In sum, if we take what should be the least complex bit of information in the typology, we encounter many potential problems of application. Our suggestion is that these problems are much greater vis-a-vis the other dimensions.

The rejoinder to this line of argument would propose, possibly, that diagnosis and classification are not easy, brief and simple matters, but necessarily must involve levels of complexity. While this may ideally be the case, our contention is that the typology may not be useful given effort, time, etc., because the variables are not coherent or operational, and that given the current and probable future quality of correctional personnel we must highly

Typologies and Treatment

objectify the process of typification. It would appear that the Gibbons' effort does not lend itself to such a system of analysis. The Gibbons' work is helpful for the reasons discussed earlier in this chapter; however, as a substantive, typological effort the mode of its construction fails to afford us with any insight into an adequate treatment typology. Most importantly, Gibbons' cavalier treatment of the "research" culminating in this book and the necessity of future research leads the critical reviewer to consider the typologies as nothing more than an unsystematic theoretical effort.

Interpersonal Maturity

The typological efforts resulting from the theory of interpersonal maturity[63] represent the most extensive and rigorous endeavors in the field of treatment typologies to date. The development of these efforts has followed an almost "classical" (in the perspective of this chapter) design: specification of a multi-level theory; observation of types specified in theory; specification of sub-types; objectification of the process of typification; analysis of the relationship between types and treatments. This is not to imply that this represents *the* typology, for the data has frequently indicated that the typology may not be as useful as was first anticipated. What we mean to imply is that in terms of procedure this is by far our best example of typology development. The locus of this work has been the Community Treatment Project (CTP) of the California Youth Authority.

Interpersonal Maturity Level Theory (IML) describes normal psychological development as following a trend toward increasing involvement with objects, people and social institutions.

> These involvements give rise to new needs, demands, and situations. Inherent in many of these new situations are problems of perceptual discrimination with regard to the relationships existing between the self and the external environment. As these discriminations are made and assimilated, a cognitive restructuring of experience and expectancy takes place. A new reference scheme is then developed; a new level of integration is achieved.[64]

At each of these levels, the personality core may be characterized as an organized set of perceptions, expectations and orientations.

In the original theory, seven levels of maturity were described, though it was indicated that delinquency[65] would be most probable in levels two through five.

A brief description of each of these four levels found in the delinquent population has been composed by Grant and Grant:[66]

Level 2: The individual whose interpersonal understanding and behavior are integrated at this level is primarily involved with demands that the world take care of him. He sees others solely as "givers" or "withholders" and has no conception of interpersonal refinement beyond this. He is unable to explain, understand or predict the behavior or reactions of others. He is not interested in things outside himself except as a source of supply. He behaves impulsively, unaware of the effects of his behavior on others, and is apt to explode or run away when frustrated or thwarted.

Level 3: . . . attempts to manipulate his environment in order to get what he wants. In contrast to level 2, he is at least aware that his own behavior has something to do with whether or not he gets what he wants. He still does not differentiate, however, among people except to the extent that they can or cannot be useful to him. He sees people only as objects to be manipulated in order to get what he wants. His manipulations may take the form either of conforming to the rules of whoever seems to have the power at the moment . . . or of the type of maneuvering characteristic of a "confidence man." He tends to deny having any disturbing feelings or strong emotional involvement in his relationships with others.

Level 4: . . . has internalized a set of standards by which he judges his and others' behavior. He is aware of the influence of others on him and their expectations of him. To a certain extent, he is aware of the effects of his own behavior on others. He wants to be like the people he admires and may feel guilty about not measuring up to his internalized standards. The conflict produced by the feelings of inadequacy and guilt may be internalized with consequent neurotic symptoms or acted out in antisocial behavior. Because the individual at level 4 tends to be uncomfortable about himself and because he is able to internalize values, he appears more amenable to treatment than previously described maturity levels.

Level 5: A person who functions at this level is able to see patterns of behavior; he may see himself and others behaving in the same way in different situations or see a continuity in his past, present, and future. Delinquency, for a person at this level, is apt to be situationally determined.

Typologies and Treatment 207

In connection with the development of the CTP (in 1961) this classification scheme was further elaborated.[67] The elaboration consists of nine sub-types found in levels 2, 3, and 4 (level 5 was omitted as a result of observations that indicated its relative infrequency). The classification presently being used follows that elaboration:

Level	Sub-type	Identifying Concept
2	Aa—unsocialized personality (aggressive type)	Demanding
	Ap—unsocialized personality (passive type)	Complaining
3	Cfm—conformist (immature personality type)	Conforming
	Cfc—conformist (cultural type)	Conforming
	Mp—Manipulator (psychopathic type)	Manipulating
4	(A) Neurotic	
	Nx—anxiety type	Defending
	Na—acting out with no felt anxiety	Defending
	(B) Non-Neurotic	
	Se—situational emotional reaction	Identifying
	Ci—cultural identifier	Identifying

In types Se, Ci and Cfc we have the emphasis on the environmental, sociological, causal factors, while in the other types we have the emphasis on other causal factors. In addition, there has been the attempt to explain development and fixation by reference to both need structures and sociocultural factors. The theory, though in certain respects psychologically reductionistic,[68] (especially the notion of the necessity of developmental movement), is overwhelmingly of the integrated or multi-level type. In addition, by definition (i.e. the selective factor) it is systemic and exhaustive. Thus, it meets the requirements established in this paper of a causal-treatment typology. It is clear that the descriptions do not seem to have the qualities of specificity and generalizability. It is to this issue that we now turn.

During the initial phases of CTP, and in earlier research, level type was determined by a semi-structured "crisis," clinical interview. The assumption behind this technique was that individuals act out higher levels than they have actually developed and that only under stress conditions would they manifest their "real" personalities. This procedure requires considerable training and very competent interviewers and thus limits the future general use of the techniques. The research to date indicates that the interview technique has high-rater reliability;[69] however, the cost of this technique in training and interview time suggests the need for a more objective and routine measurement device.

The BGOS (Beverly-Grant Opinion Schedule) represents the major attempt at IML quantification.[70] The scale was developed by analyzing the responses of 384 subjects whose IML's had been determined by 600 true-false items. The item analysis indicated that the selection of an 18 item scale could differentiate between high maturity (levels 4 and 5) and low maturity (levels 2 and 3) subjects. In subsequent research with the BGOS this level of differentiation was maintained with moderately high levels of reliability (.82), and validity (80%), where validity is defined as replication of dual-rater IML designations in terms of the high-low dichotomy. The scale cannot, to date, further differentiate the types or the important sub-types. These same problems of maximum differentiation have been replicated in the use of the Jesness Scale.[71] Presently, further analysis of the response patterns is being planned to attempt to move toward more refined measures. In addition, as the amount of time is lengthened the number of subjects will increase, thus increasing the probability of larger numbers in the sub-types and therefore the chance of identifying response patterns for these levels. To date, however, the problem of objectification of IML's has not been satisfactorily solved, though in terms of methodology, the efforts in this direction are highly commendable.

The most significant problems in IML use are those relating to the relationship between levels and treatment modes, and the related issue of efficiencies already observed in the CTP. Since 1963,[72] the project directors have been promising a "differential treatment model," and as of the most recent publication similar prospects are identified.[73] Currently, guided-group interaction is being used with randomly assigned IML's of all types, while a differential treatment unit has been created to experiment with specific treatment for each type that is also randomly assigned to the program. The most recent publications only describe this design—there is no comparative data or description of potential treatments. It is apparent from a careful review of the publications of the CTP that the typology does not readily lend itself to treatment specification. The commitment of the Youth Authority to the IML technique suggests that a treatment strategy will be developed as a result of experimentation, *if* efficient treatment specifications can be developed.

We are now prepared to note and assess the results of the CTP. Success has been measured in four primary ways: failure rates (revocation), changes in personality measures, changes in IML, and reduction in costs. In the beginning, CTP was organized to measure the effectiveness of noninstitutional treatments. All eligible subjects ("nonviolent" offenders) were randomly assigned to either a Youth Authority institution or the CTP. Since then, the IML technique has been adopted by many of the youth institutions (see the discussion of the Preston Ranch Study below) so that the controls have been contaminated in terms of treatment decisions and the movement and purpose have been toward the development of the typology itself.

Briefly, the measures of success indicate that the revocation rate of the CTP was *not* better than the institutionalized wards in the early stages,[74] but as the project has progressed, revocation rates have improved significantly for the CTP subjects;[75] there is improvement in CTP and IML measures;[75] and the CTP results in a saving of approximately $172 per month (CTP=$178; Institution=$350).

It is contended by the staff that the rates of success have improved as the understanding of treatment needs has progressed. In all cases analysis has been on less than 100 subjects which limits our acceptance of the results; but in the recent research, the direction has indicated some success for the CTP procedures. Currently, a second project is being instituted in California at the Preston Institution where six of the sub-types are being used. Here the emphasis is to be on diversified treatment for the types within an institutional setting.[76] We can expect increased reports from the California system on IML as the number of subjects becomes larger and the number of projects based on this typology increases.

In the analysis of the IML we have been minimally critical. Though we would hesitate to place the entire resources of a correctional system on one such effort,[77] we find that, as is usual, the research from California is more than adequate and that the typology effort has been unequaled in the literature.

CONCLUSIONS

We have maintained that a consistent problem in the development of treatment typologies has been the neglect of the role of systematic theory in typification. This is further compounded by the relative failure of criminologists to analyze the variety of modes of type construction and the requirements of a typology. In this chapter we have endeavored to survey these problems as well as the relevant substantive typologies.

Whether or not we accept the content of IML theory, we have maintained that the work within that perspective represents a model for the development of treatment typologies. The mode of "successive approximations" from theory to typology would appear to be our most efficient strategy.

NOTES AND REFERENCES

1. The more stimulating recent discussions include:
   P. Lazarsfeld: Philosophy of science and empirical social research. In E. Nagel, et al. (Eds.): *Logic, Methodology and Philosophy of Science.* Stanford, Stanford University Press, 1962, pp. 463-73.

   D. Martindale: Sociological theory and the ideal type. In L. Gross (Ed.): *Symposium on Sociological Theory.* Evanston, Row, Peterson, 1959, pp. 57-91.

Typologies and Treatment

C. G. Hempel: Typological methods in the natural and social sciences. *Proceedings*, American Philosophical Association, 1:65-86, 1952.
2. See, for example, the often quoted article by Robert Winch: Heuristic and empirical typologies. *American Sociological Review*, 12:68-75, 1947, where he opts for an empirical (i.e. factor analytic) approach to type construction.
3. Max Weber: *Methodology of the Social Sciences*. Trans. E. A. Shils and H. A. Finch. Glencoe, Free Press, 1949. Also, T. Parsons: *Structure of Social Action*. New York, Free Press, 1937, Chap. 17.
4. See, for example, Martindale, *op. cit.*, pp. 63-66; and Parsons, *op. cit.*, p. 580.
5. Parsons, *op. cit.*, p. 618.
6. John C. McKinney: *Constructive Typology and Social Theory*. New York, Appleton-Century-Crofts, 1966. This work includes summaries of most of McKinney's articles since 1950.
7. *Ibid.*, p. 3.
8. Howard Becker: *Through Values to Social Interpretation*. Durham, Duke University Press, 1950, p. 261.
9. McKinney, *op. cit.*, Chaps. 6 and 7.
10. Svend Riemer: The ideal type in criminological research. *Social Science Research Bulletin*, 50:138-44, 1942.
11. Don Gibbons: *Changing the Lawbreaker*. Englewood Cliffs, Prentice-Hall, 1965.
12. Theodore Ferdinand: *Typologies of Delinquency*. New York, Random House, 1966.
13. See, for example, Albert Morris: Potentialities in a suggested classification of offenders. Paper read to American Society of Criminology, 1963.
14. Riemer, *op. cit.*, p. 143.
15. Gibbons, *op. cit.*, p. 23.
16. *Ibid.*
17. There is a large and varied literature dealing with specific offense types. On the basis of the criteria of causal relevance and systemic completeness, these are to be excluded from the range of this paper. A further assumption underlying this exclusion, which may be obvious but requires explicit rendition, is that the types in a typology must be determined from the same range of characteristics. The "purpose-selection," the abstraction, must be from the same body of theory and research in order to provide us with a "closed" system.

For a further discussion of legal types, see Gibbons, *op. cit.*, pp. 24-39; Dorothy Tompkins: *The Offender: A Bibliography*. Berkeley, Institute of Government Studies, University of California, 1963.
18. Marvin Wolfgang: *Patterns in Criminal Homicide*. Philadelphia, University of Pennsylvania Press, 1958.

212 Fundamentals of Criminal Behavior and Correctional Systems

19. Julian Roebuck: A criticism of Gibbons' and Garrity's criminal typology. *Journal of Criminal Law, Criminology and Police Science,* 54:478, 1963.
20. See, for example, Julian Roebuck and Mervyn Cadwallader: The Negro armed robber as a criminal type. *Pacific Sociological Review,* 4:21-26, 1961.
21. Ferdinand, *op. cit.,* p. 55.
22. *Ibid.,* p. 22.
23. This position has only recently been expressed in sociology by authors like T. Parsons (Parsons, *op. cit.,* Chap. 19) and P. Rieff (see, *Triumph of the Therapeutic.* New York, Harper and Row, 1966, p. 6). For a more comprehensive analysis of the general problem see C. L. Morgan: *Emergent Evolution.* London, Williams, 1923; and A. Edel: The concept of levels in social theory. In L. Gross (Ed.): *Symposium on Sociological Theory.* New York, Harper and Row, 1959.
24. The discussion will omit those typologies that are derived primarily from the construction of physical types, because they would appear to be only minimally (if at all) relevant to treatment determination.
25. George Vold: *Thoretical Criminology.* New York, Oxford University Press, 1958, pp. 27-40.
26. *Ibid.,* p. 30.
27. As presented in Vold, *op. cit.*
28. Garofalo classified them as murderers, violent criminals, criminals lacking in probity and lascivious criminals. (*Criminology.* Trans. by R. W. Miller. Boston, Little, Brown, 1914, pp. 11-132)
29. In sociological criminology this tendency exists in the separation of the "insane" offender and, frequently, the "middle class" delinquent (e.g. R. England: A theory of middle class delinquency. *Journal of Criminal Law, Criminology and Police Science,* 50: 535-40, 1960.)
    There have been many restatements of the typology. For example, Albert Morris, *op. cit.,* who suggests a typology including legalistic, situational, pathological, avocational and career offenders. Also see A. R. Lindsmith and H. W. Dunham: Some principles of criminal typology. *Social Forces,* 19:307-14, 1941, for an attempt to make the "social"-"individual" dichotomy the basis of the typological effort.
30. Edwin Sutherland and D. Cressey: *Criminology,* 6th ed. Lippincott, 1960, pp. 237-50.
31. Ruth S. Cavan: *Criminology.* New York, T. Crowell, 1950, pp. 20-32.
32. Herbert Bloch and G. Geis: *Man, Crime and Society.* New York, Random House, 1962, pp. 135-37, 311-43.
33. Marshall B. Clinard: *Sociology of Deviant Behavior.* New York, Holt, Rinehart and Winston, 1963, pp. 204-92.
34. Sutherland, *op. cit.,* pp. 238-43.
35. *Ibid.,* p. 249.

Typologies and Treatment 213

36. There are numerous analyses of subcultural (i.e. gang) theories; therefore, no attempt will be made to summarize or critique them as typologies. Major problems that would be relevant to our discussion are their selectivity, their generality, and their mode of construction.
37. Ferdinand, op. cit., pp. 80-235.
38. Seymour Rubenfeld: Family of Outcasts. New York, Free Press, 1965, pp. 233-309.
39. For his most recent statement see, Clarence Schrag: Toward a unified theory of correction. In D. Cressey (Ed.): The Prison. New York, Holt, Rinehart and Winston, 1961.
40. Donald Clemmer: The Prison Community. New York, Holt, Rinehart and Winston, 1958; reissue.
41. Norman Hayner: Five inmate types. American Sociological Review, 26: 73-84, 1961.
42. Gresham Sykes: Society of Captives. Princeton, Princeton University Press, 1958, pp. 84-109.
43. Richard Korn and L. McCorkle: Criminology and Penology. New York, Henry Holt, 1959.
44. Schrag, op. cit.
45. The literature on the inmate code and prisonization is extensive and varied. Essentially, the inmate code refers to a normative system in conflict with that of the administrators of the institution; prisonization refers to the adoption of this code and other elements of the inmate culture (argot, dress, etc.). For an extensive bibliography, see G. Sykes and S. Messinger: The inmate social system. In Theoretical Studies in the Social Organization of the Prison. New York, Social Science Research Council, 1960, pp. 5-7.
46. Donald Garrity: Effect of Length of Incarceration Upon Parole Adjustment and Estimation of Optimum Sentence. Unpublished Ph.D. dissertation, University of Washington, 1958.
47. Stanton Wheeler: Socialization in correctional communities. American Sociological Review, 26:697-712, 1961.
48. Peter Garabedian: Western Penitentiary: A Study in Social Organization. Unpublished Ph.D. dissertation, University of Washington, 1959.
49. Garrity, op. cit., pp. 173-75.
50. Charles F. Wellford: Factors associated with the process of prisonization. Journal of Criminal Law, Criminology and Police Science, 1969.
51. The use of typologies is not necessarily restricted to institutional treatment; however, it does not seem appropriate to refer to the process of judicial decision-making as typology construction (as in the probation-sentenced dichtomy), though treatment potential will be restricted by those decisions. Community treatment may benefit considerably from constructed typologies as has been demonstrated in the CTP to be discussed later in this section.

52. F. Loveland, unpublished materials, 1965.
53. Classification Consultant to Eastern State Penitentiary, Summer, 1965.
54. Gibbons, *op. cit.*, pp. 146-47.
55. Stuart Adams: Interaction between individual interview therapy and treatment amenability in older youth authority wards. In *Inquiries Concerning Kinds of Treatments for Kinds of Delinquents.* Sacramento: California Board of Correction, 1961, pp. 27-44. Reprinted in *The Sociology of Punishment and Correction,* N. Johnston, L. Savitz, and M. Wolfgang (Ed.) New York: John Wiley, 1962, pp. 213-224. All further references will be to the 1962 reprint.
56. *Ibid.*, p. 214.
57. *Ibid.*
58. *Annual Research Review.* California Department of Correction, 1963, pp. 17-18.
59. Communication from John P. Conrad, former Director of Research of the California Department of Correction.
60. There is little statistical analysis of the data in the reports, which would seem to imply their acceptance of the notion of the irrelevance of statistical techniques for populations.
    The data of Phase I covers only 400 of the 1600 studied. Subsequent reviews indicate that the results were not altered by the inclusion of the remaining 1200 cases.
61. Gibbons, *op. cit.*, pp. 45-46.
62. For a summary of the characteristics of all the types see, F. Hornum and C. Wellford: Summary of the Gibbons' typology. Mimeo, Institute of Corrections, 1965.
63. Clyde E. Sullivan, M. Q. Grant, and J. D. Grant: The development of interpersonal maturity: Applications to delinquency. *Psychiatry, 20:*373-85, 1957.
64. *Ibid.*
65. The typology has been used most extensively with juveniles only; however, it is not logically restricted to this population. In our evaluation we will accept the assumption of Sullivan, *et al.* that the extension to adult criminality is not precluded by the structure of the theory.
66. J. D. Grant and M. Q. Grant: A group dynamics approach to the treatment of nonconformists in the Navy. *Annals, 322:*126-35, 1959.
67. M. Q. Grant: Interpersonal maturity level classification. California Department of the Youth Authority, Division of Research, 1961.
68. As noted earlier, we have not focused on more purely psychoanalytic typologies. These have been adequately summarized and reviewed by Ferdinand *op. cit.*, Chap. 4.
69. Ratings by the same rater at different points in time have reliability coefficients of .82 to .93; for different raters middle .80's. The measures of reliability generally used are the factor analytic-variance models. See,

Typologies and Treatment 215

M. G. Warren, et al.: *Community Treatment Project: Fifth Progress Report.* Department of the Youth Authority, 1966, pp. 35-36.
70. Robert F. Beverly: *The BGOS.* Department of the Youth Authority, 1965.
71. *Ibid.,* p. 18.
72. M. Q. Grant: Recent findings in the CTP. In *Correction in the Community.* Board of Correction, State of California, 1964, p. 40.
73. Grant (1966), *op. cit.,* pp. 23-24.
74. Grant (1964), *op. cit.,* pp. 42-43.
75. Grant (1966), *op. cit.,* p. vii.
76. *The Preston Typology Study.* Progress Report, Institute for the Study of Crime and Delinquency, 1966, pp. 12-13.
77. While in the Special Intensive Parole Project there is an emerging typology based on the degree of supervision required by parolees (see, e.g. J. Havel: The parole outcome study. Research Report #13, Department of Corrections, 1965) and in the Typology of Violence Study there is the anticipation of a violence typology based on purpose (see, 1966 Progress Report, Institute for the Study of Crime and Delinquency, pp. 12-13), neither of these have been developed to date, nor do they qualify as total treatment typology.

Chapter 10
Characteristics of the Juvenile Delinquent
MARY DEAN

Crime is the web and woof of society. It is not an accident—not just an accident. The amount, the character, and the kind of crime are socially conditioned. The good people who set out to remake the criminal, to better the police force, begin at the wrong end—and too late. The story starts earlier; it starts within the milieu in which the criminals grow up.

. . . TANNENBAUM

Introduction
Types of Delinquency
The Delinquent and Family Relations
The Delinquent and School
The Delinquent and the Neighborhood
Summary
References

INTRODUCTION

Juvenile delinquent is a catchall concept used to describe a wide range of qualitatively different youth. It has many different meanings in different social contexts. This concept includes everything from the "normal" situational delinquent to the psychopathological case. To the judge or policeman, the delinquent is one who commits an act defined as delinquent by law and who is adjudicated as such by an appropriate court although the law varies from state to state in defining who is delinquent. To the psychologist and psychiatrist reviewing the delinquent, he has a problem of a disordered personality development resulting from disordered relations between the child and significant persons in his psychological field. The sociologist puts greatest emphasis upon social disorganization and conditions of socioeconomic deprivation. To the "average" citizen, the delinquent may be a delinquent because of his appearance. To the property owner, the delinquent may be the youngster who does not respect his lawn. To the parent, the delinquent is not a delinquent but just a mixed up rebellious "kid."

With such diffuse definitions of delinquency, an exact determination of the extent and nature of juvenile delinquency is impossible. However it might be helpful to see what most studies indicate about that type of delinquent who comes to the attention of the juvenile courts. It must be recognized that many of these delinquents were delinquents long before they are brought to court and that many are never brought to court. The adjudicated delinquent is more likely to be a boy than a girl. He is generally 14 or 15 years old when referred, although he exhibited behavior problems considerably earlier. His attitude is hostile, defiant, and suspicious. He is from the lower social class, is usually retarded in school work, especially in reading ability, and shows a chronic history of truancy.

TYPES OF DELINQUENCY

While, technically speaking, a delinquent is one who has been declared so by a juvenile court, those so adjudicated represent a relatively small and nonrepresentative sample of the juveniles who commit delinquent acts. Further, just as there are numerous types of delinquency, there are different types of delinquents, each tending to commit certain types of delinquent acts and each receiving different treatment. Many studies of juvenile delinquents classify delinquents by type. From these studies, it is possible to describe four types of juvenile delinquents.

The *first* of these, the middle-class delinquent, usually is not considered a delinquent since his class standing protects him from the juvenile court adjudication process. While this group accounts only for a minute portion of adjudicated delinquents, it accounts for a large portion of the delinquent acts committed. Middle-class juveniles are implicated in a large amount of hidden and usually less serious lawbreaking, but this is not to say that there are not instances of serious criminal acts on the part of these youths. They seem to be over-represented in juvenile court for offenses such as traffic, liquor, curfew, incorrigibility, vandalism and car theft cases, while their working and lower class counterparts are over-represented for more serious offenses such as robbery, larceny, truancy and loitering.[1] It has become more evident that in many cases middle-class offenses are generally absorbed by the community; e.g., parents and children working it out with each other, except for the most flagrant violations of the law. Middle-class delinquents known to the police tend not to be involved in repetitive, career patterns of misconduct and once brought to the attention of the police are absorbed back into the community without referral to juvenile court. Only serious forms of middle-class delinquency such as auto theft, joyriding and aggressive behavior end up in juvenile court.[2] Recently much attention has been given to middle-class delinquency and a number of theories have been put forth. It is interesting to note that most theories of middle-class delinquency deal only with boys, perhaps since most middle-class delinquency reported is with boys.

Second, the occasional delinquent or one-time offender is usually charged with a minor violation. These delinquents usually participate in group acts of petty theft or vandalism. Researchers who have examined this type of delinquent find that, relative to more serious delinquents, they tend to come from unbroken homes with little family tension and have average grades in school. Several writers have pointed to types of delinquents in many ways analogous to the description of the occasional delinquent. Adolescents in a slum where racketeering or organized gambling flourishes often become assimilated into the existing adult criminal subculture, a process which usually involves normal boys from intact homes. These boys may be delinquent in a legal sense but are not considered as such by the norms of the neighborhood. An excellent picture of the occasional delinquent is given by William T. Whyte in *Street Corner Society*. His "corner boys" were well socialized to the society they lived in. Even though they were involved in occasional drug and alcohol use and minor offenses, they were usually nondelinquent.[3]

The *third* type, the habitual gang delinquent, is the one who usually is involved in more serious infractions, is more likely to be sent to juvenile institutions, and most likely to continue in a pattern of semi-professional criminal behavior as an adult. This group has been described as loyal; from poor residential areas; from families that are more often large, broken and with other delinquent members; poor students in school; antisocial; and from large families with lax discipline. They described themselves as smart, excitable, stubborn and not warmhearted. These descriptions fit with Miller's description on the focal concerns of the lower class, excitement and smartness and toughness. This type of delinquent is further described as a defective superego type who does not internalize the norms of conventional society and who experiences little sense of guilt over his delinquent acts. Rather he accepts the content of and membership in a delinquent peer culture.[4]

The violations of the *fourth* type, the maladjusted delinquent, stem from personality disturbances rather than involvement with a gang or residing in a slum area. This type of delinquent is characterized by high-tension homes, small families, school retardation, and generally are loners. Studies have shown that this type of delinquent suffers early and severe parental rejection. They were also found to have poor peer relationships and to suffer from social isolation. On a self-description inventory, they describe themselves as "disorderly, nervous, confused and not dependable." This group has been labeled as "neurotic" and with parental repression and lack of warmth in their background. It should be noted that other research done by several subculture writers indicated that there may be a form of delinquent subculture analogous to the maladjusted individual delinquent. Cloward and Ohlin identify a "retreatist" or drug-using subculture which they suggest arises when adolescents, out of frustration or lack of opportunity, seek to escape reality.[5]

Not all delinquency is rooted in tangled pathology, discrimination and deprivation of the slum. For at least a portion of the delinquent population, delinquency may be in part an immediate response to an immediate situation. While it may be true that deeper forces may be operating, the youngster may be seizing upon the opportunity of the moment (perhaps illegitimately), the pressures of others, or in response to a situation for which there are no legal or legitimate responses. This may be termed situational delinquency, an example being auto theft—predominantly a teenage crime.[6]

THE DELINQUENT AND FAMILY RELATIONS

The family is the most basic institution for developing a child's emotional, intellectual, moral, physical and social potential. It is in the family that the child learns to control his desires and accept societal rules such as the restrictions on the time, place and circumstances where personal needs may be met. Of all the variables which have been shown to be related to delinquency, family variables such as parental affection and parental discipline are among the most important. For the most part, sociologists and anthropologists have focused on social class and delinquent gangs as etiological while psychiatrists and psychologists have focused on family and personality variables. Neither approach by itself is adequate, although each may be more relevant than the other for the explanation of certain types of delinquency.

Family patterns vary by social class. Failure to account for the interrelatedness of social class, family variables and delinquency has resulted in a considerable amount of confusion. One reason for this is that studies based upon officially adjudicated delinquents exaggerate the relationship between class and delinquency because of biases operating in police and court procedures. Nevertheless, there are some characteristics of lower class families which seem to be related to delinquency. Growing up in a lower class family involves social, economic and occupational deprivation. This in turn results in lesser attraction for the family and for the father, given the emphasis that is placed upon the man's occupational position and earning power. This is related to a lower concept of personal and family worth. The parents in a lower class home have limited resources with which to manipulate rewards and punishments and thus maintain external control over their children, especially in anonymous urban areas.

This is further complicated by a lesser degree of attractiveness of community agencies such as schools and churches, therefore their lesser ability to maintain external controls. Lower class families are also characterized by more family disharmony and instability. There is a greater likelihood of lax or inconsistent discipline, and discipline focused upon the child's actions rather than intentions stemming in part from the constraining situation represented by lower class occupations. There is also less affection within the family stemming from pressures imposed upon the family by the need to adapt to deprived circumstances. All of these factors lead to a lesser degree of identification with parents and the subsequent internalization of parental norms. These variables are reflected in the wide range of research that has demonstrated a relationship between delinquency and broken homes, ordinal position, family maladjustment, parental discipline and affection or rejection by family.[7] Each of these will be discussed briefly.

The most consistent pattern observed by the individual who is working with adjudicated delinquents is the high incidence of broken homes. This is not easy to determine exactly the relationship as it is next to impossible to determine the extent of delinquency in the nonadjudicated control group. With the juvenile court operating under the *parens patriae* principle, the court is most likely to assume supervision of the child in a case where both parents are not available. Broken homes seem to be more closely related to female delinquency than to male delinquency and to delinquency in younger children than in older children.

Delinquency has also been associated to ordinal position and to family size. Generally, delinquents tend to come from larger families and from intermediates, that is children having both older and younger siblings. One study showed that over 50 percent of the glue sniffers, for example, came from families with more than eight children, compared to 18 percent in the control group. Family size is closely related to social class and ethnic background and these must be taken into account.

Family adjustment has been associated with delinquency. Parental and marital happiness and family cohesiveness are as closely related to delinquency as the broken home. Perhaps even more important than parental marital relations is the quality of parent-child relationships. Lax and erratic disciplinary techniques, unfair discipline and harsh physical punishment are all associated with delinquents. Most of this research was based on the perceptions of delinquents and, while these may be important, they may not represent actual conditions.

Another aspect of the child-parent relationship often associated with juvenile delinquency is the presence or absence of parental affection. The Gleucks reported that the most important factor seemed to be the father's affection for the boy. The bulk of the evidence seems to support the contention that at least one loving parent, coupled with consistent parental discipline, tends to mitigate delinquency producing forces. Affection seems to be closely related to the child's internalization of parental values. Assuming that these values support conventional behavior, an affectionate parent-child relationship promotes internalization of conventional values and thus insulates a child against delinquent behavior.

There has been more research on the relationship between delinquency and family than the relationship between delinquency and any other class of variables. Much more effort is needed. Most of the family variables associated with delinquency are also associated with social class. The selectivity of the process by which a juvenile becomes classified as delinquent has not been accounted for adequately in this research but strong relationships have been demonstrated.

THE DELINQUENT AND SCHOOL

Since Albert Cohen's classic work was published in 1961, there has been a steadily increasing body of literature on the relationship between delinquent behavior and the school. Generally the literature maintains that success in school is difficult for working and lower class children. At the same time success in school is requisite to occupational rewards which are emphasized and held forth as being available to everyone. School failure characterizes the vast majority of adjudicated delinquents. This condition appears to be the cause of early juvenile institutions' stressing educational programs almost exclusively and this was evident in calling them learning, reform, or industrial schools. School failure on the part of delinquents results from conditions which are deeply anchored in prevailing conceptions and organization of the school system. These conditions include emphasis on middle-class values and behaviors which working and lower class youth are not prepared to meet, irrelevant curriculum, hasty and thoughtless labeling, economic and racial segregation, low commitment on the part of the youth and school intolerance for misconduct on the part of selected students.[8] The juvenile delinquent consistently follows a pattern of school difficulty, truancy, and then delinquency. This relationship, like family organization, is complicated by the fact that boys from the lower and working classes are most likely to experience these difficulties.

THE DELINQUENT AND THE NEIGHBORHOOD

The delinquent disproportionately is likely to be from a neighborhood that is low on the socioeconomic scale of the community and harsh in many ways for those who live there. The child growing up in this neighborhood experiences few of the advantages and comforts which are taken for granted by his suburban counterparts. In these slum neighborhoods, population is extremely dense, families are large, parental attention scarce, legitimate recreational opportunities infrequent and criminal opportunities at a maximum. When a juvenile court has to make a decision about whether to release a child, place him on probation, or institutionalize him, the latter form of treatment is far more likely if the child lives under these disadvantageous and unhealthy conditions.

SUMMARY

Juvenile delinquency includes a wide range of behavior which varies so greatly between jurisdictions that a general definition is impossible. Juvenile delinquents are equally as difficult to describe. The adjudicated delinquent however is far less heterogeneous. The selectivity of the juvenile adjudication process is such that the lower classes contribute vastly more than their share. The typical adjudicated delinquent can be described as a 14½-year-old urban male from a broken or disorganized home, who has experienced difficulties in making an adequate adjustment in school and who subsequently has violated laws while in the company of other youth of similar circumstances. Planning programs for prevention or treatment of delinquency requires altering not only the juvenile but also those conditions which made it seem necessary to the court that he be so labeled and treated.

REFERENCES

1. Roland J. Chilton: Middle-class delinquency and specific offense analysis. In VAZ, *Middle-Class Juvenile Delinquency*, pp. 91-101.
2. Don C. Gibbons: *Delinquent Behavior*. Prentice-Hall, Inc., Englewood Cliffs, New Jersey, 1970.
3. Task Force Report: Juvenile Delinquency and Youth Crime—The President's Commission on Law Enforcement and Administration of Justice, U. S. Printing Office, Washington, D. C., 1967.
4. *Ibid.*, pp. 203-204.
5. *Ibid.*, p. 204.
6. *Ibid.*, p. 205.
7. *Op. cit.*, Task Force Report on Juvenile Delinquency and Youth Crime, p. 195 ff.
8. *Op. cit.*, Task Force Report on Juvenile Delinquency and Youth Crime, p. 259.

Chapter 11

Characteristics of the Female Offender

CLYDE B. VEDDER AND DORA B. SOMERVILLE

Introduction
The Incorrigible Girl
The Sex-Delinquent Girl
The Probation-Violator Girl
Observations, Conclusions and Recommendations
References

INTRODUCTION

There has been a paucity of published research in the area of female delinquency and crime. Most studies have concerned themselves with male delinquency and criminality since males predominate in crime by about five to one at the juvenile training school level and by nearly thirty to one at the adult prison level.

The pioneer research on the female offender was done by Lombroso[20] just prior to 1900. This Italian anthropologist and physician contended that the female offender including the prostitute was less likely to be born a criminal type than the male offender and was more likely to display the characteristics of an "occasional" offender who today might be termed a "situational offender" or an "offender of opportunity." Her "reluctant crime" may have originated in the suggestion of a lover, husband, father, or even a female companion. Lombroso cited parental neglect and desertion as highly causative factors leading to early female thieving and prostitution.

Another important female-offender study was made by Fernald,[13] who used the inmates (mostly prostitutes) of the New York Reformatory for Women in her sample. This study presented no theory; it merely emphasized the women's impoverished backgrounds, limited schooling, employment at an early age, meager industrial training, and a relatively inferior mentality.

In 1923, in a less factual but more systematic way, Thomas[31] viewed the sexually delinquent girl as an "unadjusted" girl, somewhat on the amoral side, who, by using sex as capital, attempts to satisfy her dominant wishes for security, recognition, new experience and response. Thomas postulated that human motives could be reduced to these four basic wishes, generated by the social circumstances and personalized by the individual's definition of the situation. In his view the wishes are, for the most part, on the conscious level.

Glueck and Glueck[13] assembled the case folder data on a consecutive sample of five hundred Massachusetts Reformatory for Women inmates. The Gluecks' research did not proceed on the basis of testing any theory or hypothesis about the female offender. It did, however, single out five factors bearing the highest association to nonrecidivism: (1) retardation in school, (2) neighborhood influences with a year of commitment, (3) steadiness of employment, (4) economic responsibility and (5) mental abnormality. The Gluecks characterized their sample as a "swarm of defective, diseased, antisocial misfits which a reformatory and a parole system are required by society to transform into wholesome, decent, law-abiding citizens."

A more recent definitive study on the female offender was undertaken by Pollak.[22] He attempted, in a systematic way, to explain why female criminality was so much less frequently reported than male criminal behavior. Pollak found that female criminality was especially underreported in such areas as shoplifting, thefts by prostitutes, thefts by domestic servants, abortions, perjury, disturbance of the peace, offenses against children, and homicide. He also noted that offenses such as homosexuality and exhibitionism go practically undetected if committed by women. Pollak points out that the woman's public image as homemaker, child rearer, nurse, mistress and other related roles puts her in a good position to commit and screen her crimes from public view. Female criminality is largely masked criminality, as women use deceit and indirection in committing their offenses. The real measure of female criminality must be sought from unofficial sources.

Characteristics of the Female Offender

In his analysis of the delinquent male subculture, Cohen[6] commented on the female delinquent. Implicit in his theory is that the female delinquent is less likely to be involved in delinquency simply because of her adjustment to males, since the bulk of her behavior is sex-connected, unlike the stealing and malicious hell-raising of her male counterpart.

The "occasional offender" theory of Lombroso, the "wish satisfaction" theory of Thomas, the "masked behavior" theory of Pollak and the "boy's girl" theory of Cohen represent the principal attempts to explain female criminality. However, since 1955, additional attempts have been made to clarify the social significance and implications of female criminality.

Barnes and Teeters[3] reject the thesis that women commit fewer crimes than men because they are inherently more moral and innocuous. Women are protected in a male-dominated world. Women generally fear social disapproval more than men and therefore tend to observe prevailing mores to a greater extent than do males. Reckless[24] calls attention to some of the specifics which characterize female criminality. To think of the criminality of women in the same order of phenomena as crime in general is to cloud the issue. Theories which attempt to explain criminality in males fall short in explaining criminality in females, due to the biological makeup of women and still more, because of the role women play in male-dominated societies. The woman must not only be herself, but must also "play up to, for, or with men," the latter role giving her a "second self to an initial self."

Since the theories of Lombroso, Thomas, Pollak, and Cohen were not supported by data collected to test a hypothesis, Kay[16] designed research to test specific hypotheses regarding components of the self-definition (concept) of females in crime. She sought to explain the chief aspects of the female prisoner's self as she perceived it in the institution, to assess her direction of socialization, to measure the extent to which she perceived herself as being alienated and, finally, to approximate the way in which she perceived the institution was affecting her. This research revealed that the younger inmates were veering toward poor socialization with more frequency than older inmates. Women who began delinquent careers before they were fourteen years old were more poorly socialized than those who started delinquency after fourteen. No significant socialization differences were found regarding the number of arrests or the length of incarceration. As to alienation, no important variations were found between inmates according to age, number of previous arrests, the length of time already spent in the institution and age at the initial onset of delinquency. However, Kay found that the alienation of the women inmates was not much more pronounced than that experienced by professional women, factory workers and shopgirls. This is conceptualized by Kay as "role lag."

Because of their role in a male-dominated society, according to Kay,[16] women generally, including female offenders, feel more helpless in society than do men. Role lag refers to the discrepancy between what is conceded to be the equal position of women in the United States today and their actual status; women are categorically discriminated against as members of the "weaker sex" much as are other minority group members. The judicial process metes out differential sentencing for the female, and all this to the benefit of womankind if the price paid for the privileges is not considered. Today's woman has to wear a variety of hats. She must change roles frequently and the roles may lack consistency and continuity. The girl who finds no suitable adult to emulate and arrives at physiological maturity without having learned to cope with the duality of roles is especially vulnerable to deviant behavior. If her control system is lacking or deficient, she will feel dissociated from society, powerless to control her destiny and hopeless as she drifts through uncontrollable situations. Heretofore, researchers have tried to understand the woman's concept of her being by observing her "looking-glass self"— beauty culture, the hairdo, a nice dress. Needed now is an endeavor to reach the innerself perceived by oneself without a mirror.

This subordination of the feminine role in a male-dominated society is not without some advantage. As Smith[28] indicates, women are more sociable and warmer than men. But although these are qualities related to being a poor judge, women have more motivation for understanding others and are, therefore, likely to be better judges than men. The typical woman in our society finds that the attentions she receives depend less upon her objective accomplishments than upon her personal conquests. The ability to recognize subtle indications of favor, disfavor, rivalry and defeat are vital to her.

Among the more recent, significant contributions toward understanding the delinquent girl is the study by Trese.[30] He concluded that (1) there is a need to detect as early as possible in the life of the child, the signs of potential delinquent behavior, otherwise the task of modifying patterns of behavior becomes progressively more difficult and discouraging; (2) mere words are futile in changing delinquent behavior—a perceived love is the line over which the spoken words must travel; what is true of words is doubly true of punishment; (3) the girls, however they may vary from one another in their feelings towards adults, are without exception, heavily loaded with negative feelings towards their mothers—all of them are greatly in need of a worthy mother figure with whom to identify.

For deeper insights and a greater understanding of the delinquent girl, it is necessary to review some major aspects of the female role in American culture. It is important, also, to consider some basic psychological principles as they apply to women.

Kluckhalm[18] states that in reviewing the history of the woman's role in the United States, it becomes evident that for many years a central issue has been her demand for the right to participate more fully in all those activities in which dominant American values are expressed. Because of the kind of education women of today receive, the issue has become more acute in recent years.

> Girls are no longer trained in markedly different ways or for different things than are boys. Throughout childhood and youth the girl goes to school with boys and is taught very much as they are taught. From babyhood on, she learns the ways of being independent and autonomous, and she is expected to know how to look after herself all through adolescence and beyond—forever if need be. The hope is expressed, of course, that she will not have to remain independent

and will not therefore need to use much of what she has learned. Instead, and this is the truly great problem, she is expected upon her marriage, or certainly after the children are born, to give her attention to all those things which are defined as feminine and for which she has not been well trained at all.

The author concludes that "it is not to be wondered that the strains in the feminine role are numerous and make for serious personality difficulties in many women."

According to Pratt,[23] certain feminine qualities make most women less susceptible than men to addiction to narcotic drugs. Most female addicts are prostitutes. Many prostitutes turn to drugs to make their lives more bearable and, once addicted, are forced to remain prostitutes to support their habit. The authors observe that although both sexes have the same inherent impulses to enhance pleasure and relieve pain by artificial means, females, on the average, are more sensitive to the taboos of society and less likely to indulge in practices that are socially condemned. The fact that women appear to have respect for, as well as fear of, the law was evidenced when there was a marked decline in the proportion of female addicts in 1915 when addiction became a federal crime with severe punishment for convicted offenders.

The fact that larceny has increased among female offenders is related to the social forces affecting women. Most forms of larceny involve little physical danger, force, and daring. In crime, women tend to be influenced by society's rule that women should not engage in violence or should not be aggressive.

Shoplifting and petty theft from employers, by a household maid for example, are typical thefts for women. Teenage girls constitute a significant number of the shoplifters and, as in other activities, they usually work in twos or threes, acting as a clique. They concentrate generally on stealing accessories, small leather goods and clothing. With the increasing use of coin-operated devices and the self-services display, the incidence of shoplifting has risen among women, who, in general, are the primary shoppers in our society.

In the case of murder, it is reported that motives of jealousy, frustration, humiliation and emotional sensitivity are frequently observed. The victims traditionally have been members of the murderer's family, usually husbands when the security of the woman within the home is threatened by a rival. The second most frequent type of homicide committed by the female is infanticide—the illegitimate child most frequently is the victim.

Pratt[23] summarized the following points in particular:

1. Women are less likely than men to commit most types of crime and to indulge in most types of antisocial behavior.
2. When women do commit crimes or socially deviant acts, they are more likely than men to carry them out furtively and secretly, and also more likely to be protected from the consequences.
3. Social change is affecting both the incidence and the character of women's delinquency. In the main, women have derived enormous benefits from the social changes of recent decades. There has been a very real liberation from ignorance, drudgery and confinement. However, as women moved into the mainstream of community business, education and political life, they have come to experience the frustration, aggravations and abrasions that were formerly absorbed by men.

In institutions the female counterpart of the male informal group is the make-believe family, which is peculiarly suited to meeting ingrained dependency needs and temporary aspirations of delinquent girls. Punishment only intensifies and solidifies its anti-staff function. A more positive approach stresses group incentives of the make-believe family, utilizing it as a treatment force in changing delinquent values. The outstanding value of this study is the fact that the information comes from those "on the firing line," from those closest to the problems under consideration.

In her study of several hundred adolescent delinquent girls, Konopka[20] concluded that these girls had in common: fear and distrust of adults and authority figures, poor self-images, a deep sense of isolation, and lack of communication with others. Four key concepts proposed as basic to these common problems are as follows:

1. The unique dramatic biological onset of puberty for which these girls are unprepared. Although some adolescent girls in the middle socioeconomic class communicate among themselves and sometimes with adults about the facts and meaning of these

biological changes, girls in the lower socioeconomic group have less communication with both peers and adults and often associate puberty with physical injury and other fear-generating events. The task of bearing children influences the girls' total attitudes toward sex. The experience of pregnancy appears to change the girl but generally there is an attitude of "let's get it over with fast."

2. Complex identity problems differ from those of boys in intensity and scope in the traditional way, but are aggravated for girls in low-income families by the inferior, undesirable status of the women they know and the frequent absence of a father in the home or his brutal treatment of his wife. While some girls are helped to understand and make positive use of the process of separating from their mothers by establishing an early love relationship with the father, many girls have no such help and this influences their attitudes toward both sexes for the rest of their lives. This becomes a strong factor in the girls' attachment to peers, male or female. Some girls remained attached to other girls because they had never been able to move into a heterosexual relationship. This was due to fear of men because of their fathers' treatment of the girls' mothers or inability to compete with other girls for the attention and affection of young men because they had so little self-confidence and harbored low estimates of their self-worth. Another factor affecting the amount of homosexuality among the girls was the comparative safety of a homosexual relationship, which could not produce an unwanted child.

3. Rapidly changing cultural patterns give today's adolescent girls no tradition of preparation for vocational roles, including those of wife and mother. Emancipation of women was stepped up during and after World War II, but society has not yet fully accepted this change. The adult world of the United States is still highly conflicted about the position of women in it. For instance, while the girl is educated to choose her place in the working life of the community and is encouraged to become a participating citizen, she finds frequent job discrimination and is often urged to reject her intellect. All of this produces value conflicts of an extremely intense nature at the time when adolescent girls are forced to deal with many other value conflicts that are expected in the maturation process.

4. A faceless adult authority seemed to prevail in the lives of these girls. They exhibited little confidence in adults. Most of them could not name one adult with whom they could relate and in

whom they had confidence and trust. An unwed mother spoke with surprise about her ease in talking with strangers in contrast to her difficulty in talking with her parents. Others said they found they could talk with parents only after they were in trouble. Girls in conflict with the law said they did not know anyone in authority who was not ruling. Help in handling authority was alien to most of the girls in the study and they resented it intensely. The girls did not blame their parents for improper or inadequate upbringing. Instead the girls saw their parents as a part of the adult world which was strange and hostile to them. The most frequent and telling criticism the girls had of adults concerned adult hypocrisy. Discriminatory attitudes toward race elicited universal attack from the girls whose value system in this case was absolute.

The girls were enormously lonely and felt they were completely rejected by adults as well as by most of their peers. Their only outlets for overcoming loneliness were to join an anonymous crowd where there was no need to relate, or to enter into a sex relationship where feeling and warmth could be anticipated for a brief time at the least.

Butler[4] describes an empirical classification system which was based upon an analysis of a California delinquent-girl population. The systematic classification of delinquent girls into three primary types was accomplished by a Q-factor analysis of a psychological inventory.

A representative sample of all girls who were ever placed in a particular institution constituted the sample. At intake each girl filled out a Jesness Psychological Inventory of 155 items concerning attitudes toward such diverse factors as family, school, police and "self." In summary, the three major types derived from this analysis were as follows: Type I—disturbed-neurotic, Type II—immature-impulsive, and Type III—covert manipulators. The descriptions of girls in each type were accomplished by evaluating differentiating items and by the operational staff's perceptions of the three groups of girls.

Type I (disturbed-neurotic) appears to be concerned with procedures, regularity, order and law, and a readiness to accept cultural norms. Over-internalization of rules and standards may be involved. Self-control and ritualism are primary dimensions, but these have been put aside by delinquent acts and there is evidence of guilt feelings and neurotic reactions. Independent evaluations by staff members of the institution include such descriptions as passive-withdrawal, anxious, depressive, and conformer. One operational staff member states that the Type I girls appear to be those who have become delinquent as a result of some interpersonal situation with which they cannot cope, and they react through delinquent behavior. The delinquency pattern in this type is seen as being of relatively recent origin and presumably of short duration.

With the Type II (immature-impulsive) there is a rejection of ritualistic behavior and external controls. Immediate gratification is of primary importance and impulsive behavior results in punitive sanctions. Behavior patterns appear to reflect manifest attitudes. Immaturity, impulsiveness, and lack of internal integration and control is the emerging picture in this group. These girls rebel against authority. Evaluations by staff members include descriptions of aggressiveness, impulsiveness and overt manipulation, with evidence of immaturity and sociopathic tendencies.

Butler[4] found that girls in Type III (covert manipulators) are self-assertive and attempt to control their environment. They are ritualistic and are overly concerned with external appearances and reputation. Overt behavior is oriented toward the expected, but latent attitudes are at variance with behavior. Conforming behavior is observed as long as expectations and structures are given. However, covert manipulation is continuous. These girls are described by the institutional staff as clever, intelligent manipulators, with sociopathic and aggressive tendencies. When first institutionalized, these girls are "hidden" or covert manipulators. Once their manipulative activities are discovered and countermeasures taken, these girls become aggressive, snarling and hostile. This type of girl proves to be the most provocative. She falsifies the test and gives expected answers—responses that do not reflect her attitudes, but responses that make her appear "good." The author stated that this girl can confuse an institutional staff with a facade that may take months to penetrate.

In a study made in a court clinic which serves an essentially middle-class suburban population, Ames, Rosenwald, Snell and Lee[1] found that of the entire caseload of 293 adolescent girls brought before the court during a ten-year period, 162 (55%) had run away. The girls' ages ranged from 13 years to 17 years and 6 months, with a mean age of 15 years and 3 months. Their study excluded those who had not stayed away overnight and those who denied the intent to run away.

They emphasized the running away, far from being a childish escapade, is almost always indicative of some severe individual or family pathology and may result from a wide variety of intolerable home situations. The cause most frequently observed in their study was the unconscious threat of an incestuous relationship with the father, the fear of the resultant dissolution of the family and the concurrent depression.

Basic to the etiology of running away was a consistent pattern of family interaction which included a disturbed marital relationship, inadequate control by the parents over their own and the girl's impulses, deprivation of love of the mother and subtle pressure by her to have the daughter take over the maternal role.

Prior to the onset of adolescence, this role can be managed in most cases. However, with the breakdown of the prepubescent defenses, the girl becomes involved in an increasingly bitter attitude of rebellion against her role and finally runs away.

The authors of this study contend that the act of running away, which legally is a form of delinquency, is often treated lightly by the parents, the police, and the courts, unless it becomes chronic or appears in conjunction with sexual acting-out or other associated delinquent behavior. They conclude that running away is the result of a complex neurotic interaction between the parents and the daughter in a "triangle" situation. Its seriousness as a symptom calls for far greater concern than is presently given by most parents and law enforcement officials.

Several studies have probed the backgrounds of high school students, socially accepted and playing the role of nondelinquents. In one study, high school and correctional school students were compared as to frequency and seriousness of delinquent acts, including running away from home. Questionnaires were anonymously filled out by high school students in three small western communities and by inmates in a western training school for delinquents. A much higher percentage of the training school girls checked offenses. The comparison of high school and training school youth is significant for repeated offenses. In their study on reported delinquent behavior among girls in high school and correctional school, Short and Nye[27] revealed that 11.3 percent of the high school girls admitted running away from home, while 85.5 percent of the correctional school girls admitted running away from home. Only 1 percent of the high school girls admitted running away from home more than once or twice, while 51.8 percent of the correctional school girls admitted running away from home more than once or twice.

In a more detailed analysis, the authors indicated that in their sample of students, a small percentage of both boys and girls exceeded the training school groups in delinquency; but that, in general, the boys and girls sent to the training school were more persistently and seriously delinquent than the high school students.

Girls typically act in a delinquent manner less often than boys. Nevertheless, 30 percent or more of the high school girls had driven a car without a driver's license, skipped school, defied parents' authority, taken little things worth less than two dollars and bought or drunk beer or wine, including drinking at home.

In the list of offenses which lead to the commitment of girls, running away heads the list.

THE INCORRIGIBLE GIRL

What is the exact meaning of "incorrigibility"? There is no consensus on this term; it can mean all things to all people, much as does the interpretation of "incompatibility" when used as grounds for divorce. Incorrigibility as a term may include "ungovernability," "uncontrollability," "beyond control of parents," "being obstinate" and/or "defying parental authority," to mention but a few. As an illustration of judicial latitude and penal sanction in terms involving moral judgment, one offender, a sixteen-year-old boy, received a five-year prison term from the judge of an adult criminal court. The Jacksonville, Florida *Times Union* reported on February 5, 1951, that this was the first case tried under the new Florida Court Act which permits the judge to send to adult criminal court juveniles whom the judge considers "obstinate."

"Incorrigibility" strongly suggests a family disorganization symptom. Elliott[11] believes that the "virtues of honesty, faith and trust form the web, woof, and pattern of responsible family life," quite important to the average woman; hence, lower female crime rates reflect a social situation pushing, to a greater degree, the males rather than the females toward crime.

The girl's case is more likely to be seen as a family disorganization symptom and less likely to be punished as such. Petitions relating to girls are most frequently made by parents, and those relating to boys usually by law enforcement officials.[7]

Incorrigibility may stem from sister-sib rivalry. Smith[28] relates a case in which the older sister chose to wear blue, the favorite color of the favored younger sister, despite the color's unsuitability to her own brown eyes and hair. Since the little sister was always dressed in blue, which was becoming to her light complexion and fair hair, the older sister unwittingly adopted the blue garments which seemed to be so successful when worn by her sister. Matters worsened between the two girls to the point that the older sister avoided family reunions where the younger sister was to be present and even took a trip to escape being a bridesmaid at her wedding.

Incorrigibility may expand to include actual violence, burglary, arson, even kidnapping. One girl entered a home and abducted a seven-month-old baby which she dropped "accidently." She kept the baby hidden six hours before returning it to its parents, who notified police. The baby was taken to the hospital where it was found to have a fractured skull, lacerations and bruises all over the body. The girl then led a group of five other girls who committed more than ten burglaries of homes, following which they set fires to destroy the evidence.

Mother-daughter "feuds" may result in incorrigible behavior, for among some girl delinquents there is a subtle and potent interaction between mother and daughter. In many cases the mother is the person who makes the complaint to police or court. A portion of the motivation, not always unconscious, for the daughter's offenses is spitefulness; she enjoys being a source of disgrace to the family and especially to her mother.

Responding to mother's provocative combination of nagging and suspicion, the daughter clutches the suggestive signs of sophistication and uses them to goad her mother. There are no laws against makeup and clothing fads, but smoking and drinking may be the obvious next moves. Almost inevitably the girl gives substance to what were, initially, groundless suspicions. She may stay out all night or even run away. In either case, there are almost certain to be sex episodes and often promiscuity. In one way or another the mother learns of what is happening. The notation on the official papers may be "ungovernable behavior," "incorrigbility," "truancy from home" or "immoral behavior."[31]

Incorrigibility may manifest itself in ungovernable temper and lack of restraint. One girl assaulted her sister's 61-year-old landlady, striking her with her fist and tearing her clothing, causing lacerations on the woman's face, breaking her glasses and ripping her coat to shreds. As a reason for this outburst, the girl stated that she was provoked when the landlady slammed the door in her face. When arrested, she attempted to escape, kicking and scratching the arresting officers.

It is unfortunate that the terminology embracing offenses committed by girls lacks preciseness in definition. In many respects, "incorrigibility" is a weasel term, a blanket type of nomenclature that includes other offenses which, to the casual reader, may seem to be more serious than the term "incorrigibility" itself.

THE SEX-DELINQUENT GIRL

The breakdown of traditional sexual mores and the drift and diversity of changing opinion about sexual morality affect individuals in different ways. Differences in sexual orientation and practice, however, may reflect differences in socioeconomic and class standards. For example, Ehrmann[9] found that 61 percent of the men and 91 percent of the women "draw the line" within conventional moral limits in their current dating behavior. This finding is fairly consistent with Kinsey's surveys of the sexual practices of women, in which he reports class and educational differentials indicating that sexual intercourse itself is engaged in at an earlier age and more frequently among the less educated who, however, tend to avoid the "petting" preliminaries that are so prevalent among college youth.

Ball and Logan[2] confirmed Ehrmann's findings. The girls involved in this study were aware of the middle-class norms, knew promiscuity was socially undesirable, were not hostile to such social norms, but were motivated by the desire to maintain status within their own adolescent subculture. The majority of the girls lost their virginity while on automobile dates and the principle reason given was that "they liked the boy very much." Nearly a fourth of the girls admitted it was the first date. Subsequently, sex was a part of dating as "the boy expected it," or there was "nothing else to do," for fun or pleasure. Other rationalizations included "had been drinking," "would be considered chicken otherwise," or "everyone was doing it." At least 70 percent of the girls questioned admitted that they knew it was wrong, and all of the girls questioned were slightly below average intelligence. They had dated actively from age 13 and had no interest in supervised recreation.

Many juveniles, despite rather extensive sexual experiences, may be incredibly naive in many aspects of biological import. Sessions in group therapy with both boys and girls in institutions seem to confirm this observation. Some delinquents have astonishingly childish notions about sex. Dressler[8] reports an instance of a youthful parolee who didn't drink coffee because "it gets you syphilis." He explained: "Yeah. You drink coffee and you get noivous; coffee leads to smoking, smoking leads to drinking, drinking leads to goils and goils give you syphilis. No coffee for me."

Partly as a reflection of the contemporary cultural accent on sex, the public is easily titillated by accounts of sexual escapades—

a fact on which the newspapers have capitalized. Many notorious sex cases have tended to overemphasize sex as an offense. One club of four girls admitted that their activities were devoted to the "seduction of bus drivers." Our culture permits the female to be more demonstrative toward her object of affection, while any open display of affection by men, even the young male child, is discouraged. As compared with male delinquency (stealing, assault, robbery), female delinquency is largely sexual delinquency and running away. The juvenile male delinquent tends to hurt others, while the female delinquent tends to hurt herself.

There are interesting sex differentials that should be taken into account when handling juvenile offenders. A 15-year-old girl is more mature than a 15-year-old boy. The boy may not know whether he is a man or still a child, but the 15-year-old girl knows she is a woman. Girls feel the loss of status with peers more than do boys. Girls are far more dependent than boys on the status furnished by the family, any family, even the "make believe family," so frequently found in informal groups in girls' institutions.[21] If a girl is caught in delinquency, other girls' mothers will not let their daughters associate with the "bad" girl; hence, the female offender has a "bad girl" role. Many sex offenses of juveniles are relatively unimportant and are often due to a fixed morbidity or adolescent experimentation. Although society is upset by the promiscuous girl, the promiscuous boy is regarded with tolerant amusement as only "sowing wild oats." Female delinquency may also be affected by premenstrual tension or postpartum reaction.

The extent of adolescent sexual experimentation by girls, both delinquent and nondelinquent, was noted by Short and Nye[27] as they compared this activity among girls in high school and girls in a correctional school. As part of the reported delinquent behavior, 14.1 percent of the high school girls admitted to have had sexual relations with a person of the opposite sex, while 95.1 percent of the correctional school girls admitted to the same offense.

In some instances the mother of the girl may be gaining some vicarious satisfaction from her daughter's misdeeds. In one case, the investigating policewoman said the mother greeted the girl the morning after each date with the taunting question: "Are you still a virgin?"[31]

In some disorganized areas and families, opportunity for sexual exploitation may include homosexual as well as heterosexual contacts. Influenced by promised financial rewards, boys have been known to aid and even seek out older males who prefer them as sex objects. There is also the problem of females who use youngsters for normal, as well as deviational, sexual gratification; a practice which is often known to the police of metropolitan areas. Lesbianism may be found at all age levels. According to Short and Nye,[27] 3.6 percent of the girls in their high school sample admitted having sex relations with another person of the same sex, and 25 percent of the correctional school sample of girls admitted having had sex relations with another person of the same sex. Only 0.5 percent of the high school girls admitted committing this offense more than once or twice, while 12.5 percent of the girls in the correctional school sample admitted to having had sex relations with another person of the same sex more than once or twice.

As pointed out by Elliott and Merrill,[10] studies of women and girls who were inmates of correctional institutions have shown a large percentage to be sex offenders, whether or not they were committed on that charge. Apparently, judges are more apt to sentence women with a record of sex delinquency, irrespective of their current offense. More recent analysis of women serving federal offenses at the U. S. Reformatory for Women at Alderson, West Virginia, also bears out this conclusion. Even though none of the women in the federal reformatory are committed for sex offenses, about 75 percent apparently have some record of prostitution.

Novick[21] has summarized in a most succinct manner how the female delinquent may become almost hopelessly enmeshed in a social maze of cultural expectations and conflicting roles and statuses. Social pressures tend to foster a dependency role for the female; a need to be loved, accepted, protected—best achieved through marriage and a family; a necessity to develop special techniques so that she may cope with her male environment; and a tendency to place much emphasis on narcissistic attributes that render her more attractive to men, but which still permit open expression of affection toward members of her own sex.

In order to analyze the behavior of sexually delinquent girls, one must first have some understanding of the "normal" stages of sexual development which are a part of the maturation process of all children. The conflicts which accompany the various stages of sexual development and the ways in which the child learns to cope with or resolve them influence the patterns of behavior it adopts. Furthermore, in relation to these, the child's perception of herself, her parents, and human interpersonal relationships are formed. In early childhood, when the child is three or four, she usually experiences what is called the electral conflict. It is a phase during which the child becomes aware that her parents have a personal love of which she is not a part. Prior to this, she has been aware only of the close mother-child relationship. With the recognition of the father in her life, the child begins to fantasize that she can compete with the mother for the love of the father. This is the first unconscious sexual attraction that the child experiences.

This conflict is usually resolved when the child must face the fact that although the father loves her, she cannot take him from the mother. She finds that his love is not sexually motivated and that he acts with the mother in a "caring, protecting way" toward her. Then she learns to respect and love him as "caring adult" and she places this love in a category of "father love" which is different from "romantic love" as it is not contingent upon or affected by her actions or attractiveness. The father becomes a model for her to use in her choice of a sex-love object when she is older.

However, as she reaches puberty and begins to undergo physical changes accompanying maturation, her earlier conflicts and feelings are usually reconsidered because of her uncertainty about this new adult sex role that she is about to enter. The earlier insecurities as well as the unconscious hostility, anger, and sense of failure and inadequacy engendered by her earlier failure to win her father cause her to doubt her femininity and her ability to succeed as a female and be found desirable by males.

Usually the girl works through these insecurities by learning social skills and successfully experiencing acceptance and popularity with her peers. This acceptance reassures her that she is capable of filling the adult female role. As she gains confidence that she will be able to participate in heterosexual relationships and eventually fill the role of wife and mother and begin to develop more maturity, she is able to make judgments as to the standards of behavior which she will set for herself. Feeling that she is an adequate female, she can incorporate socially acceptable modes of behavior as her other needs of belonging are met in other areas of life.

THE PROBATION-VIOLATOR GIRL

Probation for the juvenile offender is a form of court-disposition of the child following his adjudication. Although it is a nonpunitive method of treating offenders, it should not be interpreted as leniency or mercy. In England and in the United States, probation developed out of the various methods for the conditional suspension of punishment, as attempts to avoid the cruel precepts of a rigorous criminal law. Among these Anglo-American judicial expedients, the direct precursors of probation, are the so-called "benefit of clergy," the "judicial reprieve," the release of an offender on his own recognizance and the provisional "filing" of a case. However, probation is America's distinctive contribution to progressive penology, because the development of probation has been entirely statutory, insofar as the system is an expression of planned state policy.[20]

In deciding a case involving a girl who is not insane or feebleminded, most juvenile or criminal courts will adopt one of the following alternatives: (1) return her to her home on probation; (2) refer her to such welfare services as exist in larger cities; (3) place her in a boarding or foster home; (4) send her to a correctional house; or (5) confine her to jail. For chance offenders and for first offenders, it is generally believed that the most sensible disposition of the case is to return the girl to her home on probation, under court supervision. There are many advantages of probation as compared with commitment to an institution. As detailed by Reinemann,[25] probation is an individualized form of treatment; it applies the methods of social casework; it leaves the child in his own home surroundings; it enlists the help of community resources; it is not considered punitive and therefore is free of social stigma; and, as in the case for probation of adults, it is much less expensive than incarceration.

Not every girl adjudicated a delinquent is eligible for probation. There are no real criteria for use in deciding upon probation; it is a matter of grace and not of right. In many states probation is impossible to obtain if the offense is "repugnant" to society, such as offenses against morals or against the government. In Illinois, for example, the offenses of murder, incest, rape, perjury, and arson preclude consideration for probation.

Most probation laws provide that the probation agency make a presentence investigation and prepare a report for the court, although the judge is not bound by law to consider the report. The defendant, as a rule, cannot view the report made by the probation officer, nor can he offer testimony in his own behalf. For these and other reasons, the use of presentence investigation reports and recommendations for or against the use of probation as part of the court process raises some serious issues concerning "due process."

It has been estimated that it takes about three years to rehabilitate a serious child offender, at a cost of several thousand dollars. But, it will cost society even more to retain the same child in a state training school, from which she may emerge more at odds with society than ever. Therefore, few steps would be more economical—as well as beneficial on other grounds—in the improvement of the administration of criminal justice, than the wise extension of probation and the raising of the quality of probation services.

However, for some children and youths in trouble, probation does not appear to be an appropriate practice. To return to her home and neighborhood, a girl of any age who has become habituated to delinquent practices or who has deep-seated maladjustments or whose delinquent behavior springs from brutality or immorality at home or from the breakdown of satisfactory relationships in the family, may involve a disservice to the girl herself, to society, and to the cause of probation as well.

As indicated by Cavan,[5] the child placed on probation remains in the community, usually in her own home, and carries on the normal activities of children of her age and sex. Although there may be a slight stigma connected with being on probation, it does not condemn a girl as does commitment to a correctional school. The Children's Bureau defines probation as a "process of helping the girl accept and live with the limitations required by society by developing her potentials." A more limited definition is that the purpose of probation (or function of the probation officer) is "to help the offender comply with the order of the court."[15]

Unfortunately, the way probation is practiced differs in various courts and in different states; therefore, it is impossible to estimate accurately the total number of children on probation in the United States. The number must be several times the number of correctional school graduates, which approximates 30,000 annually. If one were to guess that 65,000 to 100,000 children are placed on probation each year, it would not be an overstatement of the facts. In a summary analysis by England,[12] of probation and postprobation studies, it appears, from the available research, that probation is an effective correctional device on both juvenile and adult levels.

Probation is an enlightened attempt to cope with a crisis in the life of an offender who possesses rehabilitative potential. It is often misunderstood and underrated by the public because the press coverage is so frequently negative. Probation is less dramatic than commitment to a state training school, and neither probation officers nor successful probationers make "good copy." Ideally, probation services are dignified. Probation is social casework with the power of the law behind it. According to Kay and

Vedder,[18] probation is the only really promising rehabilitative technique for use with violators of the law.

An analysis of the girl probation violator is most difficult because she does not present a particular or distinct pattern of behavior. In the probation process, a variety of offenses can bring about commitment if one engages in these activities while on probation. Consequently, violations may include truancy, sexual delinquency, incorrigibility, and runaway behavior or a combination of several of these. The commitment results because it is obvious that the individual is not responding to this type of service and apparently is unable to become rehabilitated in the relatively unstructured probation situation.

Most of the girls who violated their probation did not appear to have any insight into their behavior. The most common characteristics detected in the stories written by probation violators were an awareness that what they had done was "bad" because they did not obey their parent or guardian, and a general lack of respect for their probation officers. While there was no evidence of strong dislike for them, the girls, in general, were little affected by the words and counseling of the probation officers and usually attempted to manipulate them. Apparently, the relationship was not constant or close enough to fulfill whatever needs these girls were attempting to meet.

OBSERVATIONS, CONCLUSIONS, AND RECOMMENDATIONS

The authors have noted the lack of consensus and lack of preciseness in definition of terms describing the offenses which lead to commitment. While the anticipated variation of recorded offenses among states and the fluctuations of offenses from year to year within states were observed, nevertheless, offenses dubbed the "big five" appeared most consistently. These are (1) running away, (2) incorrigibility, (3) sexual offenses, (4) probation violation and (5) truancy, often in that order. Approximately 75 to 85 percent of the offenses leading to commitment of delinquent girls are found in the "big five" grouping. The underlying vein of many of these offenses is sexual misconduct by the girl delinquent. However, in most instances the most innocuous charges of "running away," "incorrigibility," "ungovernability" and the like are used on the official records. It is for this reason that sexual offenses are in third place.

The offenses leading to commitment, as defined by the courts, are limited to various types of delinquent actions and antisocial behavior. The training school or central agency is confronted with the necessity of making a thorough analysis of the factors which have contributed to the development of the antisocial behavior in order to plan an effective treatment and rehabilitation program directed toward the return of the girl to the community. In communities where the courts have clinical services, clinical reports are helpful to the schools or central agencies in gaining deeper insights into the dynamics of the problem. Refinements in clinical services of the courts and the availability of specialized services in all juvenile courts would be an invaluable resource in diagnostic evaluations and placement of children in accordance with their needs. Sharper focus on the gaps in available community resources would be revealed. The necessity for planning an action-coordinated community program for the needs of these children would contribute much to the prevention, treatment, and control of juvenile delinquency and crime.

The importance of having knowledge and understanding of sociological, cultural, psychological and physical factors in the delinquent behavior of the girls is clearly demonstrated. The need for a thorough diagnostic evaluation, drawn from experts in the various disciplines, is essential to the planning of an effective treatment and rehabilitation program. The important role of social workers, psychologists, psychiatrists, educators, chaplains, cottage parents, work supervisors and parole officers is reflected. The courts, police, community agencies, schools and social agencies give evidence of the importance and the nature of these contacts with the girl and her family prior to the adjudication and commitment process.

Also pointed out was the importance of a broad, diversified institutional program to cope with the various areas of difficulty encountered by these girls. It is evident that some girls responded to external controls and the milieu of the institutional setting; while others, whose problems were primarily psychological and internalized, responded to the individual professional services offered. The recognition that the needs of all committed delinquent girls cannot be met within the institution should be evident.

Since all persons working in the institutions affect to some degree the rehabilitation of the delinquent, efforts should be made to coordinate all services so that consistent philosophy, attitudes and treatment are employed in working with each girl and her particular problem and needs. Since most offenses leading to commitment are usually the culmination of a series of difficulties which began at an early age and, in part, reflect some disturbance in the child's primary relationship with her parents, particular attention should be given to the selection and training of cottage parents. Living with a group of girls in a 24-hour real-life situation, these persons must be able to cope with all of the various patterns of behavior which serve as releases for the girls' frustrations, hostilities and anxieties. It is, therefore, extremely important that each cottage parent has some understanding of psychodynamics and receives professional help in working with these girls.

Since most of the institutions have predominantly female personnel, serious consideration should be given to involving more males in the programs. Few of the girls seem to have had the experience of a positive relationship with an adult male. Such an experience could greatly increase their ability to cope with heterosexual social situations when they return to the community.

This chapter has pointed out the frequency of the pattern of avoidance and the related problems associated with leaving the structure of school and/or home, such as sexual offenses, drinking, and other acts. This suggests the need for a closer attention to the preventive aspects of delinquency through early detection and counseling in the community for the runaway girl. The significance and importance of community programs in the area of delinquency and prevention of juvenile delinquency and crime has been widely documented.

While the home is the first and most important influence in shaping the personality and character of the child, other community and environmental forces such as the school help to determine them also. It goes without saying that since the school reaches practically all children at a relatively early period of their growth and development, it is the most strategic community institution in all efforts to prevent delinquency and to help in the rehabilitation of the delinquent child.

It is recognized that the many problems students, especially low-income students, bring into schools are not the primary responsibility of the schools. But they must be dealt with if effective learning is to occur. Although the school is in a strategic position to identify problems, it is not equipped to handle the underlying contributing conditions. Therefore, the school must join other community agencies in a team effort to work on these problems.

Staff members in institutions should recognize that close friendships between adolescents are necessary and desirable. They should recognize that whenever children are isolated in a closed institution, some sexual activity between members of the same sex will inevitably take place. Understanding this phenomenon is extremely important to the well-being of the girls as well as the morale of the staff members. They should recognize that there are very few true homosexuals and the so-called "honey business" is an expression of normal needs to seek friendship and acceptance in whatever manner the girls can in an alien environment such as the training school, where they have been isolated from family, friends, acquaintances, and familiar surroundings. They are emotionally deprived girls seeking attention. The vast majority of homosexual activities of girls are situational, since only a few are lesbians in the community. Most of the "butches" and their "lovers" are not true homosexuals; when they leave the institution they immediately return to normal relationships, some to promiscuous sexual activity.

Halleck[15] has so ably stated that there is always some danger that staff members in institutions will increase the problem of homosexual behavior by becoming obsessed with it. He concludes that the institution which takes a firm but casual attitude toward homosexuality and attends to the more urgent problems of establishing a treatment program will reap the rewards of stability and therapeutic success. Homosexual behavior is more prevalent in those training schools which do not have adequate treatment programs. An increase in such behavior in any institution usually indicates some breakdown in the program and greater distrust between the adolescents and the staff.

The commitment of pregnant girls to state training schools has long been a controversial subject. Differential treatment according to class is clearly evident in the commitment of pregnant girls, oftentimes because of lack of other resources. It is generally true that our society is inclined to treat sexual deviation as a form of illness or immaturity if it occurs in middle- or upper-class people, and is a crime if it occurs in lower-class people. Even in the lower-class, the double standard operates—the girl is punished by being sent away and the male usually remains free. The authors recommend greater efforts be made to establish and to strengthen programs at the community level for working with unwed mothers.

REFERENCES

1. Ames, R.; Rosenwald, R. J.; Snell, J. E.; and Lee, R. E.: The runaway girl: A reaction to family stress. *Am J Orthopsychiat*, 1940, p. 651.
2. Ball, J. C., and Logan, Nell: Early sexual behavior of lower-class delinquent girls. *J Criminal Law, Criminology and Police Science*, 51:209-214, 1960.
3. Barnes, H. E., and Teeters, N. K.: *New Horizons in Criminology*. New York, Prentice-Hall, 1959, pp. 61-64.
4. Butler, Edgar W.: Personality dimensions of delinquent girls. *Criminologica*, 3 (No. 1):7-10, May, 1965.
5. Cavan, R. S.: *Juvenile Delinquency*. Philadelphia, Lippincott, 1962, p. 287.
6. Cohen, A. K.: *Delinquent Boys. The Culture of the Gang*. Glencoe, Illinois, Free Press, 1955, p. 45.
7. Cooper, Robert: Comparative analysis of the nature of crime and delinquency in girls as compared to boys. In Frank H. Cohen (Ed.): *Youth and Crime*. New York, International Universities Press, 1957, p. 70.

8. Dressler, David: *Parole Chief.* New York, The Viking Press, 1951, p. 144.
9. Ehrmann, W.: Influence of comparative social class of companion upon premarital heterosexual behavior. *Marriage and Family Living,* 17:48-53, 1955.
10. Elliott, M. A., and Merrill, F. E.: *Social Disorganization,* 4th Ed. New York, Harper and Row, 1961, p. 157.
11. Elliott, Mabel: *Crime in Modern Society.* New York, Harper & Brothers, 1952, p. 201.
12. England, R. W., Jr.: What is responsible for satisfactory probation and post-probation outcome? *J Criminal Law, Criminology and Police Science,* 47:667-677, March-April, 1957.
13. Fernald, M. R. et al.: *A Study of Women Delinquents in New York State.* New York, Century, 1920, p. 525.
14. Glueck, S., and Glueck, E. T.: *Five Hundred Delinquent Women.* New York, Knopf, 1934, p. 288.
15. Halleck, S. L.: *Psychiatry and the Dilemmas of Crime.* New York, Harper, 1967, pp. 141-142.
16. Hardman, D. G.: The function of the probation officer. *Federal Probation,* 24:4, September, 1960.
17. Kay, B. A.: Differential self perceptions among female offenders. Unpublished Ph.D. thesis, Ohio State University, 1961.
18. Kay, B. A., and Vedder, C. B.: *Probation and Parole.* Springfield, Thomas, 1963, p. 92.
19. Kluckhalm, F.: *Personality in Nature, Society and Culture.* Clyde Kluckhohn, Henry A. Murray and David M. Schneider (Eds.): New York, Knopf, 1953, pp. 346.
20. Konopka, G.: *The Adolescent Girl in Conflict.* Englewood Cliffs, N. J., Prentice-Hall, 1966, pp. 120-128.
21. Lombroso, C., and Ferrero, W.: *The Female Offender.* New York and London, Appleton, 1916, pp. 109-111.
22. Newman, C. L.: *Sourcebook on Probation, Parole and Pardons.* Springfield, Thomas, 1958, pp. 60, 69.
23. Novick, A. G.: The female institutionalized delinquent. In Donald D. Scarborough and Abraham G. Novick (Eds.): *Institutional Rehabilitation of Delinquent Youth.* Albany, N. Y., Delmar Publishers, 1962, pp. 158-170.
24. Pollak, O.: *The Criminality of Women.* Pennsylvania, University of Pennsylvania, 1950, pp. 1-7.
25. Pratt, L.: Women in trouble. *This Week Magazine,* Chicago Daily News, July 31, 1965, p. 5.
26. Reckless, W.: *The Crime Problem.* New York, Appleton, 1957, pp. 98ff, 148ff.

27. Reinemann, J. O.: Probation and the juvenile delinquent. *The Annals of The American Academy of Political and Social Science,* 216:109-119, January, 1949.
28. Rosenheim, F.: Techniques of therapy. *Amer J Orthopsychiat,* 1940, p. 651.
29. Short, J. F., and Nye, F. I.: Extent of unrecorded juvenile delinquency tentative conclusions. *J Criminal Law, Criminology and Police Science,* 49:296-309, Nov.-Dec., 1958.
30. Smith, H. C.: *Personality Adjustment.* New York, McGraw, 1961, pp. 3 and 68.
31. Thomas, W. I.: *The Unadjusted Girl.* Boston, Little, 1923, pp. 1-69.
32. Trese, L. J.: *101 Delinquent Girls.* Notre Dame, Indiana, Fides, 1962, p. 77.
33. Wattenberg, W. W.: Psychologists and juvenile delinquency. In Hans Toch (Ed.): *Legal and Criminal Psychology.* New York, Holt, 1961, pp. 251-252.

Chapter 12
Not Less than Two nor More than Six
WRIGHT STUBBS

I see no reason to attempt to explain the reasons or give any particular excuses for the above sentence I received in 1958 from Travis County, Austin, Texas, for misappropriation and theft of approximately $40,000. The purpose of this chapter is to give a factual account from an inmate's viewpoint of prison conditions, particularly one unit of the Texas Department of Corrections at Huntsville, Texas. As it will creep in naturally, I will state that prior to my conviction I was an attorney, primarily in the practice of criminal law.

In order to keep from giving opinions as I progress so as to retain this account as factual, I think it proper to state at the beginning that the reason for my interest is to try to have something written about prison conditions that is not entirely fictional or biased with the conclusions of a writer, but is rather a straight presentation of facts. There is a great opportunity in rehabilitation work in prison but not for any other fundamental reason than the fact that 90 percent of all inmates believe it is stupid to steal because they eventually get caught and have to return to a "joint." There is no greater myth than the one presented by some so-called experts that the old offender teaches the young one to steal. It is the young kids (punks) who are the stupid pop-offs, and if they can be segregated from each other and placed in the company of some older persons they might be taught that 95 percent of the time crime pays only the ones who participate legally such as lawyers, bondsmen, etc.

I arrived at Huntsville, Texas, home of the main unit of the Texas Department of Corrections in February of 1959 with a sentence of six years. (Legal definition "two to six years.") The procedure at that time was to place all new inmates in a separate unit called "Quarantine." I was assigned a cell together with several other prisoners and was getting ready to settle down when I was called back to the front and told to prepare to go to another location. I was escorted (this means walking in front of a guard about six feet tall) to what was known as "12 Row." This was the old Death Cell Row which had been abandoned when a new separate execution chamber and quarters had been completed. It was used as a place of confinement for inmates who for some reason or other were not permitted to mingle with the others. These particular inmates were isolated usually because they were considered dangerous to the main operation of the prison. I was told this by my first contact with my neighbor on my right who stated he was termed "The Green Dragon" and specialized in starting riots in the dining halls on the slightest pretext. He told me the man on my left was an escape artist having "punched it," six or seven times. These cells faced out in a main room but had no communication between each unit because of the solid walls between each cell. We had a little pulley going along the front upon which we exchanged things we could not throw down the line by hand. And so began 23 months flat time working on a six-year term. The two-to-six sentence means nothing in Texas since it is superseded by other laws regarding parole, but more of this later.

My first instruction was from my neighbor to the left of my cell. He was the one with the escape record whose name I have forgotten. He found out I was just coming into the penitentiary and he told me that I would have to learn two things: (1) how to cut meat with a spoon, and (2) call everything that moved a m . . . f . . . SOB.

This particular cell row had twelve cells and hence was called "12 Row." I discovered it had a variety of inmates; not only the ones who caused the guards trouble but also those that were to be protected. Just as in most prisons, Texas had abolished any sort of corporal punishment and a recent incident had resulted in a guard being convicted for beating an inmate, so the matter of disciplining the inmates was a little sticky. The "Mulligans" came up with a solution that was pretty cute, I thought. It was to promote in the name of "inmate government" a goon squad who would be given access to the cell of the rebellious inmate and would proceed to "strum his skull" (beat him with homemade black-jacks). The members of this squad were given special privileges, mostly early recommendations for parole. However, the inmates would retaliate and would in time mark for attention certain of these "finks" and it would be necessary for them to be transferred to a place of safety, so this was one of the sanctuaries provided by the guards. The conversation along 12 Row was certainly interesting, particularly when they brought in a homosexual named "Susie." He/she bitterly complained of the salty language used in her/his presence. But I must move along to my next assignment or placement.

About ten days after I arrived, I was taken before a committee composed of the warden, assistant commissioners, education director and others including the clinical psychologist for the prison system. It was their duty to screen and place the inmate in his proper work section and locality. By this I mean that the Texas Prison System extends nearly 180 miles and includes at least ten different units, the majority being farms and processing plants. It so happened that the clinical psychologist was in the middle of a course of study to attain a degree in law from a night school in Houston. He had decided that psychology was rather restricted and that the practice of law was more to his liking. My coming into the prison system was just what he needed. He gave me a rather soft job. His clerk known as "bookkeeper" by the inmates was in the process of being discharged, and, in return, I was expected to help him with his law studies. This worked out quite well; I kept my part of the bargain and the psychologist is now a Houston attorney as well as the prison psychologist. It is because of the contacts with the inmates at my job there that I feel I have the information for this chapter.

The inmate staff of the psychology department consisted of five of us: Jack B. who specialized in holding up poker or dice games, doing twelve years; Dr. Jim G. doing it all (life imprisonment) for murder; Fred C., a former president of an insurance company who sold insurance but neglected to turn in the money collected, the one "graduating"; Modesto M., also a person who collected

256 Fundamentals of Criminal Behavior and Correctional Systems

money with a gun, convicted for holding up a motel, fifty years. This collection of talent gave various tests, including the Minnesota Multiphasic Personality Inventory (MMPI), and even the Rorschach (reading the ink blots) to each of the new arrivals for the purpose of determining their ability etc. for job placement.

We put on quite a show all dressed up in starched whites for the new inmates. Quite often various newspaper reporters would observe our activities and word would be published about the modern way the Texas Department of Corrections was functioning. Wardens got substantial pay raises and all of the guards had to wear shoes and socks, but actually it was known when a new inmate arrived just where he would go and what job he would get. If the new arrival was young and strong, he was screened for a job in Huntsville (The Walls) which was considered the country club of the prison system, or he was sent to one of the modern semi-farm units where there was available some semblance of training in construction work as well as ordinary farm labor. However, should the new man be a repeater (recidivist—a term all the guards loved to use), then he was sent to one of the so-called tough farms, the toughest being operated by a warden known as "Bear-tracks." We would dutifully take in all of the grades of the inmate to the classification committee and they would carefully place them in the folder and make a note on a scratch pad, then say, "Send this one down to the Bear." This unit was located in the southern part of the system, and the activities were primarily agricultural. Let me stop a moment—I am falling in my own trap and apparently criticizing the Texas Department of Corrections in the same manner any inmate doing time would do without giving any credit whatsoever. This is not the picture. It is a far cry from the old days in the Texas Penitentiary. Now, inmates are not abused nor maimed and practically every one discharged comes out in good health. Remember, there are some good people in prison but also collected there are the lowest both in mentality and morals to be found. So where discipline is maintained without undue force, it is a good prison, in my opinion. This is shared by a lot of people who have served time in other similar institutions.

After I received my work assignment to the office of the psychologist I was moved from "12 Row" to Dormitory O in the lower part of the prison at Huntsville. This was known as the "Trusty Shack" by the inmates and housed about one hundred fifty men. Beds were in tiers of uppers and lowers, and had pretty good mattresses and ample bed clothes. I was taken to my new quarters by Jack B., who was a young, strong fellow about twenty-eight years of age and very popular among the other inmates. He took a "liking" to me and it was due to him that I became known as a "convict's convict," or as "good people," which was the common term given for anyone who is approved by the inmates. Jack showed my bed space to me and also pointed out a locker I could use. He said I could get a lock if I wanted but it was not necessary. I told him that it would be necessary as I did have a few valuable possessions and, after all, the big majority of those around were thieves like me. He told me that was true but that I could leave my gear, cigarettes, etc., around near my bed and be sure they would not be disturbed. Occasionally something was taken, but the culprit was discovered usually; and the "Bosses" turned their heads until it was time to send him to the prison hospital. It is strange that punishment normally does not deter crime, but the kind given one inmate from his fellows sure kept down theft in our dormitory. Time will not permit a description of life in detail of my stay in prison, but I will briefly mention the routine at my location during the next twenty months.

There were two meals served three times a day, Regular and Short-line. The Short-line was for those who worked in the so-called responsible jobs and were "Trusties" for the most part. It was considered quite a status symbol to be on the Short-line. All five of those employed, or rather assigned, to the psychology office were in this class. Also, certain inmates were permitted to wear starched whites, another mark of distinction, and I had that honor. The food was usually plentiful and good, being prepared by inmates (there being no shortage of cooks and bakers in the prison population). The food was raised on the prison farms and was as good as could be found. This food was pure as far as nature was concerned because the farms were state owned and never particularly overplanted. They easily produced sufficient food for the population of the system and employees. We worked each day except Sunday yet reported to our office on the Yard even then, as we met most of those at the Walls Unit during Saturday and Sunday. I made many contacts with a large number of people who had been sent there to pay for their crimes. This last sentence may sound a little grim but strangely most inmates said the reason they were there was because of some crime they had committed. They would start out by saying "I got caught for the crime of paper-hanging (hot-checks)." The next sentence to me usually was, "I would like to talk to you about throwing a writ for me because I was told. . . ." This was because it was known by them before they even saw me that there was a lawyer over at the office of the Classification Committee, and this was when I found out about why I was locked up over on 12 Row for so long.

As everyone knows, it was in the early 1960's that the higher courts began enforcing the rights of persons convicted of offenses to have lawyers, have their confessions processed in proper order, etc., and a number of prisoners were being released, through original applications for *writs of habeas corpus* sent from the prisons. The heads of the Texas Department of Corrections did not know just how to cope with this situation. At first they refused to permit the inmates to have writing material; after this was discontinued, they attempted to stamp out what they described as professional writ-writers (other inmates who had sufficient education to write up applications to the courts). They were in the process of locking up anyone caught writing writs for others. It was during this stage that I arrived. (It was during the time the writs were just starting.) I was turned out to work on the yard, through some court order, after the prison officials were told to stop interfering in any way with the prisoners' sending requests to the courts. I thought they were keeping me secluded because they wanted to shield me.

I helped a number of inmates but this is another story. The important part of my prison confinement occurred at about this period when I decided that regardless of being able to get myself reinstated in the law, which was not a sure thing, I would never be considered anything but second-class. I would have to spend too much of my time persuading the court that I was honest and then to have him consider my client favorably after this was accomplished. So I decided to work in the field of alcoholic rehabilitation since alcoholism was the reason for most of my troubles. Also I was an arrested alcoholic at this time. From then to the present time, my occupation in life has been and will continue to be the observation and possible participation in the changes of those around me from being a loser to a winner. I am not a dedicated person. First the pay is pretty good, and the thrill in seeing an old boy come out from the "joint" or from under the bridge and turn into a respected citizen is as great as any I have ever had regardless of what I might have done in the past. It is from this angle that I looked at and shall attempt to describe some of the people I knew in prison so that possibly a new or better approach may be taken.

Any organization or person at the present time who states that he has an alcoholic rehabilitation program that is quite successful either is misinformed or is just lying. Some help is being received but not enough, and the percentage of recovery is not at all what it should be. From the first day to the day I left I was allowed to get out into the mass of prisoners from my security cell. I heard daily from inmate to inmate the refrain, "If I ever get out of this stinking place, there is no way they are ever going to get me back. The only law I will ever break will be singing too loud in church." Unfortunately, I would see them back in their same state clothes without them even getting dirty. A few recognized this fact after they had been back several times—one was a "hot check" addict. During his present stay someone had told him that the only way he could stay out of the pen was to change his ways. He took them literally and changed his habits entirely; did everything differently, ate with his left hand, put on left sock first, etc. This was known and

260 *Fundamentals of Criminal Behavior and Correctional Systems*

one day when he started into a urinal located in the rear of our office, Jack told him, "Wait, Joe, remember you have to squat."

At about this time the alcoholism program made its first appearance in the Walls Unit. It had been tried out over at the Wynn Farm and seemed to promise some good publicity at least. So, an arrested alcoholic was admitted on the staff and permitted to hold meetings within the prison. The warden brought him into our dormitory one night and announced there was to be an AA meeting the next night. All who wanted to go should congregate at the entrance of the guard's cage and would be released to go. When the time came to leave not a person, including me, had the nerve to brave the catcalls and other names called out concerning "winos," etc. I thought this would end this little effort but the alcoholic counselor had other ideas.

The next day two of our notorious "hard case convicts" who had led riots and been locked up most of their stay for fighting guards, (and naturally were highly respected by the other inmates) were transferred to our quarters. The next night, Nick C. the counselor, came in and again announced the AA meeting. Both of these outlaws spoke up saying they sure wanted to go. Nick told them that someone might make fun of their being alcoholics, "winos," etc.; and one of them, Crazy Red, just looked around and asked if anyone had any remarks to make. Naturally, this was the end of all comment and a number of us regularly attended AA thereafter. This seemed to be the beginning of a good operation, but the staff decided to start giving merit points for AA and church attendance to count on parole. This caused practically the entire population to join up, and it became obvious that they came merely with the hope of getting out. The only thing ever discussed was the probability and possibility of getting their time cut or a favorable parole application sent to the governor.

We also had an educational program in Huntsville. A number of the inmates participated as teachers and a high school equivalency test was given. The teaching process was pretty sound, I was told; but it was on a voluntary basis. The inmate was at times excused from heavy work if he participated and this got a number of pupils. It will be noted that practically every attempted rehabilitation effort that was and is made at Texas Department of Corrections seems to be ridiculed by me. I am attempting to state the facts. We are not going to change the thinking of inmates in a penal institution by some hocus pocus lectures and teaching even with gimmicks. Perhaps the following illustration might be of constructive help. During the second year of my term served, they abandoned the auditorium above our office and made a dormitory which housed "construction workers." These were inmates who earned double time but their work was much harder than say a laundry worker or kitchen help. They were carried in trucks throughout the system wherever there was new construction. When it became known that a new bunch of workers were to be recruited and housed due to a new project to be erected just north of the Walls at Huntsville, a very large number of inmates with rather soft jobs came to the Classification Office and wanted to enroll in construction work. After a number who were already trusties and earning double time also applied, we began to screen for the reasons. Invariably it was because in this work, a trade of bricklayer, carpenter or carpenter's helper or other trades could be learned. One said to me, "Stubbs, do you know what a bricklayer makes outside?" This idea of learning a new trade had not been advertised by the staff. The inmates figured it out and a number of those outside had learned their trades this way without the formal teaching as such by a teacher but while working and doing their time.

I may have said this before but I will repeat—the inmate in any penitentiary knows he was sent there for punishment for his crime and if in the process of accepting that punishment he can learn a trade he will jump at the chance, ordinarily, that is, if he is the normal convict. Of course, there are many who are mentally deficient, etc. Whenever someone comes out with the statement that they are there for rehabilitation, they think some chaplain or other do-gooder is sounding off and it will not help them in the long run, so they just tune him out.

A lot has been said about the tricks of evading the law that are passed from one inmate to another. I am sure a lot of this is true, but all I ever heard along this line always ended up with the statement that sooner or later the thief is going to get "busted." However, one thing passed around among inmates is worth repeating, and that is how to get a job outside with a prison record. If an inmate has learned a trade inside or knows one already and applies for a job, he should go to the person hiring and state, for instance, "I am a good carpenter and a good man but you won't hire me so I guess I am just wasting your time." The "square-John" will immediately jump at this bait and demand just why—"Because I am an ex-con." That gets his attention and he usually says he will hire whoever he damn pleases provided they can do the job and then, usually, leans over backwards to hire the applicant. Other prison lore is how to conduct yourself if questioned about anything. Look the man in the eye and answer firmly with whatever story you are using. *Do not* make the mistake of saying, "If you don't believe me, I can prove it by thus and so or someone." Down the line of questioning if you have a witness who can help you, mention that casually but do not fall into the trap of saying someone can prove the truth before it is even doubted.

Because I never preached or posed as superior, I believe I gained the confidence of most of the inmates I came in contact with—particularly my immediate associates. Modesto M. did most of the testing and, being a pure Chicano, made no bones about the discrimination practiced by the Anglos in the prison. I will discuss this no further because that has now been remedied somewhat, but it is interesting that Modesto felt as he did concerning the Anglos to the extent that one day he completely quit and disassociated himself from the Catholic faith. He had always been a Catholic, but he became a strong believer and a disciple of Christian Science after meeting a well-dressed and financially solvent Reader who was visiting our section for local color for an article he was preparing. Modesto dropped the Catholic priest for this man and immediately began following his advice including no smoking and a rather strict diet without dessert, etc. There is so much hard concentration on projects by inmates that it must be logical that if properly channeled this energy could go towards their rehabilitation. It seems as though the inmate must find it himself, yet he looks with disfavor upon anything attempted to be pushed on him by some social worker. This is not to say that the judgment of the inmate has improved particularly because of his being in prison. An example of this is the performance of four inmates in "punching it" (escaping).

A number of inmates were used outside the Walls to clean the streets around the buildings and these work crews were passed out through three different sets of locks. Briefly, the first checkpoint merely saw the inmates with rakes, hoes, and tools in their hands so he passed them to the next point who then checked for identification, passes, etc. They then passed to the final gate who checked again, before letting them out. All of these actions were timed over and over to see just how long each movement took to the second. Then the four inmates presented themselves to the first gate with tools they had secured. Some trusty clerk called the second guard imitating the warden's voice telling him to pass the four to the third gate, and then to present himself immediately at the Warden's Office. The same voice called the last guard to tell him that the four had already been cleared and for him to pass them outside and then report to the office of the warden—double quick time as it was an emergency. While this took only a short time to execute, it took weeks and weeks of planning. It was not discovered how the voice imitating the warden was cleared through the central switchboard. The operation was a complete success! The four inmates found themselves outside the prison just as they had planned; but this is as far as they had planned, and they had no place to go. Naturally, they were picked up within a short time and returned to segregation and solitary confinement with loss of good time. The point of this incident is that direction must be given to inmates' thinking to have anything constructive result. They must be directed in some manner—just how to direct this thinking is what we are working on in the writing of this text.

The above episode was the talk of the Walls for a short time, more humorous than particularly alarming or dangerous as are some attempted escapes. When there was violence involved, the situation can become quite "uptight" as far as the guards are concerned.

The Texas Department of Corrections at Huntsville, like most other penal institutions, requires the guards that mingle with the inmates in overseeing their work to go unarmed. This is inside the Walls; on the farms, guards are mounted and carry guns. If you have kept up recently with the news, it has described numerous prison riots in which guards were held hostage. This can easily be done if planned by the inmates as there are only a few guards to hundreds of prisoners. Every time a new guard is placed on duty, the inmates begin to try him out. They use approaches which try to discover if he can be bribed to bring in illegal merchandise (usually alcohol). Sometimes they find out he is frightened by them, and then they really have a ball telling him of what they have heard about some pending riot and the proposed assassination of the guards.

The Texas parole system is one of the poorest in the nation, I think. All inmates come up regularly at certain times during the time of their sentence, but they have no way of knowing whether they will be considered favorably or not. It is known that certain things must be done in order that the inmate will have a place to go and a job, or the promise of a job to go to, before he is given a parole. However, if all necessary steps have been taken prior to the time of the action on his case by the Parole Board, there is no definite certainty that clemency will be granted. A member of the Board who may not like the inmate or his offense might be one that prejudices the majority. I don't particularly ask for an easier parole policy (that can be determined by lots of study as parole procedure is quite a profession in itself), but for the rehabilitation of the man, the parole procedure should be changed. I know that all of the worry and sleeplessness that precedes whether or not parole may be granted and then the despair when he is told he will be put off for a time is not necessary to his punishment. It could be set out definitely just what requirements need be met prior to parole being granted and then the inmate could be working towards that goal. I make this statement not as any authority from study but as an ex-inmate who had to go through the procedure described above; came up and was put off, then came up and refused but manipulated a parole despite the refusal.

If a person beginning his sentence is told that after a certain time he will be considered for parole provided he has either mastered a trade or perfected himself in a legitimate operation so that he may go out into society and be able to earn a respectable living, then you will see dedicated workers in the prison. To have some friend or kinsman secure the promise of some mediocre job such as working in a service station (this is the most common) is of little help to the total rehabilitation of the convict. But I repeat, if his job is one of skill and he is being paid because of his ability, it is then easier to become law abiding than to get up in the middle of the night to "boost" something; the pay not being any better if as good. The chances are overwhelming that a parole system like this will result in a reformed citizen.

There are lots of problems in the operation of a state penitentiary and to merely criticize without offering something constructive is stupid. These may be the thoughts of the reader of this chapter but it is only for the purpose of outlining the problem that critical mention is made so often. We have an old saying that "anything good in prison will soon be messed up by the convicts," and this is too true. Many things are done just to violate rules for sport. There was a minor fire on the unit next to ours and the fire extinguishers were turned over and opened up. Fortunately the blaze was minor because "Chock" beer, made from canned fruit, came out. During Christmas week a number of patients in the Walls Hospital got drunk despite daily searches for bottles (empties were found in garbage cans). It so puzzled the warden as to where they had been hidden that he publicly promised some reward with no punishment if someone would tell him how the trick was worked. It seemed that each time the search was made for liquor, some of the bed patients had to be sitting on a bed pan. The guards neglected to have them get up so the contents could be inspected.

It seemed everything was exceptionally quiet and no disturbance of any sort had occurred. I could not understand why all of the captains and assistant wardens were running around so excited. Jack B. told me that when everything was going too smooth it was a sure sign a caper was going to be pulled. The warden, being an old hand, was aware of this and was trying to find out in advance. The next day, Jack said we were going to work overtime that night. I didn't know of anything that needed to be done in a hurry, but Jack said he would show me as he had cleared it with our immediate boss. That night while we were over at the office working, a tunnel was opened under our dormitory and several inmates "punched it." The whistle blew; the guards all got out in regalia in their pursuit with the dogs; and as Jack said, everybody enjoyed a good old-fashioned "punch out." The inmates were caught, of course. The dormitory was restricted for about a week; that is, it was locked up and rather than to go to meals, all inmates were confined except those of us working out that night. We could not have participated in the "punch-out," so we were excused. Strangely, the others did not resent this; they merely admired Jack B. for arranging our working overtime during the action.

The punishment of being locked up in the dormitory was more than it may sound; within the Walls at Huntsville there were a number of open facilities, an exercise yard, a canteen, a library, and general access to all other prisoners at meal-times and recreational periods. The fact of being imprisoned was not particularly evident; a person considered himself to be in a small town, unless you were locked up in an individual cell, or even a dormitory. I am not saying that this creates a home away from home. No inmate will admit anything but hate for "this stinking place," but the facts show that some have found friends there and are able to carve out an enjoyable existence better than in the free world. The head of classification knew this and would send some old offenders back to their friends when they brought in new time. Life imprisonment meant at least ten years flat time (actual time served) and these inmates were usually sent to one of the units where they could develop into trained technicians or clerks; whereas, the short term man usually would be sent out to labor in the fields. As in all places, there were easy jobs to be had; these were called "political jobs." The one I held there was so styled.

I am aware that the name of this game is to rehabilitate the offender so that he will no longer be an expense to the state but be an asset to society. In order to make any progress the counselor had better know well just how the subject under investigation thinks, and acts under the stress of daily life. The naive counselor who accepts the inmate on his representations as to character, work habits, drinking, and values not only is wasting the time of his client but also has stamped himself as being a "stupid square who can be made," just as a guard who can be bribed or threatened in some manner. It is worse to be known as a "hard nose," as the offender will either tune him out or will plan how he can beat him for something. I think the word is "acceptance" and that is hard to come by.

Fred C. was on his way out having served all of his short two-year time. All inmates received *good time* which was 80 percent over the regular time, provided they cooperated and obeyed orders. One year was done in seven months and fourteen days. He was due to get out a month before he made it, but was "busted" for operating a poker game in the dormitory. Enough of his good time was taken to cause his discharge to be delayed thirty days. He also received the standard punishment at the Walls which was to stand on a box, usually a soft drink carton, in the Bull Ring—a sort of cage at the entrance of the unit used to process new arrivals. The prisoner was required to stand on this box for several hours at night, sometimes all night, and meditate on his sinful ways. Fred received no particular attention from anyone in the prison because he was reasonably well educated and his offense was more by mistake than deliberate. I am not talking now about rehabilitation, but rather the history and method of operation (M.O.) carefully catalogued by the Department of Public Safety in Texas with a copy to the FBI. It is anticipated that over 80 percent of the inmates will repeat; and by keeping an active file, they may be more easily apprehended. This fact is known and resented very much by all ex-convicts that are sharp; however, the facts are that the 80 percent return is unfortunately accurate. A particularly hot number (repeater several times over) will be questioned over and over about his habits and people he knows outside. He is told that this is for his own good but, actually it is to get a picture of his trail so he can be picked up "for questioning" as quickly as he is discharged. The inmate knows all about this; and as a result, now that there is some work being done in Vocational Rehabilitation, the prejudice against the "fuzz" has to be overcome. Fred C. came by to see me after I was released; he was doing well, but the only job he could find was a door-to-door salesman for a Bible publishing company.

I think it proper at this time to discuss the manner in which money is passed in prison. I presume all are alike in that no cash is permitted but scrip for canteen use may be purchased each week up to a certain amount. In Texas the inmate has to present his scrip book personally to the canteen runner who takes out the coupons. The coupons themselves are not transferable from person to person. As a result, merchandise becomes the method of bartering and settling debts. Cigarettes are the most common commodity used among the inmates. For some reason, Camels were the most common brand used at Huntsville; perhaps because they were more securely packaged. Practically all inmates smoked Bugler tobacco and rolled their own or had them rolled by others. This was true because, regardless of the amount of money one had on deposit, only a certain amount could be drawn (I believe it was $6 weekly); this was not sufficient to purchase ordinary rolled cigarettes and the other necessary articles of comfort. I saw many cartons of Camels passed around from inmate to inmate, but rarely did I ever see one of them opened and smoked. They were used as stakes in poker and bridge; those who had draws available usually paid with cigarettes for maid service (another inmate's making up your bed and mopping and sweeping around it). Also they were used to pay for haircuts and laundry services performed by other inmates. Strangely, an inmate was not looked down upon because he performed these services. The row-tenders, as the maids were called, were usually the leaders in the dormitory. Those that had money and did not hire these services were the ones who had a hard time until they caught on to the routine. If you would want to analyze this practice, it could be said that this was the convict's way of sharing the wealth.

Life in prison is brutal at any place I am sure; at the Walls I will mention just one incident concerning the punishment of a prisoner who was supposed to have "snitched." About four of his associates fixed razor blades in soap so the edge would protrude and then attacked him in the shower. He was not a pretty sight when led off to the hospital. This leads to one phase of convict life that is hard to cope with and that pertains to the duty expected of one convict from another.

If a certain inmate has been placed in charge of supplies, particularly food or drugs, or if he may, by use of ingenuity, secure access to these, he is expected to steal and share with his fellows. He doesn't have to indulge himself if he does not wish but he must provide for the others that do. There is no excuse accepted for this and the wise warden will know the practice and never expect his inmate clerk to be above this demand. Life is real cheap in a modern penitentiary. You may read about some prominent prisoner being killed or otherwise abused, but did you ever read about a Grand Jury investigation and the trial for murder of an inmate who was supposed to have killed another? Sometimes there may be such a trial if an inmate kills a guard, but usually the inmate is taken care of by guards (known as a Mexican Escape)—in the back! The blacks have it better now than the whites because of their insistence upon investigations of their civil rights. This has caused the authorities to watch all guards and to avoid anything that might bring down the federal agents.

Note: This chapter is designed to give an inmate's view of life in the corrective setting. It is not a story in that it does not have a plot or an ending. However artificial it may seem, we have ended it at this point since we feel it has accomplished its purpose.

Chapter 13
Effects of Incarceration
ROBERT G. LAWSON

| Personality and Other Factors
| Challenges and Approaches
| Inmate Hierarchy, Peer Group and Other Effects
| References

It is generally believed by the lay public that society acts normally when it subjects individuals to periods of incarceration. The same society does not understand that despite the effectiveness of any presently used rehabilitation programs, the subjection of persons to periods of incarceration is abnormal for those persons. Incarceration effectively restricts deviant behavior and prohibits it from having further immediate undesired effect on society; it also effectively constrains the individual from having the normal experiences to which he was accustomed. Living in a free society requires adjustments of every person; institutional living requires additional and major adjustments. Penal institutional living requires even more. Having thought about it, one can understand that confinement, with its deprivation of any heterosexual relationship, its enforced contact with homosexuals, and its mandated conformity, is foreign to people who have experienced a free society. Even having thought about it, one can hardly conceptualize the dehumanizing erosion that results from constant surveillance, the absence of privacy and the loss of personal identity. The imprisoned person is really the only one to testify on the basis of experience about the effects of imprisonment. This chapter then is obviously an effort to construct a picture, neither pleasant nor adequate, on the basis of observation and the experience of others.

The effects of imprisonment are as variable as the persons subjected to it; however, certain effects can be considered in relation-

Effects of Incarceration

ship to several major identifiable factors, but we must bear in mind that no single factor is operative alone. This chapter is limited to three factors. The first factor includes those characteristics personal to the inmate, such as age, sex, health, education, family experience, cultural background and personality. The second factor covers the inmate's experiences with other inmates and the institutional staff. The third factor relates to the systems in society that the imprisoned person encounters after release.

Of the many changes which occur as a result of imprisonment, very few are physical. Unless an inmate is confined for a number of years, he will probably emerge without outward signs of change. In keeping with this line of thought and, contrary to popular belief, physical abuse by staff members is a relatively rare occurrence (in part, because of its lack of effectiveness). Corporal punishment tends to result in increased hostility. Likewise, other "negative incentives," such as a denying or taking away privileges more often produces increased misbehavior and further "acting out." The tool most often used to control people in confinement is additional confinement or "lockup." The most often heard justification for this is the prevention of aggressive acts, relaxation of tension, or in many cases both. Physical abuse from fights or beatings by inmates is a more serious problem. No one in an institution is far removed from potential danger, and actual confrontation is not uncommon. Overriding the physical damage is the resulting incrimination and fear which are intricately involved and which cannot be separated. No inmate is immune from fear. Because of this fact he must use whatever recourses are available to create a place for himself or be constantly subjected to the influence of others whose positions in life are more secure than his own.

PERSONALITY AND OTHER FACTORS

Institutionalized people (both juveniles and adults) develop quite similar personality characteristics. These traits include being immature, extremely insecure, easily confused, susceptible to following leaders, and having anxiety about the future. The inmate is often bewildered by his situation and simply cannot understand, at least emotionally, why he is paying a debt to society. Of even more significance is the idea that generally inmates just cannot accept responsibility for their own actions especially as they relate to any question concerning guilt or innocence. As a part of his situation the inmate learns to be quite adaptive often through using rationalization. All these things have post-institutional carry over effects. An illustration may help to explain.

Many inmates develop a tremendous need to dominate and control others. This is noticeable in most conversations among inmates and also in discussions involving inmates and staff. This problem appears to represent a failure to develop adequate self-confidence and a failure to accept others on an equal basis. No professional person should be surprised in a discussion with an inmate to realize that the real issue to be resolved is whether or not the inmate will dominate the situation. Also noteworthy is the fact that once this issue is resolved then it probably will not reoccur. Another personality development, primarily but not exclusively experienced by the juvenile delinquent is the formulation of a concept about his home and family that may border on delusion. It is quite common for the younger inmate to "forget" the horrible home and way of life he experienced. In place of his real home life, he visualizes an image of warmth, security and love for his family and friends. Extreme care must be taken in dealing with this kind of situation. While it is necessary to help the individual face up to and then cope with reality by developing inner strength, it is also vital to protect him from a severe emotional shock. Current thinking indicates that the best method to avoid this occurrence is to provide treatment and training close to the individual's home, hopefully within his own community utilizing small regional facilities and day care or outpatient techniques especially for the less dangerous prisoner.

CHALLENGES AND APPROACHES

Two basic challenges face penologists today that directly influence the effects of institutions. One is the philosophy of the institution staff and their needs and the other concerns how more inmates can be meaningfully involved in their own rehabilitation.

The first question which centers around philosophy basically is, should an institutional program be oriented in a more permissive, individualistic, open environment anticipating that self-reliance and confidence will evolve; or, should the treatment approach be more controlled, with encouragement of conformity and suppression of unusual behavior with the expected result being self-discipline and stamina? It is accepted that both schools of thought can produce living examples as positive proof of success. Proponents of either way of thinking can likewise point out the flaws in the opposing approach. The point is that all too often the inmate is confused and victimized by a real lack of consistency. He would be better off with either approach than he is when he is constantly caught among staff who are playing by differing sets of rules. In effect, he must learn both the "hard and soft" approach; be able to adapt to each staff member differently and expect to suffer the consequences whenever the blades of the scissors decide to cut. It would seem that adequate understanding of each individual and a consistent approach by staff would alleviate much of this dilemma.

It is generally accepted by most institutional staff that desirable changes in behavior result when successful experiences and positive rewards are gained. It also is true that the likelihood of successfully rehabilitating an inmate will depend in large part on whether or not the inmate becomes an active participant in his own treatment program. It is one approach to assemble a group of staff members, discuss personal history of the inmate, educational and social data, psychological and medical information, and then formulate a treatment plan. It is an entirely different proposition to have him realize his role and that he must play an integral part in the process of his own rehabilitation. Without his involvement the lasting success of any treatment process is questionable. While there are many ways of accomplishing this goal, one of the most effective is obviously to include the person (counselor, teacher, maintenance worker, guard or secretary) who has developed the best personal/professional relationship with the inmate on the team. This "contact person" can more readily solicit the confidence and support of the inmate in taking an active part. One of the most perplexing problems facing progressive institutional personnel is that of minimizing the adverse effects of group living. So long as the prevailing economic and social climate dictate that inmates be housed in large numbers with high inmate-to-staff ratios, the institution staff will be hard pressed to create favorable conditions for psychological and social growth. Inside or outside prison walls, greater population density gives rise to more social friction. The response to such friction is to establish more rules and more interpersonal barriers in an attempt to reduce friction.

Since most inmates suffer from failure in incorporating normal and essential rules of social conduct and from a lack of skill in establishing and maintaining constructive social intimacy, it is obvious that the institutional environment is, in many ways, presenting them with a confusing clutter of additional artificial obstacles. They are given a mandate to adapt to an environment which bears little resemblance to real life. They have little opportunity to learn to make decisions, to make mistakes and to recover from poor decisions, to assume responsibility, to set goals, to try their wings on new attitudes and values. All of these behaviors are needed if they are to adjust outside the walls. Ideally, an institution might be a safe, somewhat cushioned place where this kind of learning and experimentation could occur. The very word institution as derived from the Latin implies setting up, introducing, founding; so the original idea was to give people a place where change could occur and where new habits could be established. Society has not yet, however, given adequate concern to what kinds of changes are desirable and to what methods and costs these positive changes entail as opposed to the costs of present methods.

The level of emotional maturity and the inmate's age make a decided difference on the effects of institutionalization. Generally, adolescents and young adults seldom exhibit signs of extreme despair; they always have hope and are optimistic about the future. This statement is true even though they may not have realistic methods planned for obtaining their goals. This premise is valid even in the case of young adults who may be facing an extended period of incarceration. Only the elderly who have been institutionalized for a number of years and the severely emotionally disturbed with a tendency toward depression admit feelings of hopelessness and despair. It is also notable that this group is extremely fearful of facing life outside the protective environment of the institution, and they frequently fall victim to the pressures of free society when released. It seems that the most severe punishment for these individuals is to be released from prison.

Effect of Time

There is a definite correlation between the length of time incarcerated and the effects it has on the individual. Simply stated, the longer a person resides in an institution, the more difficulty he has adjusting to society and taking care of himself. It would seem that most of the convicted, if they understand the time element involved, can adjust to confinement. We are all aware of newspaper reports of escapes by inmates who were scheduled for release within a very short time, weeks or just days. Analysis of these cases, however, reveals a number of circumstances contributing to these seemingly illogical acts. These elements, when examined, have been of sufficient force and influence to blot out consideration of an early release. A frequently overlooked fact is that inmates suffer from a lack of mobility while imprisoned. Those simple freedoms such as being able to take a walk, visit a friend, go for a drive or go out for a meal seem to have tremendous effect on inmates. There can be improvement in permitting these or other activities that would alleviate much of the associated discontent.

Sex Factors

While most statements concerning inmates apply equally well to both sexes, there are notable differences. The adult female offender will frequently admit to guilt feelings about being institutionalized. This should not be confused with admission of guilt for the crime. They simply more openly express personal shame over the experience. The degradation of having been committed has a more devastating effect. There seems to be a reluctance by court officials to sentence females to institutions. This fact is especially true of young girls and consequently, institutional records reveal repeated court appearance for numerous offenses before sentencing. This means in many cases the female offender, especially the juvenile, has experienced more opportunities for failure and the resultant psychological damage prior to reaching the institution. There is a debatable assumption that society is less willing to readmit a female following release from a correctional facility. The writer's opinion is that women do experience more difficulty primarily because of their own personal emotions.

It is universal truth that juvenile and adult offenders develop a hostile attitude toward authority. Having been placed in a very structured environment they have been forced to deal directly with authority figures. Respect for authority occurs only when the individual feels that he has been treated equitably. The most notable exception is the respect for policemen. The attitude toward him can be very nebulous and quickly changing. Authority figures are universally mistrusted. Questioning has revealed that one reason for this is the result of the ability of the police to apprehend lawbreakers. In short, "If the policeman can catch me, he must be a capable person." Here again, however, this attitude is centered around individuals and not the police in general.

Some Cannot Be Rehabilitated

Society has to come to grips with another unpleasant reality. A small percentage of inmates are hopeless in terms of rehabilitation, at least within present technology. This is a fact which overzealous professionals and penal reformers may have obscured in their perfectly legitimate and justified pleas to improve conditions in order that more inmates can hopefully be rehabilitated. Unquestionably, most delinquent and criminal behavior can be modified and many can be returned to society. Just as unquestionably, some cannot be safely restored to the society. This fact has probably been ignored because recognition of it would pose some knotty issues for many professional persons and the society. For example, to whom will society be willing to entrust such an awesome judgment? What would happen to the legal fabric of the justice system were it to try to cope with permanently removing some citizens and what safeguards and reviews would be necessary to protect the individual while protecting society? What alternative, perhaps in the form of a sheltered community, could society develop, between mere incarceration and release, which would allow such persons to live as productively as they can in a setting that is an benign as possible? Some few of those who cannot be rehabilitated appear hopeless out of functional causes such as having experienced a completely devastating, brutalizing childhood which helped create an individual unresponsive to modification. However, most of those in this untreatable category are persons whose dangerous or grossly incompetent social behavior arises from organic causes, such as central nervous system dysfunction, suspected biochemical imbalances, and similar handicaps (often multiple ones) for which present medical and behavioral sciences have no remedies. Such people exist briefly on the fringes of society and blunder repeatedly in and out of both mental hospitals and correctional facilities. Until such time that research may provide means to prevent or effectively treat such conditions, society must come to grips with their existence and design some humane and sensible concepts for their care and custody.

INMATE HIERARCHY, PEER GROUP AND OTHER EFFECTS

Considerable criticism has been leveled at institutional officials for their apparent inability to control or even effectively monitor inmate cliques or subcultures which develop in all institutions. No person experienced in correctional work or any former inmate will deny the influence of the inmate controlled hierarchy (social order). Its terrorizing effect can, however, be minimized if constructive programs are being implemented. There have been isolated instances in which the presence of various group pressures has had a positive effect in helping inmates realize the importance of others and their rights. More often it produces fear of association with others and a reluctance to get involved or to develop interpersonal relationships. There is speculation that former inmates never cast off their fear of organizational power and influence. One result of this system is the production of the "loner," who is easily recognized by his hermit type characteristics.

Most authorities agree that institutionalized people do obtain useful technical skills. With few exceptions, the inmate improves his level of educational development, vocational skills, and knowledge of the world around him. These skills when released appear to off-set, to some extent, the public negativism regarding "ex-cons." While this idea is encouraging, the recidivist seldom reports a lack of ability to apply these skills as his reason for failure on the outside. Further study shows that his inability to develop adequate relationships with people proves to be his downfall. All too often, institutions develop a "good inmate" who, on release, turns out to be totally unprepared to cope with society as a free man. We must learn to determine the success of programs, not on the basis of how well they serve themselves, but on their ability to produce an individual who can adjust in an unstructured or free community.

A relatively recent phenomenon is the realization that inmates generally are the products of an extremely complex social order. They are in the first place rejects from a society of forced conformity. A number of inmates from a fast-paced society encounter staff who are generally less sophisticated than they. This situation may occur frequently with staff responsible for custody. When we add the militancy associated with racism and the newly defined group of inmates committed to revolution, anarchy and destruction, we have an extremely turbulent situation. As yet no one knows how to deal effectively with this problem. Prison officials and society in general have been unable to react in a meaningful way. It is only speculation at this time to attempt to answer the question concerning how these clusters of factors will affect the inmate who is a part of the system. We can only speculate concerning whether or not the staff members themselves will be able to understand the changing society and be able to help the inmate learn to adapt to it.

The therapeutic attitude of the institutional staff is quite important in developing an atmosphere where constructive personality changes can occur. Personal relationships which develop between inmates and staff, either wholesome or otherwise, are not readily discarded. In essence, if the inmate has experienced an ability to develop self-confidence and acceptance by others, he will likely develop a pattern of more socially acceptable behavior. On the other hand, his failure to gain confidence in himself or to lessen his distrust of others will reinforce his asocial tendencies. Given an adequate opportunity for change, almost all who are committed are pliable, flexible individuals with the potential to be damaged or benefited by their institutional experiences.

The most overlooked dilemma facing the former inmate after release concerns how he lives in a society that really never forgives or feels that it has been repaid. Every state has legal restrictions that deprive the "ex-con" of obtaining equality. The most notable examples include loss of the right to vote or hold public office, restrictions from serving as a juror, obtaining insurance and the loss of property rights. Former inmates also suffer loss of employment opportunities due in part to being ineligible to qualify for occupational and technical licenses. These civil disabilities have been examined and many of the restrictions can and should be removed. Society screams for penal reform and then blindly accepts social injustice.

Information necessary to determine what is happening to released offenders is extremely sparse. Most of the data available are from recidivists who are products of correctional system failure. Most former inmates who are able to avoid returning to an institution also avoid any further association with the penal system and "lose" themselves in society. They are reluctant to respond to requests for interviews, questionnaires, or other means

280 *Fundamentals of Criminal Behavior and Correctional Systems*

of obtaining follow-up information. There is indication that the former inmate fears to be associated with the system. It is inconceivable that any individual could escape unaffected by a period of incarceration. The combination of experiences will be either helpful or harmful as determined by a variety of factors. By now, it is realized that not all of these factors can be controlled. It is, therefore, a matter of being aware of those factors that can be manipulated and utilizing professional skills to bring about the desired results.

REFERENCES

Ramsey Clark: *Crime in America*. New York, Simon and Schuster, 1970.
Neil P. Cohen and Dean Hill Rivkin: Civil disabilities: The forgotten punishment. In *Federal Probation*. Washington, D.C., Administrative Office of the United States Courts and Bureau of Prisons, Department of Justice, June, 1971.
Karl Menninger: *Crime in America*. New York, The Viking Press, 1968.

Chapter 14
Psychiatry in Corrections
CHARLES E. SMITH

Introduction
Psychiatry and the Courts
Prevalence of Mental Disorder Among Criminal Offenders
Relationships Between Mental Disorder and Crime
Scientific Examination of the Offender
Vocational Rehabilitation Services
Goals and Problems for the Future
References

INTRODUCTION

The involvement of psychiatry in the criminal justice system has a lengthy background. The practical need to involve psychiatry in the law enforcement process is immediately apparent when one considers the extent of mental illness occurring among the offender group. As behavioral scientists began to see a closer correlation between crime and abnormality of function, the role of medicine in this area has become increasingly important. Thus, today, increasing emphasis is being placed on the contributions which medical specialists, particularly psychiatrists, can make toward the improved understanding and treatment of the criminal offender. All of this is consistent with society's traditional expectation that medical men will interest themselves in behavior problems such as crime, knowing that the profession has always employed its great technical knowledge for the greatest public good.

Jails and prisons continue to receive many mentally ill persons whose impulsive, adverse behaviors have led them into conflict with the law, either by chance, or circumstance. The likelihood of a mentally ill person's being imprisoned is determined by several factors, such as the commission of an unlawful act; the nature of the unlawful behavior; and the dispositional alternatives and treatment resources which may be available at the time. It is generally recognized that considerable discretion exists at all levels of the criminal justice system in the handling and disposition of the mentally ill offender.

At the turn of the century, when there was a dearth of mental hospital facilities, no doubt the percentage of mentally ill persons among jail and prison populations was much higher than it is today. However, the problem of the mentally ill offender is still far from resolved, either in terms of generally accepted social policy, or in terms of the necessary resources to implement such a policy, once agreed upon and adopted.

In this chapter, some aspects of the problem of the mentally ill offender will be examined, including the scope of the problem, some known relationships between mental disorder and crime, and the legal and medical methods which have been employed in dealing with the problem. Emphasis will be placed upon the ways in which available dispositional alternatives can be integrated with contemporary vocational rehabilitation programs and practices. Finally, some of the unresolved problems and issues involved in this endeavor will be identified, hoping thereby to point the way toward future directions in this difficult and important area.

PSYCHIATRY AND THE COURTS

A review of the historical development of the present role of psychiatry in the criminal justice system reveals that there are substantial precedents for such involvement.[1] The earliest, and, perhaps, traditional role of the psychiatrist, which won him the title of "alienist," was the direct outgrowth of the law's attempt to separate out those offenders who appeared to be grossly disordered to an extent that they might not be responsive to the forces of punishment and deterrence. It is quite significant that the law's interest and concern with the mentally ill antedates by many centuries any development which can be identified as clinical psychiatry as it is known today. In the Anglo-Saxon common law there are decisions relating to "madness" which go back to the 13th century, while contemporary clinical descriptive psychiatry had its beginnings less than 150 years ago. Certainly, this should lay to rest any feelings that psychiatry has any claims to originality in this field. The expertise of psychiatry is an ancillary to the implementation of the common law, and not a substitute for it.

The traditional concern of the law with the role of mental disorder in criminal behavior is evidenced in both the common law proceedings for determining competency for trial, and those designed to determine criminal responsibility. A representative statute dealing with the determination of competency for trial asks whether the defendant *may be presently insane, or otherwise so mentally incompetent that he is unable to understand the proceedings against him, or to properly assist in his own defense.*[2] The classical M'Naghten case rule (1843) asks *whether the defendant was so mentally unsound as not to know right from wrong in respect to the act charged.*[3] The irresistible impulse test asks whether the defendant was capable of adhering to the right concerning the act charged.[4] The Durham case rule, which was enunciated in 1954, asks whether the defendant was *suffering from a diseased or defective mental condition* and, if so, was the act charged *the product of such mental abnormality.*[5] A more recent innovation, the American Law Institute test, which has been adopted in several jurisdictions, provides that "A person is not responsible for criminal conduct if, at the time of such conduct as a result of mental disease, or defect, he lacks substantial capacity either to appreciate the criminality or wrongfulness of his conduct, or to conform his conduct to the requirements of law."[6] At the present time, most states follow either the M'Naghten rule or the American Law Institute rule, or some modification of one of them.

In actual practice, the medico-legal approaches to questions surrounding possible relationships between mental disorder and criminal behavior, as formulated in the tests for fitness for trial and responsibility, continue to be surrounded by controversy. Also, it becomes increasingly apparent that these procedures offer very little to the solution of the overall problem of the mentally ill offender, since they are applied to only a small number of the 10 percent or so of offenders who stand trial. There is little doubt that many defendants who could make these defenses choose not to do so, some because they lack the necessary resources, others because they regard mental illness as more stigmatizing than criminality, and, perhaps, others because they see the possible duration and conditions of treatment in a correctional institution as more attractive than those in a mental hospital.[7]

PREVALENCE OF MENTAL DISORDER AMONG CRIMINAL OFFENDERS

Currently, there are about 300,000 prisoners in confinement in this country. Roughly two-thirds of these are confined in state and federal correctional institutions for adult offenders, while the balance are confined in local jails and workhouses. In attempting to estimate the prevalence of mental illness among this group, it is revealing to apply data obtained in several studies which have been made of selected offender groups. For instance, a review of the findings in examinations of offenders carried out in Massachusetts under the Briggs Law over a 14-year-period showed 15 percent to have a significant psychiatric disorder.[8] In their analysis of findings made in examinations of 10,000 consecutive cases seen in the psychiatric clinic of the Court of General Session in New York, Bromberg and Thompson reported significant psychiatric illness in roughly 20 percent of these defendants.[9] Both of these studies showed something less than 2 percent of the examinees to be psychotic. Several years ago, I found 15 percent of 500 consecutive commitments to the Federal Bureau of Prisons to have some recognizable mental disorder. A more recent study of over 1,000 prisoners confined at the Federal Penitentiary, Lewisburg, Pennsylvania, showed the psychiatric morbidity within this group to be about 20 percent. Several other surveys of prison populations have shown the incidence of mental disorder to be in the range of 15 to 20 percent.[10] All of these surveys tend to suggest that the prevalence rate for mental disorder is about the same in the prison community as it is in the community at large, which might come as a surprise to some who wish to equate criminality with mental illness.

Some idea of the magnitude of the problem of the mentally ill offender may be gained by applying the 20 percent figure to a representative state prison population. For instance, in North Carolina, where there are about 10,000 in confinement any day of the year, and where approximately 13,000 new commitments were received last year, the 20 percent rate would have given 2,600 prospective mental cases, or ten each working day. This is enough caseload to provide material for several thriving outpatient clinics and a small mental hospital.

Because of the seeming proneness of certain mentally ill persons to become involved in minor offenses such as vagrancy, trespass, simple assault, petty theft, public drunk, and a variety of minor offenses which are often carried out while under the influence of alcohol, special attention needs to be given to misdemeanant and jail type populations. Such data as we do have suggests the prevalence of mental disorder among jailed minor offenders may be much larger than that found in representative prison populations. For instance, in a recent study of 50 randomly selected misdemeanants referred for pre-sentence diagnostic study in North Carolina, 82 percent were found to have a diagnosable psychiatric disorder.[11] Many of these cases can be viewed as relative failures of the health and welfare services which are available in their respective communities.

As it turns out, this fairly substantial caseload must be handled for the most part in institutional systems which have inadequate and limited physical facilities, as well as severely limited staffing patterns. The last survey with which I am familiar showed less than 60 psychiatrists employed full-time in the approximately 230 adult correctional institutions in this country.[12] Of these 230 correctional institutions, only 26 can be identified as having specific treatment programs for mentally disordered offenders. With few exceptions these treatment programs have the services of only one full-time psychiatrist and, perhaps, one or two more who work part-time.[13]

Assuming that it takes four to six hours of intensive psychiatric interviewing to begin to understand the dynamics of an individual offender, and, assuming this small number of psychiatrists available to examine the large potential caseload which we have already described, perhaps no one should be surprised if there is still no substantial body of case material available for scientific comparison and analysis. Also, recognize that the very transient nature of the clinical contacts with cases in this category tends to preclude the possibility of doing the kind of long-term observation and follow-ups which are so essential to the development of any meaningful predictive criteria.

RELATIONSHIPS BETWEEN MENTAL DISORDER AND CRIME

At this point it should be of interest to review some of the observations which have been made concerning the relationships between mental disorder and crime. While only about 2 percent of all offenders are found to be overtly psychotic, these are the offenders who tend to achieve the greatest notoriety because of the regressive, primitive, and, often, needlessly aggressive characteristics of their offenses. Thus, it is common to suspect psychosis in the cases of certain unusual and bizarre offenses. The most frequent disorder observed in this group is schizophrenia, a disease manifested by confused and delusional thinking, along with inconsistent and inappropriate feelings. When persons with these disorders act out in response to their deluded fantasies, the results are ordinarily predictably unique, and even, occasionally gruesome.

Neurotic and sociopathic types of mental disorder, which occur amongst approximately 15 percent of offenders, are associated with a variety of offense groups. The impulsive auto thief, and the compulsive check writer are common examples. The behavior of certain sex offenders, notably the exhibitionist, that of some arsonists, and that of some shoplifters, can often be seen as related to underlying neurotic disorder.

Those offenses which mentally defective persons commit are usually marked by qualities of suggestibility and poor judgment which tend to set them apart. Individuals with psychopathic personality, those with manic types of illness, and alcoholics, often reflect underlying impulsivity in the offenses which bring them to the attention of the courts. Finally, in offenses involving threatening and assaultive behavior, it is not uncommon to find an underlying paranoid mental disorder. In the federal courts a high incidence of paranoid mental disorder has been observed among individuals charged with mailing threatening and obscene letters.[14]

From this brief consideration of some known relationships between mental illness and personality disorder and crime, it is possible to begin to formulate a listing of some indicators of pathology which can be employed in the task of separating out the emotionally disordered offender.[15] Some of these indicators are as follows:

1. The apparently motiveless crime
2. The bizarre offense
3. An offense which seems to represent a significant departure from the offender's usual behavior
4. Seemingly senseless repetitive criminal behavior
5. Certain sex crimes, arson, and other apparently compulsive behaviors
6. Offenses in which drugs and/or alcohol are implicated
7. Instances in which the defendant has a known history of prior mental illness, and instances when the defendant seems emotionally disturbed, confused, or perhaps depressed
8. Apparently dangerous behaviors

In its recent report, the President's Task Force on Prisoner Rehabilitation has recommended that "any offender who can safely be diverted from incarceration—or in some cases even adjudication—should be."[16] This conclusion stems from the growing feeling that there are substantial numbers of offenders coming through the criminal justice system who could be handled more effectively in a variety of social and medical agencies, assuming that these programs and facilities had the capability to deal with this potential increase in caseload. The discovery and diagnosis of suitable cases for such diversionary treatment will require a wider application of a variety of scientific examination procedures.

SCIENTIFIC EXAMINATION OF THE OFFENDER

All models for the scientific examination of the offender designed to determine the presence of mental disorder are of comparatively recent origin. Perhaps the earliest systematic approach to the identification of the mentally disordered offender was the technique of employing a three-man study team composed of a psychiatrist, a psychologist, and a social worker; a plan which was introduced in juvenile court practice around the turn of the century. More recently, psychiatric clinics have been developed to serve courts which deal with adult offenders. Among the cities which have adult court psychiatric clinics are New York, Chicago, Philadelphia, Detroit, Baltimore, Boston, Cleveland, Pittsburgh and Washington, D.C.[17] Also, diagnostic centers, which provide psychiatric examinations for offenders, have been established in several state departments of correction, as, for instance, New Jersey, California and Florida.

The Pre-sentence Diagnostic Procedure

In my opinion, the most promising route toward individualized treatment we have today is by way of a comprehensive diagnostic study which, at its best, brings to bear all that we know about the scientific examination of the offender to the case in hand. Basically, such a diagnostic study is designed to answer two questions; what led the individual to commit the offense, that is, what social and personal factors may have influenced him in making his decision to commit the offense, and, what measures are necessary to lessen, or to prevent, the offender's tendency toward crime, and to safeguard the community.

Two viable, working examples of these diagnostic procedures are the observation and study procedures employed in the federal system,[18] and the pre-sentence diagnostic studies employed in

North Carolina.[19] In both these jurisdictions these examinations are made on a selective basis, at the discretion of the court, after trial and conviction, but prior to sentence, in those cases where more exact knowledge is required. In some other jurisdictions, such examinations are also made prior to trial, and may be incorporated in the pre-sentence investigation report.

Under the North Carolina statute, which is modeled after the federal statute, defendants selected for this procedure may be committed to the Department of Corrections for a period of from 60 to 90 days for these special examinations, which include a comprehensive social study, physical examinations, psychological and psychiatric examinations, educational, vocational and aptitude appraisals, a religious interest survey, and extensive observations of behavior during the period of the study.

These pre-sentence diagnostic studies involve not only an evaluation of the defendant's personality and his capacity for adaptation in the institutional environment, but an evaluation of the ways in which he adapted in the community. The community aspect of the evaluation involves an assessment of the defendant's resources, both personal and material. For instance, one wants to know something about his associates, his friends, his family and, in particular, the durability and strength of his interpersonal ties. Where his resources appear to be deficient, and when it appears that his ability to cope in the community might be improved through involvement in new and different interrelationships, one wants to know what kinds of resources may be available to implement indicated change.

Essential information on these factors may be obtained through an appropriate pre-sentence investigation conducted by a probation officer in the defendant's community. Such an investigation can provide valuable information concerning the community's attitude toward the defendant, and it should disclose those questions and problems which will require further exploration in the course of the pre-sentence diagnostic study. For these reasons, the pre-sentence investigation is an essential prerequisite in all cases referred for pre-sentence diagnostic study.

After all of the various studies have been completed, the study group then meets to review the results and to formulate an understanding of the dynamics of the offender, and his offense, and to develop an acceptable treatment plan, consistent with the interests of the community. In North Carolina, the staffing procedures have been developed administratively, since there are no statutory guidelines. Here it is the practice to have a caseworker assigned to each case, to be responsible for the study of the defendant's social history, and to coordinate all other special studies which are undertaken. When the case is staffed, the caseworker presents the study findings to the staffing group, along with a discussion of the various alternative treatment approaches which have been identified. After discussing this presentation, the staffing group, which now has available all of the information which has been garnered, customarily interviews the defendant. This unique feature of the staffing procedure allows each member of the study group to make his own assessment of the defendant's personality in terms of a variety of relevant considerations, such as his mental state, his reliability and perhaps, most important, his motivation. Following this, the staff enters into a discussion directed at seeking a consensus as to the course of treatment to be recommended to the court, weighing the alternatives and the resources available to implement each alternative. The results of these deliberations are then transmitted to the court in summary form, along with copies of the essential supportive data which the group employed in reaching its decision.

In summary, the aim of the scientific examination of offenders is to evaluate medical and psychosocial factors which may have contributed to the offender's delinquent behavior. It is not intended to say that all offenders are sick, but rather to recognize those who are, and, hopefully, to be able to implement appropriate treatment to remedy underlying emotional illness which has contributed to delinquent behavior. There is reason to hope that some of these same treatment techniques may be employed to good advantage in the modification of behavior of offenders who are not found to be obviously mentally ill or emotionally disordered. Thus, treatment techniques which improve motivation, enhance initiative, and lead to the adoption of more constructive attitudes, should have some utility in correctional treatment programs for all offenders.

VOCATIONAL REHABILITATION SERVICES

Offenders whose examination reveals medical or psychosocial dysfunction may be eligible for vocational rehabilitation services. These services are available to offenders who are substantially handicapped for employment because of mental or physical disability. Vocational rehabilitation services seek to develop activities programs which will affect life style in desirable ways, and they seek to re-educate handicapped persons through exposure to concrete creative experiences.

Two brief case histories are presented to illustrate the complementary way in which vocational rehabilitation services can facilitate the restoration of a public offender whose disability has been identified in the course of an appropriate study. The first case was committed for observation and study under the pre-sentence diagnostic procedure:

Case 1. This 18-year-old girl was convicted of possession of marijuana. She was alleged to have given some marijuana to a younger sister, who was arrested when she tried to sell some of the drug to one of her friends at school. When the younger sister revealed her source of the drug, a search of their home uncovered an additional quantity of the drug in the older sister's room.

This girl's parents had been separated for several years. She described difficulties in her relationship with her mother, particularly a feeling that she had never been able to live up to her mother's expectations. While still in high school she began using drugs, presumably for the relief of the intolerable tensions which she was experiencing. A few months prior to her arrest her mother had sought treatment for her at a mental health clinic. After graduating from high school she had had no significant employment.

Both the psychological and psychiatric examinations showed this girl to have good intelligence. These examinations showed her to be an anxious, passive person, who was having serious difficulties in her relationships with others. She verbalized angry feelings toward her mother and observed that she did not feel that her mother really understood her needs. She gave the impression that she had enjoyed using drugs and she seemed somewhat uncertain about her ability to abstain from drugs in the future. The study group recommended that she be placed on probation with the understanding that she would continue under supervision of the mental health clinic to receive individual and family counseling, and either attend school or be regularly employed. Under the sponsorship of vocational rehabilitation services, this girl was continued in treatment in a community mental health clinic and counseling services were provided to the mother. At the same time, she was enrolled in a training course at a nearby community technical institute on an interim basis until she could be enrolled in a college program. During this training, efforts were made to determine her true vocational potential. She has responded well to the supervision and guidance which has been provided and the prognosis for continued acceptable adjustment in the community appears to be favorable.

The second case illustrates the use of vocational rehabilitation services in the corrective treatment of an institutionalized delinquent:

Case 2. At the age of 17 this defendant was sentenced to an indeterminate term as a youth offender on charges of breaking and entering and larceny. He was the product of a broken home and had been raised by grandparents. He was expelled from school while in the eighth grade and was subsequently committed to a training school, where he adjusted poorly and ran away on several occasions. He seemed to be very prone to come in conflict with his supervisors. He was easily angered and he was soon classed as a potential behavior problem and security risk. Initial testing showed dull intelligence, suggestive of borderline mental retardation. However, this finding was not consistent with the achievement level which was considerably above his claimed education. Subsequent examinations and retesting revealed normal intelligence and a sociopathic personality disorder.

Initially, a combined approach to this youth was made by the institutional vocational rehabilitation counselor and the academic staff. These efforts were directed at motivating him to complete his high school equivalency in preparation for entering a vocational training program. Eventually, he was enrolled in a community technical school in study release status and there he completed the requirements for his high school equivalency. Following this he was conditionally released to a halfway house where he obtained part-time employment as an electrician's helper and was enrolled in a training course at a local technical institute, all under the sponsorship and guidance of vocational rehabilitation services.

GOALS AND PROBLEMS FOR THE FUTURE

In cases of this type, the primary aim is to determine the best possible course of treatment for the individual offender. Although most authorities agree that individualized treatment is the desired goal, there continue to be significant impediments and obstacles to the achievement of this aim.

Traditionally, the treatment of offenders has been carried out in closed institutions, often at some distance from the offender's community. More recently, courts have been making increasing use of study procedures to identify offenders who may be safely diverted from incarceration, or in some cases, even adjudication. This trend has required the development of more community treatment facilities. It has also served to facilitate the recognition of areas of mutual interest and concern in which correctional agencies, the courts, and the community can cooperate in arranging effective treatment for the offender. A parallel development has been the implementation of training programs for law enforcement personnel to improve their ability to identify mentally ill offenders.

Earlier in this chapter reference was made to critical shortages in manpower and facilities. Paradoxically, the implementation of new techniques and procedures often aggravates already existing shortages in personnel and facilities, and such seems to be the case with increased use of the scientific examination of the offender. George Dession stated the following over thirty years ago:

> All too frequently the comprehensive and searching picture of an offender revealed by psychiatric case history and diagnosis will serve chiefly to bring out in bold relief the essentially primitive character of all alternatives open for his disposition within existing institutional frames.[20]

Although there seems to be some trend toward improvement, recent surveys of correctional institution staffing patterns continue to show a shortage in the various categories of skilled personnel who are required to implement effective study and treatment programs.[21] Perhaps the greatest shortage is that of psychiatrists, who have been gradually moving away from institutional practice over the past two decades. Clinical psychologists, who are essential to this effort, are also in short supply, though perhaps more ready to accept institutional assignments. Social workers and counselors are also in the shortage category, largely because their contribution has tended to be undervalued by correctional administrators. Finally, the contribution which sociologists and social psychologists might make continues to be essentially unrecognized.

Fortunately, these manpower shortages are being eased to some extent through increasing use of community agencies, and through intensified efforts to recruit specialists who will serve institutions in part-time and consultative assignments. The current emphasis upon community treatment, with its concurrent impetus to develop liaison with a variety of community agencies and institutions, should eventually facilitate the interchange of the available pool of specialists between these organizations and the correctional institutions which they serve. Furthermore, personnel who have gained experience in both areas will achieve a better understanding of the continuum of the treatment process, which should make for improved treatment, as well as more effective prevention.

Among the conceptual and theoretical problems there are several which deserve special attention. Correctional institutions are still steeped in the traditions of the past, so that their approach to their charges often remains rather primitive in basic philosophy. Thus, one must accept the fact that the need for punishment and retribution continues to operate effectively in shaping institutional policy. Emphasis upon custody tends to encourage distance between inmate and staff, a condition which runs counter to the closeness which is essential to any therapeutic endeavor that is intended to improve interrelatedness. Traditional institutional adherence to standard operating procedures encourages rigidity in program design, and thwarts the development of the kind of flexibility which is essential in the treatment of human problems. Segmentation of the correctional process tends to interfere with continuity in treatment programs, which most authorities agree could be better achieved under a unified system of corrections. Continued resistance to the application of the medical model in the treatment of offenders, perhaps for valid reasons, has, nonetheless, often resulted in treatment programs with inept and inadequate design, there being as yet no really viable alternative to the medical mode.

Emphasis upon penal reform has resulted in substantial improvements in the life style of prisoners in confinement. The newer emphasis upon human development will, no doubt, be accompanied by the development of more effective correctional treatment programs. Meanwhile, it is clear that social policy toward the criminal offender remains somewhat unsettled, ambivalent, and even at times, contradictory. Until the nature of the problem of criminal behavior can be more explicitly defined, it seems essential that we continue to pursue a variety of alternative courses in dealing with the problem, hopefully influencing social policy to support those programs which provide measurable results in ameliorating the crime problem.

Finally, it is important to recognize the occurrence of certain ethical and moral problems which inevitably occur in the implementation of programs designed to provide for the study and treatment of offenders. For instance, at times, in the course of an examination, an offender may be required to disclose information which may bear on his culpability. Under such circumstances, there is some risk that the examination may evoke increased anxiety in the offender, even to an extent requiring treatment, which, of course, must be available. This consideration raises questions as to the nature of the setting in which the examination and study is to be made. Where specific psychiatric treatment may be required, something more than the usual custodial institution may be indicated.

Another problem is to determine the extent to which information obtained in these examinations should be disclosed to the public at large. To achieve the kind of "doctor-patient relationship" which would facilitate these examinations would seem to require that the offender have some assurances that his disclosures will not be employed to his disadvantage. The question of how to achieve such a doctor-patient relationship, devoid, insofar as possible, of strain and suspicion, and, at the same time, satisfy the needs of program administrators in the context of this kind of inquiry, remains for practical purposes essentially unresolved. One can only hope that, as we continue to perform these examinations, we will maintain a continuous regard for human dignity and human rights, striving at all times for the highest possible ethical and moral standards, with periodic review of our procedures to insure that these standards are met.

REFERENCES

1. Smith, C. E.: Psychiatry in corrections. *American Journal of Psychiatry, 120* (No. 11): May, 1964.
2. 18 U. S. C. Sec. 4244 (1949).
3. 8 English Reports 718 (1843).
4. *David v. U. S.* 160 U. S. 469 (1895).
5. *U. S. v. Durham,* 214 F. (2) 862 (C.A.D.C., 1954).
6. *American Law Institute Model Penal Code,* Sec. 4.01, 1962.
7. Goldstein, A. S.: *The Insanity Defense.* New Haven, Conn., Yale University Press, 1967.
8. Overholser, W.: The Briggs Law of Massachusetts: A review and an appraisal. *Journal of Criminal Law, Criminology and Police Science, 25* (No. 6): March-April, 1935.
9. Bromberg, W., and Thompson, G.: Relation of Psychosis, Mental Defect and Personality to Crime. *Journal of Criminal Law, Criminology and Police Science, 28* (No. 1): May-June, 1937.

10. Guttmacher, M. S.: *The Psychiatric Approach to Crime and Correction, Law and Contemporary Problems.* Duke University School of Law, 1958.
11. Hobgood, Martha: The Adult Misdemeanant Pre-sentence Diagnostic Referral in North Carolina: A Study of 50 Cases, Unpublished manuscript. University of North Carolina at Chapel Hill, 1971.
12. Wille, W. S.: Psychiatric facilities in prisons and correctional institutions in the United States. *American Journal of Psychiatry, 114* (No. 6): December, 1957.
13. Eckerman, W. C.: *A Nationwide Survey of Mental Health and Correctional Institutions Providing Comprehensive Psychiatric Care for Adult Mentally Disordered Offenders.* North Carolina Research Triangle Institute, 1970.
14. Smith, C. E., and Strawberry, K. R.: Mental Competency Proceedings in Federal Criminal Cases. *Public Health Reports, 75* (No. 7): July, 1960.
15. Smith, C. E.: Recognizing and Sentencing the Exceptional and Dangerous Offender, *Federal Probation Quarterly, 35* (No. 4): December, 1971.
16. *The Criminal Offender—What Should Be Done?* The Report of the President's Task Force on Prisoner Rehabilitation. Washington, D.C., U. S. Government Printing Office, April, 1970.
17. Guttmacher, M. S.: The Status of Adult Court Psychiatric Clinics. *National Probation and Parole Association Journal, 1* (No. 2): October, 1955.
18. Smith, C. E.: Observation and Study of Defendants Prior to Sentence. *Federal Probation Quarterly,* June, 1962.
19. N. C. GS 148-12, GS 148-48 (1967).
20. Dession, G. H.: Psychiatry and the Conditioning of Criminal Justice. *Yale Law Journal,* 47:530, 1938.
21. Scheidemandel, P. L., and Kanno, C. K.: *The Mentally Ill Offender: A Survey of Treatment Programs.* American Psychiatric Association, 1969.

Chapter 15

The Role of Higher Education in the Rehabilitation of the Public Offender*

CRAIG R. COLVIN

Overview
History of University Involvement in Correctional Education
Rationale Supporting Prison College
Implementation of a Prison Education Program
Acceptance of College Programs in Correctional Institutions
Virginia Commonwealth University's Role in the Rehabilitation of the Public Offender
Future of University and Corrections
References

OVERVIEW

The charge of this chapter will be to investigate the role of higher education in the rehabilitation of the public offender. A brief history of university involvement in correctional education will be presented, followed by the rationale supporting prison college programs. The next topic will be concerned with implementation of prison education programs. Here, an analysis of the various components will be surveyed such as the determination of inmate eligibility for such college programs, the types of instruction offered, types of courses offered, and different funding mechanisms utilized to carry out these programs.

A discussion will follow regarding the acceptance of college programs by the various groups of people associated with the inmate population and the roles that vocational rehabilitation, the community, and junior colleges play in the social integration of the inmate into society.

―――――
*Note: This chapter has been developed further from a paper presented to the Canadian Congress of Criminology and Correction held in Ottawa, Canada, on June 13-18, 1971.

The Role of Higher Education of the Public Offender 299

Next is a description of Virginia Commonwealth University's correctional education project. This university has been involved actively in a pilot program at Virginia State Penitentiary in Richmond, Virginia. The potential success to which such an endeavor eventually may lead must now be reviewed critically so that future program development will be realistic and will meet ever-changing societal needs.

Lastly, the future role of university and corrections' involvement will be examined, followed by concluding remarks and a summary.

One cannot talk specifically about a specific program of correctional education which purports to have all the answers; it is, therefore, necessary to draw upon several of the more widely acclaimed prison college programs and then pursue a discussion of their ramifications.

As so with programs, the same applies to individuals responsible for initiating the interest or arousal for the need for college programs and their association with correctional institutions. This chapter will employ many of the philosophies developed by such men as Dr. Stuart Adams who is director of research and planning with the Washington, D. C., Department of Corrections; Dr. Delyte W. Morris, president of Southern Illinois University; Dr. Daniel Glaser, professor and head of the Department of Sociology at the University of Illinois; Dr. George Beto, director of the Texas Department of Corrections; and Mr. Ernest A. Cote, Deputy Solicitor General of Canada. This is only a partial list of important leaders associated with correctional education and philosophy, and the reason for mentioning them is that they are cited most often in the literature pertaining to higher education and the correctional institution.

The underlying premise weaving throughout this section will be directed toward attitude and attitude change within the inmate and, specifically, his motivation toward a better life. Everyone needs to analyze the role that the university can play in effecting attitude change in the public offender and its resultant influence on him, the correctional system, the university, and the community.

HISTORY OF UNIVERSITY INVOLVEMENT IN CORRECTIONAL EDUCATION

Before examining where we are today and in which direction we will be heading, it is important to summarize briefly the historical development of correctional education as well as a survey of programs which are presently in operation.

The historical development of education in prisons carries us back to the 16th century where religious and vocational training were first instituted.[22, 23] In North America the first school system for public offenders was established in Maryland during the 1830's. New York State followed soon thereafter operating under the premise that illiteracy among prisoners was an important factor leading to incarceration. It was felt that if this void could be filled with appropriate education, the prisoner could deal more effectively with the society he previously had rejected. During these early years, the emphasis was placed primarily on vocational training in areas that would help the various prison units to function more smoothly and to benefit financially from the trainees' work.

A name which stands out in American correctional education prior to 1900 is that of Zebulan Brockway. In 1861, he developed an industrial program at the Detroit House of Correction where the United States' first grading system based on prisoner attitudes rather than pure administrative guidelines was enacted.[22]

From this crude beginning, education at the primary levels advanced rather rapidly.

> In 1932, educational personnel in prisons and correctional institutions began convincing their administrations that, although important, academic instruction, library facilities, recreational activities, and religious guidance had no direct connection with the more serious problems a prison released man ... would encounter in his return to society. Something more was needed—something which would help to rectify the many misceptions the offender has about life and the complexities involved in carrying out normal daily activities. The serious business of adjusting to the demands of society, the ability for self-direction, and the knowledge that each individual has the potential of directing his own behavior is extremely important to all of us, and [especially] to the offender.[23]

Continuing with Vukcevich's article,[23] a New York State commission in 1936 stated that "only when vocational training, religious training, academic work, and physical education together with many other institutional influences and contacts are focused on the socialization of inmates can a program of total rehabilitation be effective." They defined socialization as "a process achieved by providing a series of worthwhile experiences which may lead to desirable changes in the attitudes and behavior patterns of offenders so that they will be willing and able to live efficiently in society."

Throughout the United States today, prison educational activity is in wide variance. A number of different programs are in operation including compulsory education through the eighth grade, high school training, and a wide variety of vocational courses. In relation to the entire spectrum of penology, the most recent form of education is that which involves the academic community at the university level. A brief description follows of current programs in the United States where universities and correctional institutions have joined forces in an effort to provide rehabilitation services for selected groups of inmates.

Eastern Michigan University has a program underway at Milan, which is a federal correctional institution. The University furnishes the prison with consulting services, classes for inmates, instructors, and overall program development advice.[10, 16]

Northern Illinois University has established a college degree program at Statesville Penitentiary at Joliet, Illinois, "to offer inmates an opportunity to complete a bachelor's degree program behind prison walls."[10]

A two-year college curriculum is being presented by Chicago's Wright Junior College via television. Since 1958, more than 100 inmates have graduated from this college program while serving time at Statesville Penitentiary. The governor of the state of Illinois supports this program 100 percent; and he is confident that "as instruments of the State, the university and the penitentiary can work together to improve the educational facilities without in any way diminishing the primary objective of either institution."[10]

302 *Fundamentals of Criminal Behavior and Correctional Systems*

Probably one of the first institutions to establish a large scale college program within its walls is the Illinois State Penitentiary at Menard. This endeavor began under the guidance of Southern Illinois University in 1952. Success of the program was such that further emphasis was placed in developing an expanded college curricula in 1962. Since that time, over 500 inmates have participated in a full-scheduled college program in prison.[10]

Several impressive papers have been written by Adams regarding the San Quentin State Prison college program under the auspices of the University of California.[1, 2, 3, 4, 5, 11, 12, 13] Even though funds for this program have diminished, the impact on the academic community, especially in correctional education, has been tremendous. Some effects of the San Quentin project will be discussed later in the discussion on rationale and implementation of college work within the correctional setting.

Several other college prison programs should be mentioned. The United States Penitentiary at Leavenworth, Kansas, is working in cooperation with Highland Community Junior College which is located in a nearby Kansas town;[14] Washington State Penitentiary and Walla Walla Community College have established a working relationship;[14] Oregon State Penitentiary and the University of Oregon have a similar program;[15] the United States Penitentiary at Lewisburg, Pennsylvania, and Pennsylvania State University have recently established college-level courses through an extension program;[17] the University of North Carolina and the State of North Carolina in conjunction with the local community colleges have undertaken a massive program to provide college-level instruction to the inmates of that state. (Another section of this chapter will deal exclusively with Virginia Commonwealth University's role at the Virginia State Penitentiary in Richmond, Virginia.)

One should not get the idea that these institutions are the only ones involved in higher education work in the correctional setting. This is not true. In an exploratory survey made by Adams regarding college-level instruction in U. S. prison,[1] 36 of the state's 46 prison systems had initiated some form of academic work. Since his report was written in 1968 this number has increased, thereby pointing out that more than 80 percent of all prison systems in the United States have some degree of university involvement in their correctional programs. This truly is impressive when one considers the fact that less than 20 years ago only 5 percent of the prison systems had any type of college-level instruction provided for their inmate population.

After perusing the above material regarding the history of university collaboration in correctional education, it is logical for one to ask what the outcome of such endeavor has been. Unfortunately, statistics bearing out the success of each state's higher education program are not available. The reason is that adequate follow-up and research had not been initiated during the initial stages of program planning, and we now are relying on hearsay and gross approximation. However, all is not lost; we have been able to make adequate estimates which justify the continuation of college-level programs within institutional settings.

RATIONALE SUPPORTING PRISON COLLEGE

Before embarking on an endeavor as complex as college instruction in the institution, one must be familiar with the type of inmate the program will serve along with the rationale supporting such a prison college. Several estimates have been given that roughly 10 percent of the approximate 250,000 inmates in the American correctional system could profit from coursework offered by an accredited college or university.[2, 3, 4] Also, regarding inmate intellect, it should be obvious that we are primarily concerned with a group of inmates who would usually score in the normal-to-superior range on selected intelligence tests.

Most professions working in corrections are well aware that there are numerous problems confronting the rehabilitation of the public offender such as provision for adequate housing and appropriate counseling and guidance, vocational training and some type of remedial education, and a host of other variables compounding the inmate's chance of reintegrating himself into the community. The objective of this chapter is to discuss the role of higher education in the rehabilitation of the public offender. This is definitely a small area on which to concentrate in relation to the vast problem facing those working in correctional rehabilitation; but those functioning in the area of correctional education feel that their role is important enough to warrant additional research as well as appropriate expenditures and personnel to carry out the responsibilities inherent in the job.

The small population of inmates eligible will be discussed further along in the chapter, but every inmate within the institution must be given attention if we expect to say that services are comprehensive. Why should we not provide courses which are college level when we are providing remedial reading and writing for other inmates at the opposite end of the intelligence continuum?

To continue with the justification supporting this involvement, strong evidence derived from the various prison-college programs has indicated that prison education does, indeed, reduce recidivism, especially among the younger inmates.[4] Also, academic involvement increases the morale of those participating in the program and, surprisingly, those not fortunate enough to qualify for admission into such courses, as well as inmates in other types of schooling at the high school and vocational level. Further support is evidenced in comments made by prison administrators in which they state that total management of the inmate population within most units becomes easier, and there is an overall reduction in tension as well as an improvement in the entire prison environment.[10]

Regarding the need for more research in correctional education, Waldo[24] mentions the following:

> In spite of some rather dubious statements practitioners and academicians sometimes make concerning the effectiveness of correctional programs, unless the program has been effective in reducing recidivism, in the final analysis we cannot say we are achieving our goal in corrections.

No matter how much we improve the reading ability or language skills of an inmate, unless recidivism is reduced and he becomes a more acceptable and productive member of society, the product of our correctional education program is simply a better educated criminal. This implies that we are not achieving the primary goal of "correcting" inmates.

The purpose of correctional education is not to train inmates to be better inmates; the purpose is to train inmates so that they are able to remain in society without returning to the correctional system at a later date. There is no appreciable demand on the streets of America's cities for a good inmate. What is in demand is an individual who can adapt to society and make a good community adjustment.

> Unless we are able to accomplish this, we are kidding no one but ourselves when we say we are being too stringent in using recidivism as our primary measure of success. We normally use this excuse as a "cop-out" when our figures indicate we have not been successful in reducing recidivism.[24]

Also, let us not forget that failure is inevitable. Don't expect that every man released from prison after completing a prescribed academic program, and for that matter, continuing on with his schooling in the free community, will become a "success." Prior urgings of the "easy life" will consume some men, while others will falter when tempted by the proverbial wine, women, and song. We must contend with these failures as best we can and then proceed to our ultimate objective of helping inmates who show the greatest potential. We can help some of the people some of the time but not all of the people all of the time. The same applies here in correctional education; we expect failure with a percentage of those people living in the free community. Yet, when failure descends upon an ex-inmate, we somehow get hung up on his failure syndrome without examining all possible variables. It is essential to prevent the same thing from happening again. We must not close down all programs for the mere reason that one of the participants has failed to meet predetermined "success criteria."

IMPLEMENTATION OF A PRISON EDUCATION PROGRAM

This section will define some of the variables consistent in the majority of prison college programs currently underway within specific correctional facilities in the United States.

306 *Fundamentals of Criminal Behavior and Correctional Systems*

The following are comments by Morris regarding Southern Illinois University's association with the Illinois State Penitentiary:

All would agree that education cannot be effective without systematic curricular planning at all levels. Courses may be offered because they develop skills needed in prison work programs. This is useful, but the curriculum should also develop skills, goals, and habits of social responsibility needed by the inmate upon release. But, there is more. Counseling and guidance, in a social sense, are essential to education. Inmates, especially, need realistic appraisal. This guidance may come from group or individual conferences, but a broader behavorial guidance comes in education with the teacher as the model. Therefore, planning is more than a series of organizational steps; this includes the instructional personnel so that teachers and guidance counselors—all persons involved—become important cogs in planning.[22]

Continuing with Morris's discussion (his comments are based on the American Correctional Association's *Manual of Correctional Standards,* 1959), the following categories apply to the planning of courses of study offered by universities in prison situations:

1. *Competent personnel.* To a great extent, the quality of any educational program derives from the type of teachers, the number in relation to students, their emotional stability, and their concern for intellectual and personal growth. As noted in the American Correctional Association *Manual:* "It must not be overlooked that the frequent association of inmates with men of intelligence, skill, and balanced personality, is one of the recognized means of achieving desirable changes in inmate personalities."

2. *Institutional setting.* In the sense that every living experience is a learning experience, all men who serve time in an institution require learning of a sort. What kind of education it is depends in a large part on educational planning. For better development of students, surroundings are important. They must be conducive to study, to thought, to communication.

3. *Scope of the program.* The extent and intensity of the schedule will be governed by the institution, its size, and the character of the trainable population. For the university, planning must

include usefulness to the prisoner when released. Prison vocational programs have one set of circumstances and rules; the secondary school's preparation another; the candidates at the higher level of education also must have an awareness of their intended direction.

4. *Defining the educational program.* The university must be aware of its formal relationship. What are the elements which make the university's contribution important? They are well-stated objectives; teachers for suitable purposes, sound texts, equipment, environment, a balanced offering for a well-conceived end, a regular schedule of meetings, proper measurements and records, excellent guidance.

5. *Library coordination.* The prison library usually does not contain the necessary resources for the college courses. The university must furnish or have in the prison library adequate supplementary reading and other materials needed by the educators and students.

6. *Special education.* The university's cooperation should include physical, cultural, and social training. The physical is self-explanatory. The cultural should include concerts, exhibits, performances, etc.—all of which are geared to the aims of the course schedule. Social education works in a less definable area, but it is ultimately the most vital. Its aim is to rehabilitate, that is, to develop acceptable human behavior. Included are group or individual therapy and special programs for the handicapped. Within the United States, this usually is where vocational rehabilitation actively becomes involved.

7. *Orientation, guidance, pre-release advising.* None of these activities can exist in a vacuum. The ultimate goal is adjustment through intellectual means toward social responsibility.

Criteria Used for the Selection and Determination of Eligibility for Prison Courses

After the initial planning stages have been finalized, it is then necessary to select inmates for the various academic courses being offered. Since we are dealing with a rather unique population, it is necessary to alter the traditional eligibility requirements found within the free-college system. Ordinarily, the most obvious criterion would be that the individual must possess a high school diploma or hold a general education development certificate (GED). But again, we must consider the uniqueness of this experiment and rely on other criteria such as whether or not the individual has had prior college experience.

Within this age of affluence, even the prison population is undergoing radical changes. Another reason for supporting a prison college system is the increasing number of inmates convicted of violating civil codes, problems with drugs and addiction, along with an array of other problems considered social in nature. Many of these people come from high schools, junior colleges, and universities prior to their incarceration. Possibly through previous academic work, coupled with the discipline of the institution and appropriate medical treatment, the cycle of crime, maladaptive social behavior, or addiction may be broken.

Age is another variable which must be considered. Since our prison population approximates the normal distribution in relation to age, this variable probably will not have the impact of others previously mentioned. As an example, if an individual is young and rather bright and is a high school dropout with a GED, he may be considered for college-level work. On the other hand, a man who has spent 20 years in prison and who has benefited educationally from the prison school program might also be considered for advanced work. We cannot underestimate the individual's interest in attending university courses if they are offered. His motivation, his confidency, and his responsibleness must be evaluated before formal course registration.

One of the traditional criteria used is an individual's mental status. This is based on tests provided by the correctional psychologist or the public offender's past academic records. Achievement and personality, as well as intelligence tests, can be used as an index of intellectual maturation.

If an individual is a security risk as far as the correctional administration is concerned, he may not be eligible for academic work; this is especially true if such courses are offered outside the prison walls. Prison officials may be withholding the privilege of attending higher academic coursework as a means of negative reinforcement for an inmate's past behavior.

An inmate's length of sentence must be discussed as well. If he has a relatively short period of time remaining prior to release, one might hesitate in recommending him for college courses within the prison setting. On the other hand, if there is a possibility for him to initiate a course within the prison and then be paroled to a university program on the outside without interrupting his academic work, such a plan should be developed accordingly.*

If an inmate does not seem to fit any of the descriptions described previously, those people responsible for inmate selection may ask him to write a paper stating why he is interested and why he should be considered for prison college work. The material that he presents may be a better indication of potential success in further academic work than any of the other criteria thus far discussed.

Another factor to be considered is the location and screening of qualified inmates in an attempt to find the best applicants for college courses. The most prevalent places to look for inmates who might qualify for advanced academic work are in administrative areas, hospital and physical therapy departments, prison education departments, and in records and bookkeeping sections. Obviously, many inmates with higher I.Q.'s gravitate toward these jobs within the correctional setting since they do require a higher level of intelligence. But do not overlook such departments as maintenance, carpentry, baking, and cooking since men of superior and very superior abilities have been found in all major assignment categories.[4] It should be kept in mind that these assignment designations are not descriptive of the intellectual abilities of the applicants.

---

*Programs of this nature have been developed at several correctional institutions in conjunction with participating universities. An article by Murphy and Murphy (*Federal Probation*, March 1971, p. 45-48) outlines the social implications and current trends of parole as a college plan.

Types of Instruction Offered

In one of Stuart Adams' several studies regarding college-level instruction in U. S. prisons,[1] he outlines several of the most prominent types of instruction offered within the correctional setting. Of those prison systems responding to a questionnaire which he distributed in 1968, approximately 80 percent completed the report. The most accepted form of college instruction offered within correctional institutions was correspondence courses. The reason for this should be quite obvious since a correspondence course is the simplest way for someone incarcerated to procure academic material. In addition, correspondence courses involve the least amount of money and time on the part of both corrections and university personnel.

Following correspondence courses in acceptance was live instruction by visiting college staff. This type of educational involvement has gained recognition during the last several years, specifically from 1967 up to the present. With live instruction, the college instructors and professors come directly into the prison and provide lectures and demonstrations. With this arrangement, it is necessary for the university to prearrange a meeting place conducive to study and discussion, and at the same time, maintain security precautions as established by the prison administration. As in the majority of correctional units, there must be selective integration of specific coursework requirements with the somewhat rigid requirements imposed by custody and the institution's administration.

There are a myriad of details that must be worked out prior to commencing any course within the correctional setting. For example, if classes cannot be scheduled at night and must meet during the day, it is necessary to obtain permission for inmates enrolled in such courses to be released from their respective work details. If additional books are required for the successful completion of courses, arrangements must be made to procure adequate library books from the university or other reliable sources. As usual, any item entering the prison system must be checked thoroughly for contraband that might be included and missed by the unsuspecting eye of a professor.

A third type of instruction offered by some correctional institutions has been TV courses. In this kind of instruction, courses are broadcast regularly via closed circuit television from the university or by regular network television (such as Sunrise University) to the prison. The major drawback to this type of presentation is that if the inmate has a particular problem during the television broadcast, he must jot his question down on a postcard. This, in turn, will be checked by security before mailing to the professor in charge of the television course. Upon receipt of the inmate's question, an assigned graduate student will make every effort to answer whatever problem the inmate may have expressed. The response is then sent back through the mail to the inmate who probably has forgotten his original question!

Of course, one realizes that social interaction is missing in both television and correspondence courses. Such interaction is a necessary ingredient for self-fulfillment within the educational process. But as expressed to this writer by an inmate in North Carolina, correspondence and TV courses are better than no courses at all.

The fourth and final type of instruction offered to correctional units is the college furlough plan whereby an inmate is bussed to a nearby college during the day, and after classes is returned to prison for the night. This type of program has been carried out with a high degree of effectiveness and success. To give an example: An inmate in North Carolina was serving a sentence for armed robbery. After being placed in a maximum security unit for a length of time, he was eventually transferred due to his good behavior to a minimum security unit outside Winston-Salem, North Carolina. After a short period, he gained the respect of the prison administration and was placed in honor grade status. About this time the Department of Correction, the Division of Vocational Rehabilitation, and the local community college entered into a cooperative agreement whereby selected inmates could participate in the junior college academic program on campus. This young man was one of the first inmates chosen to participate in this cooperative endeavor in North Carolina.

His overwhelming success, both academically and socially, in the junior college was unbelievable.

Early in the morning, he would get up and study prior to changing into civilian clothes. He would then be driven to the junior college and let out at its entrance. For the remainder of the day, he would attend classes, mingle with the regular students from the community, and go to scheduled social events. At the end of the day, the prison car would come to pick him up and take him back to the institution. This young man gained the respect of the community college administration, faculty, and students. In fact, during his freshman year, he was elected to the student council; during his sophomore year, he was elected president of the student government association. Upon graduation in the spring of 1970 (and by the way, he graduated with honors), he contacted a prestigious southern university regarding admission into their upper division program. Tentative acceptance was granted by the university pending the outcome of a parole board decision. The parole board took into consideration his age, the offense, the length of time served under good behavior, and his outstanding record as a college student. All of these variables convinced them that parole was in order for this outstanding young man. Since parole, he has entered the university and all indications point toward successful completion of his chosen objective.

Types of Courses Offered

Thus far in the college-level instruction within the correctional setting, a wide array of courses has been presented to the inmate population. These include the traditional courses in English, English composition, sociology, psychology, personality, history, and mathematics. Some of the more interesting courses being offered in various institutions across the country have been accounting, music, art, law, calculus, physics (without the lab), chemistry (without the lab), and engineering. In the San Quentin

---

Personal communication from Jack McComas, State Coordinator, Department of Correction, Raleigh, North Carolina, May 3, 1971.

Project, two unique courses were initiated: The Prison Community and Field Studies in Criminology. In the first course, the Prison Community, inmate students were required to write term papers depicting various roles and situations prevalent within the correction setting in which they were interested. The course was conducted on a seminar basis where discussion was expected along with a critical examination of methodologies. It was stressed that the course would not be a gripe session where inmates could vent their hostilities; rather, it was to be a constructive attempt to organize one's thoughts in an effort to communicate effectively with someone else.

In the latter course, Field Studies in Criminology, individual inmates were selected to participate on their own. Usually, an outstanding student who attended the first course dealing with the prison community continued on in the second course, thereby allowing him the opportunity for additional exposure and a chance to further his thoughts that began to germinate earlier in the year. Rationale supporting his position was expressed in the form of a special project or term paper. The instructor in this course re-emphasized that this course was not going to be a pushover, so to speak, and that diligent work was expected of each participant. During that semester, several of the students involved in this unique project were advised that every possible attempt would be made to get their papers published by the university or other interested journals (one article was later published by the California University Press).

An interesting sidelight in regard to the various courses offered where term papers and projects were required was that, of the many presented, several were outstanding enough to warrant further consideration as research topics to be carried out by university and corrections personnel. This, in turn, substantiates the rationale supporting university and corrections' involvement: Through reports submitted by inmates for college credit, full-time faculty members and other researchers (including graduate and undergraduate students) could utilize this information as a sounding board for further and more in-depth research regarding incarceration and the underlying philosophies of penology.

Types of Degrees Earned

The culminating objective of any academic program is the successful completion of all requirements and the awarding of degrees or certificates of accomplishment. Since the structure of college courses within the prison setting does not parallel exactly the curriculum offered in the regular university programs, it has been difficult in the past for an inmate to earn the degree while being institutionalized. But this is not to say that degrees are not offered; correctional units in Michigan, Illinois, Kansas, North Carolina, Texas, and several other states have had inmates complete requirements for associate of arts, associate of science and associate of applied science degrees; and a few inmates have earned bachelor's degrees.

There was a unique graduation from a junior college in Alabama where five prison inmates had been released for the day so that they could attend their own commencement exercises in the local community. It seems that during the two and one-half years prior to graduation, these five men had been working diligently in academic coursework while in prison (most courses were attended in the community). At these commencement exercises, the chairman of the board praised the inmates for their conscientiousness in pursuing a higher education under such unusual circumstances. He went on to say that even though their bodies were locked up, their minds were still free; and with this freedom, these men chose to better themselves so that, upon release, they would have something to show society. One inmate put it as follows:

> I did go wrong and I realize this fact; therefore, I am serving time as dictated by the courts and society. But, I must say I have used this time wisely in study and for reflecting on my mistakes. Since there is such a high demand for college degrees in our country, I feel I now have something to contribute to society rather than detract from society.*

---

*An unidentified inmate made this statement during a commentary presented by Walter Cronkite and the Columbia Broadcasting System's "Evening News," May 10, 1971.

Even though the majority of inmates cannot earn a degree *per se* while being institutionalized, their programs have been arranged so that upon release it is simple to transfer to a college in the community without losing credit for courses completed. As an example, a research and demonstration program called "Project New Gate" is underway at the Oregon State Penitentiary.[20] Funded by grants from the Office of Economic Opportunity (OEO), the project provides college preparatory courses for inmates at the maximum security institution and enables them to continue their education upon release at a college where their tuition, room, and board are paid.

To emphasize the growth of college instruction in prisons, one correctional unit in Texas, after several years of conducting the higher education program, wanted to see if it was possible to have its program accredited by the Southern Association of Colleges. Tentative approval was given to the correctional center and the sponsoring junior college with the stipulation that the prison libraries be upgraded to meet accreditation standards. This stipulation was met during the first year after tentative approval was given. Since 1969 when the first degrees were conferred, more than 43 inmates have received associate of arts degrees from this school.

Funding Mechanisms

In this investigation of prison college programs, probably one of the more important topics has to be funding mechanisms. Without adequate justification, it is conceivable that no program would ever be initiated. The premise under which funds may be appropriated has been stated by Glaser.[18] He says as follows:

> Justification for educational expenditures is based upon the established fact that there is a high negative relationship between years of education and indices of delinquency and crime. It is reasoned, therefore, that by reducing the education deficiency of prison inmates, the needs for crime and delinquency will be replaced by more socially acceptable aspirations.

Under the present system, the majority of prison budgets do not include sufficient funds to operate adequately a college program. One reason is that the prison administration feels that monetary investments can be made in other areas where greater rewards might be achieved.

Advanced educational programs currently in progress in the United States are being financed in several ways:

1. Many correctional systems employ the support of the department of vocational rehabilitation. Under the auspices of this organization, tuition, fees, and books can be authorized to eligible inmates. One must realize vocational rehabilitation has its own eligibility criteria which must be met before an individual can receive services.

2. In a small number of state correctional systems, small educational budgets within various prisons' departments have been used to pay the necessary costs of inmate involvement in a college program. Normally, such funds are employed in the prison's remedial, primary, and secondary education programs where the greatest percentage of inmates are participating. It should be noted that as college-level instruction increases within correctional units, it will be necessary to rearrange the allotment of funds to benefit the college-bound inmate.

3. Some colleges have worked out an arrangement with the local correctional institution where they pay the entire cost of tuition and fees for participating inmates. In other colleges, only a percentage of costs have been absorbed, or tuition has been reduced so that it becomes nothing more than a token payment.

4. In the United States, OEO has initiated several demonstration projects across the country where it is paying part of the costs with the remainder being assumed by the correctional unit and the inmate.

5. Surprisingly, there are some correctional units which require the inmate to pay his own way. If he does not have the appropriate amount of money in his personal account to pay tuition costs, or if he cannot arrange for his family to help him with this financial problem, he is not considered for the program. Unfortunately, this is unfair to the motivated inmate, since in the majority of cases he is lacking in financial resources. It is imperative

that he be provided the opportunity to make arrangements for the payment of required fees.

There have been many innovative ways in which money has been raised in various correctional units across the country to help pay the costs of college work. Some of them are as follows: In Texas, the inmates sponsor a rodeo where a portion of the collected funds is allocated to those inmates considering advanced academic work. Other inmates have donated their blood in lieu of tuition payments. Still others donate their services to pharmaceutical and other scientific companies for experimentation. In the literature, there have been several references to inmates' tape recording books for Lions Clubs to distribute to blind people.

Probably the most rational approach to these funding problems would be to divide somehow the costs among the various organizations (prison correctional units, OEO, vocational rehabilitation, the sponsoring colleges, the prison's educational fund); and most importantly, let the inmate himself contribute something toward the payment of fees.

Finally, regarding the allocation of funds, one must gain support not only from state prison administrators and college personnel, but from the state's legislative body as well; these people are in a position to provide favorable input for the creation of sound academic programs that ultimately can benefit everyone—the institution, the college, the inmate, the community, and the state as a whole. This mutual sharing of responsibility is absolutely necessary if we expect to maintain and increase our involvement in prison-college programs.

Acceptance of College Programs in Correctional Institutions

As is the case with the majority of newly instigated programs within any system, there usually are varying degrees of acceptance ranging from total support to total rejection. The same, of course, holds true for the acceptance of college programs within the correctional institution.

As a result of the findings of the San Quentin Project and Virginia Commonwealth University's involvement in this type of program, it is important to examine some of the attitudes relating to acceptance by people representing various disciplines.

Generally, those people in the upper administrative levels of corrections accepted the rationale as well as the formation of college prison programs. The assumption that supervisors and line officers would accept the decision of top management is not substantiated. This writer has heard correction supervisors and officers say that the administration of college-level courses for inmates was unfair since they themselves had to pay for their education, while inmates were provided identical courses at no charge. Similar comments were made by citizens in the community who were aware of courses being offered inmates within the institution.

Education as a mode of rehabilitation received limited support from a minority of correctional personnel. These people felt that since nothing else had worked to any significant degree up to this point, why not try something new such as providing them the opportunity to take college courses. Even though there were adamant objections to providing this experience for inmates, a lack of cooperation on the part of the correctional staff was negligible.[4]

At times, those people responsible for initiation of college-level projects felt that their endeavors were being hindered or even undermined by the correctional administration; however, the typical daily procedure supposedly necessary to carry out prison responsibilities was the interfering factor. Such acts were not intentional but merely standard operating procedures, especially with the advent of anything considered new. This should be a warning or red flag for anyone interested in promoting any new project within the correctional institution—it takes time and a lot of paper work to reach fruition. Until some of the archaic security measures are changed, modified, or eliminated, there will always be delays in implementing new ideas for the correctional setting.

With only a few examples of indifference, the majority of professionals functioning outside the controls of the correctional administration—vocational rehabilitation, OEO, public welfare, and the Department of Labor—were most supportive toward the activation of prison colleges. Their allegiance is attested by the fact that support has been provided in terms of personnel, consultation, and financial contributions.

A vital member of this endeavor that has been mentioned only briefly and yet plays a significant role is the college faculty. After their initial involvement in a prison college program, almost all faculty members supported and encouraged the continuation of university participation. With minor incidences of harassment which mar a "perfect score" in acceptance of inmates as college students, I feel safe, as a faculty member myself, in considering the university's effort in correctional education as being totally worthwhile.

There is another group that deserves consideration with regard to attitudes—the community—the free community. In the majority of cases, there is no question that the community accepts the rationale for higher education within the correctional structure; however, there are many citizens who feel as do those correctional officers mentioned previously. They feel a dichotomy exists when someone convicted of a crime and sent to prison has more of a chance to do college work than their own sons and daughters who have worked so diligently toward that objective. When people have the opportunity to defend the prison-college program as a method of rehabilitating a selected group of inmates so that they do not return to a life of crime, most people within the community support the initiation or continuation of the academic program.

One of the basic questions raised by a group of laymen is, "How much will this program cost us as taxpayers?" and, "Can you guarantee that upon release, the inmate will not return to a life of crime?" Of course, one would be foolish to say, "Prison-college programs do not cost money," and, "Yes, we can guarantee the individual will not resume his previous criminal behavior." This cannot be said at all. But it can be said that in relation to cost-effectiveness, the provision of college-level instruction for selected inmates does pay off; and that with the support of organizations discussed previously, the burden does not fall solely on the shoulders of the taxpayer. Studies also have indicated that recidivism *is* reduced significantly.[21]

At the June 1971, commencement exercises of Virginia Commonwealth University, those in attendance had the privilege of hearing Dr. John Joseph Akar, former ambassador to the United States from Sierra Leone of the African continent. In his address, he told a story that is rather appropriate to relate at this time. It seems that a mental hospital in New York City had an art show where material prepared by the patients was put on public display. One painting which drew the most curiosity depicted high walls in a multitude of depressing colors—predominantly, shades of gray. At the bottom of the picture was written, "People are lonely because they build walls; not bridges." Just think of this for a moment—"People are lonely because they build walls; not bridges."

Now, if this is put in context with what has been discussed thus far in this chapter—the relationship between the academic community, the prison community, and the free community to which the inmate must return—we begin to visualize the important role the community must play in order for inmate resocialization to occur. We must bridge this gap which exists between the institution and the community—not build higher walls.

VIRGINIA COMMONWEALTH UNIVERSITY'S ROLE IN THE REHABILITATION OF THE PUBLIC OFFENDER*

Correctional rehabilitation and, specifically, correctional education requires intervention into many more areas of the individual's life than do the more conventional types of rehabilitation and education. Successful rehabilitation with a prison population generally requires changes in the individual's established life style, his self-concept and his level of interaction with others. As one approach to facilitate growth in these three areas, Vir-

---

*This section is part of a revised paper originally prepared and contributed by Dr. Robert A. Armor. Acknowledgment and appreciation are extended to Dr. Armor for allowing the basic content of his work to appear in this chapter.

ginia Commonwealth University (VCU) proposed a program of courses for the inmate population with special emphasis on developing communication skills. This proposal was based on the premise that the ability to communicate adequately and appropriately with others will substantially enhance self-concepts.

During the spring semester of 1970, VCU sponsored a course for inmates at the State Penitentiary in Richmond, Virginia. This course, the first of its kind in Virginia, was a pilot program designed to evaluate inmate response to college-level material and to discover whether special problems exist because of the unusual setting. History, rationale, and implementation of various college-level courses have been described earlier in this chapter.

Prior to the commencement of academic work at the state penitentiary, several of its representatives and the university faculty convened. The purpose of this meeting was for VCU to offer its services to the penal system. From this initial meeting, two areas of services were defined: (1) professional courses for the penal staff were to be considered, and (2) basic college courses for the several hundred eligible inmates were to be considered. It was decided that the pilot program should start in the spring of 1970. In-service training for the professional staff was to be decided upon at a later date even though adequate support had been given to inaugurate it immediately.

The first course offered was English 101, a basic composition course where the goal is to teach rhetoric and composition and to give training in basic communication skills. Two English professors volunteered to teach the course in addition to their required teaching loads on the main campus. Administrative responsibility was given to one of the faculty members.

The funding for the course came from the Virginia State Department of Vocational Rehabilitation. This agency authorized funds to help carry out the pilot course in conjunction with appropriate supervision and guidance. Thirty-four inmates volunteered for the course, and 15 were selected randomly to enroll as special students in the evening college division of the university. The number in the class was kept at a minimum so as not to cause an unnecessary burden on the professor. The class can be described as follows: All members had earned GED certificates; nine were in their 20's, five in their 30's, and one was 51 years old; eight were Caucasian, and seven Negro. From this point no further attempt was made to investigate their backgrounds.

These men should not be considered average freshmen. Their educational and social backgrounds were different; their ages and certain experiences more advanced. They had special problems and special talents, and the professor had to be flexible enough to solve the former and take advantage of the latter. All of these men could be classified as disadvantaged.

Problems Discovered in the Pilot Program

A pilot course is designed to discover what problems may exist in a full-scale program. The problems revealed in this course may be divided into two types:

1. There are two obvious problems resulting from the inmates' educational backgrounds. First, their grammar is unacceptable by common standards. They speak a prison dialect full of slang and incorrect usage. Also, many speak a dialect prevalent among the black society. A heavy emphasis on grammar was necessary; and, fortunately, they wanted to learn grammar and were quick to do so. They requested extra lessons and drills in grammar and one of the professors obliged. Second, since they received their secondary education through the GED program, they had little training in methods of research; again special emphasis solved this problem.

2. The problems that result from the peculiarities of teaching within a penal institution are more extensive:

A. *Social Security Numbers.* Many computers, including the one at VCU, are set up to file students by their Social Security numbers, thereby alleviating many problems of duplicate names and initials; but many inmates have either never had a number or have no record of it. The problem is compounded by the length of time it takes to assign a number to a man by the Social Security Administration (registration was delayed several weeks in the pilot program as a result). In the future, the problem will have to be anticipated and all prospective students encouraged to get their social security numbers far in advance of registration.

B. *Textbooks.* Textbooks can be ordered through two sources: the VCU bookstore or the prison facility. It has been recommended that the prison facilities be utilized, but the courses must be set up far enough in advance to allow for delivery of textbooks at the institution. In the pilot program, the tardiness of some books and the failure of others to arrive at all forced the participating faculty to provide alternatives. In fact, the two professors involved in this project brought personal copies of complimentary books for distribution among the inmate class.

C. *Library Facilities.* The prison has a small and useful library, but it is not extensive enough to provide research material for college-level courses. The professor must realize that a student's opportunity for research will be somewhat limited and, therefore, should make allowances.

D. *Registration and Other Red Tape.* The faculty tried to complete registration during class time to keep from making extra trips to the prison. The class time lost in this way is too valuable to be spent on red tape, even though some problems are unavoidable. It has been suggested that arrangements be made with prison authorities for time in advance to take care of the majority of these matters, including whatever publicity is deemed necessary.

E. *Individual Advising.* On a regular campus, a professor is expected to see his students on an individual basis in his office several times a semester. At the prison, there was no opportunity to hold regular office hours; therefore, it has been recommended that a certain period of time be set aside for counseling other than class hours. Trying to counsel during class hours proved unsatisfactory not only to the counselee but to the other inmates as well. The amount of time scheduled for counseling should be determined by the instructor and should depend upon the demands of the course; i.e. freshman English will require probably more individual counseling than an advanced literature course.

F. *Responsibility for Choosing Subject Matter and Textbooks.* The nature of the inmates' confinement and their psychological make-up dictates course content; and, more importantly, textbooks must be chosen with care so as not to cause undue personal problems for the inmates and the prison administration. As an example, one of the professors was advised that *The Autobiography of Malcolm X* might prove to be inflammatory; as a result, this text was not used. The prison officials probably are more conservative on this issue than most instructors; but then the prison staff must "live with the problem" once the course has terminated. Tactful compromise will solve most problems of this sort.

G. *Study Time.* Much to the surprise of most outsiders, inmates do not have an overabundance of time to study. They all have jobs that consume approximately eight hours a day. Added to this are a couple of hours a day for relaxation and recreation followed by an early bedtime. These restrictions provide the inmates with only two to three hours per weeknight for studying. Their weekends offer them several more hours of study. On this note, it would be safe to make the assumption that it would be difficult for most inmates to take more than two courses during any given semester.

H. *Number of Class Meetings.* In the federally sponsored project, Operation Headstart, it has been observed that the majority of children in this training program were returning at night to homes where they unlearned what they had been taught during the day. A similar problem exists at the prison, especially for those involved in an English course. When the inmate returns to his cell or the yard, he often forgets his lessons. The faculty observed that the longer between class meetings (often from Wednesday until Monday and over holidays), the harder it was for the students to pick up where they had left off. Basic courses might meet only once a week, but even these probably would benefit from more frequent contact with the inmates.

I. *Sudden Release.* Provisions should be made so that an inmate with a chance for release is not delayed because of his enrollment in a course. If the schedule at the prison college were to coincide with the course schedule on the main campus, perhaps arrangements could be made for a transfer from one campus to another. This is an area which deserves further consideration.

Special Techniques of Instruction

With the 15 inmate-students, there was no need for a specific remedial course (with others, the need may exist even though it is on the college level); but there was a need for some additional concentration in grammar and punctuation, as well as research techniques. Moreover, it was suggested by one of the professors that programmed instruction might be a useful device.

Through training, these men largely approach their experiences sensuously. Their intellects have not been developed highly in a systematic way; and as yet, they, like many freshmen, are unable to relate this type of experience to the intellect. To take advantage of sensuous orientation and to correct the inability to relate the two, it is suggested that a multi-media approach be integrated regarding intellectual subject matter. The more printed material they can be given, the better; they react better to printed instructions than to oral instruction. Also, including experiences in other media—lights, music, etc.—and asking them to relate these experiences to their writing, have enhanced program success. For the poorer student, this technique was helpful; but it did little for the better student. For these students, it is suggested the augmentation of films, tapes, and records will act as catalysts.

The faculty members involved in this prison college project at VCU used pre- and post-testing. This was done in an attempt to measure objectively the student's progress as compared to a national norm, as well as to diagnose specific inmate problems. The instrument used was the English Composition part of the College Placement Tests distributed by Educational Testing Services (ETS). This proved unsatisfactory for several reasons. First, most students improved on the second test. This improvement, however, is meaningless without appropriate statistics to show how much improvement occurred with students in other classes at various colleges. If one could test for several years, data could be assembled and assessment made depicting inmate progress; but with one test administered to only one class of inmates, it is difficult to derive a meaningful and valid score. Second, the ETS material did not provide the project coordinators with a national norm but only with general guidelines. Therefore, only a rough approximation of how inmate-students compared nationally with others can be inferred (even without this information, there is reason to speculate that Virginia State Penitentiary inmates scored slightly below average). Thirdly, since this test is not broken down into specific areas of writing problems, there is no way to use it to diagnose specific problems for individual inmate students. With this in mind, several other batteries of tests have been selected which can approximate the information desired.

Since the educational experience of these men is limited, faculty members decided it would be beneficial to expose inmates to several college teachers with varied backgrounds. Two professors held class discussions, met in individual counseling sessions, and delivered occasional lectures. In addition, these professors invited several prominent figures with the university into their classes. One such person led a discussion on creative writing which interested many of the inmates, especially since she was a noted authoress who had published widely. Her attention to the details of good writing gave the students insight into the more sophisticated aspects of composition.

Results

In this pilot project, all inmates passed the course. There were four A's, four B's, and seven C's. The high grades signify that some students came a long way, since they began the course at the below-average range. This success is attributed to two factors: (1) motivation—they wanted to succeed; and (2) innate intelligence that had not been tapped or trained before (when given the basic instruction that was needed, they caught on quickly and readily).

The change between the first papers required in a writing course and the last paper is usually noticeable in all students; but in these men who had little prior formal training, the change was dramatic. By comparing these two sets of papers, one can observe definite improvement in grammar, punctuating, paragraphing, and style; but perhaps the most significant improvement is in tone. In the second set, the students were more trusting, less hostile, and better able to relate personal experience without an undertone of suffering or hostility.

Most students improved the second time the diagnostic test was given. Some improved more than others, and several actually lost a few points. Cautiously evaluated, this improvement in the majority of inmates seems to show a better knowledge of basic composition.

The true success of this course or, for that matter, any college experience, cannot be found in grades or statistics alone, but in the immeasurable part the course played in the total maturation process. The realization on the part of these student-inmates that they can perform well in the competitive world outside will go far toward rehabilitating them and will make the expenditures of time, energy, and money worthwhile.

Virginia Commonwealth University will continue its collaboration with the prison because this work gives the university an opportunity to serve both the inmates and the community. Many intelligent inmates are anxious for an education that will allow them to rise above their life style. They want respect and a position in society that results from a worthwhile education. They do not want to return to the life that led them to crime in the first place. Also, it should be pointed out that such an experience with a correctional institution definitely can serve the institution, university, and individual faculty members. This is not meant selfishly but as an actuality of academic life. Research is one of the charges of any university, and this program can be used for two types of research: (1) an investigation can be made of the personalities of the deprived and the criminal, and (2) we can improve our methods for teaching the disadvantaged and at the same time be providing a valuable service to the institution.

Later, the project hopes to involve the correctional staff in some college-level coursework in an effort to upgrade the correctional profession.

Additionally, the image of VCU as a concerned urban institution has been enhanced. Thus far, almost everyone outside the prison has been impressed with the college program and the university's involvement in correctional rehabilitation.

The English course is being expanded to include a fairly complete curriculum offering the basic college courses. Speech, mathematics, history, psychology, sociology, English, and philosophy are being considered. Later, it is hoped to expand further into a curriculum leading to a two-year associate of arts degree if there is enough student demand. There may be between 300 and 400 inmates within the Virginia penal system who would be eligible for a college program; therefore, it is the consensus of this university that a community college someday will be initiated within the system.

Another problem that has been mentioned previously and must be considered is the matter of funding. Thus far, the university has committed a small amount toward the actual operation of college-level instruction within the Virginia State Penitentiary. The correctional unit staff has been cordial and extremely interested, but they have been stymied insofar as providing adequate funds for academic work. The State of Virginia has appointed a task force to study the need and feasibility of such a concentrated program. With this in mind, this writer is making an assertion that rehabilitation of the more intelligent inmates will be furthered by intellectual rather than pure vocational training.

Recommendations offered to the legislative task force regarding the university's expansion of correctional education services were as follows:

1. Serving inmates who are granted study-release to come to a campus for classes and then to return to confinement at night. The 1970 legislature authorized the program but allocated no funds for tuition. Suggestion has been made that some inmates

might be granted scholarships or perhaps loans. Others might be eligible for the university's Opportunity Scholars Program, and others could be provided some part-time jobs around campus to allow them to earn their tuition money. The number of inmates involved in this program definitely should remain small. Also, they need to be provided with an academic counselor. The director of the Opportunity Scholars Program or the director of the general studies curriculum within the university may function in this capacity.

2. Teaching courses in the prison for inmates who cannot be released to come to the campus. This financial burden should not be borne solely by the university; it should be shared with not only the institution but other state organizations and the inmate as well. The cost is parallel to that charged to any student taking one course at a time—$75 per student for tuition and books.

In Virginia as it is with the other states, a period of fiscal tightening is taking place, and government officials do not have the money to fund all worthwhile programs; but the justification for program continuation should take precedence. If the university does not provide adequate educational resources for these intelligent inmates, rehabilitation cannot take place or surely will be hindered; and, in turn, they may return to crime. Who suffers? The citizens will suffer the expense of this crime and the state will suffer the expense of police action, the trial, and reincarceration. On the other hand, if we can raise the educational level of these men and provide them with the challenge of attitude change and motivation toward a better life, the probability of them becoming productive members of society has been increased. Therefore, further education should lead to better paying jobs which would increase buying power and tax contributions.

In concluding, it is imperative that the communities as well as the surrounding areas be kept informed of the progress being made in the correctional education programs. The reason for this should be quite obvious; after the inmate's release from prison, he will be reentering the community in an effort to regain social acceptance. If the community is accepting and willing to help him overcome whatever deficits he may have, the probability of success is enhanced greatly.

FUTURE OF UNVERSITY AND CORRECTIONS

Within the literature pertaining to prison college programs, the future appears to be bright; yet in order to determine this legitimately, the future must contain research. Beto[7] and Canada's Deputy Solicitor, Ernest Cote,[9] both said at the 100th anniversary of the American Correctional Association:

> We have little evidence to show that they are successful in achieving the objectives which we have set for ourselves, namely, redirecting and restructuring the life of the offender.

Beto emphasized the following:

> Many of our programs may be good, they may be effective, but they are based on an unvalidated assumption; we have no assurance—without the measurement found in research—that these programs are effective and successful.

Empirical feedback must be gathered in order to predict program success as well as future program growth.

What we are after is a true concern for our fellow man. Within our society, we say that everyone has the right to certain benefits and this holds true even for the institutionalized public offender. The right to receive an education whether it be at the remedial, primary, secondary, or college level remains as a definite pathway in avoiding the misfortunes associated with criminal behavior. There is a definite gap existing between education provided within the community and that provided within the correctional setting; it should be our personal objective and professional responsibility to narrow this gap. Reducing the probability that the inmate receiving this type of education will return to a life of crime is a secondary side-effect that we cannot ignore. If, through further academic training, he realizes his past mistakes and is able to accept himself as an individual within the constructs as established by society, all has not been lost.

The Role of Higher Education of the Public Offender 331

Ramsey Clark,[8] former Attorney General for the United States, summarizes this quite well in his book, *Crime in America,* when he says the following:

> Within the correctional setting, human dignity is lost. As professionals, we must make every effort to restore or build this dignity within the person. A purpose in life must be found and then appropriate action taken so that they can hope to achieve this long-awaited goal. Education, physical and mental health, all add to the likelihood of inmate success upon release.[8]

As a closing statement, remember that without education, the probability is increased that they will return to lives of crime.

REFERENCES

1. Adams, S.: *College-level Instruction in U. S. Prisons.* Berkeley, University of California, January, 1968.
2. Adams, S.: Higher Education in Prison: Some Current Trends. Paper presented at the 98th Congress of Corrections, San Francisco, August, 1968.
3. Adams, S.: Education and the Career Dilemma of High IQ Prisoners. Paper presented at the Conference on Manpower Training for Offenders in the Correctional Process, Berkeley, February 25-28, 1968.
4. Adams, S.: *The San Quentin Prison College Project: Final Report, Phase I.* Berkeley, University of California, April, 1968.
5. Adams, S.: *The D. C. Prison College Project: An Interim Report.* Research Report No. 18, LEAA Grant #A110007. District of Columbia, Department of Corrections, July, 1970.
6. The American Correctional Association. *Manual of Correctional Standards.* Washington, D.C., 1959.
7. Beto, G.: Presidential address: continue work, so much to be done. *American Journal of Correction,* Nov.-Dec., pp. 6-7, 1970.
8. Clark, R.: *Crime in America.* New York, Simon and Schuster, 1970.
9. Cote, E. A.: Canada congratulates ACA on 100th birthday. *American Journal of Correction,* Nov.-Dec., pp. 36-39, 1970.
10. *Federal Probation.* Washington, D.C., United States Courts and Bureau of Prisons of the Department of Justice, March, 1966; March, 1967; December, 1967; June, 1968; December, 1968; March, 1969; March, 1970; September, 1970.
11. *Ibid.,* March 1967.
12. *Ibid.,* December 1967.
13. *Ibid.,* June 1968.
14. *Ibid.,* December 1968.

15. *Ibid.*, March 1969.
16. *Ibid.*, March 1970.
17. *Ibid.*, September 1970.
18. Glaser, D.: *The Effectiveness of a Prison and Parole System.* Indianapolis, Bobbs-Merrill, 1964.
19. Glaser, D.: The effectiveness of correctional education. *American Journal of Correction*, March-April, pp. 4-9, 1966.
20. Gordon, N. J.: Fighting crime with sheepskins. *Communities in Action.* Office of Economic Opportunity, Washington, D.C., 5:1-7, June 1969.
21. McWilliams, J. P.: Rehabilitation versus recidivism. *Junior College Journal*, March, pp. 88-90, 1970.
22. Morris, D. W.: The university's role in prison education. *Nebraska Law Review*, 45:542-571, 1966.
23. Vukcevich, S. U.: The general progress of correctional education. *The Journal of Correctional Education*, 21:16-20, Summer 1969.
24. Waldo, G. P.: Research in correctional education. *The Journal of Correctional Education*, 21:4-9, Fall 1969.

INDEX

A

Abnormal brain waves, 157
Abnormality, 23
Abramsen, D., 149
Absence of privacy, 270
Accomplice, 42
Adams, Stuart, 214, 299, 302, 310, 331
Addict, 259
Adult male, 248
Adults, 96
Aggressive-exploitative, 189
Aggressive tendencies, 234
Akar, John Joseph, 320
Alcabes, Abraham, 118
Alcohol, 8, 287
Alienist, 282
America, 10
American Association for Forensic Sciences, 8
American Correctional Association, 85, 330, 331
American Federation of Labor v. Watson, 54
American Law Institute, 35, 283
American Law Institute Test, 283
American Lecture Series In Social and Rehabilitation Psychology, ii
American Prison Association, 85
American Revolutions, 6
Ames, R., 235, 250
Amos, William E., v, 176
Amputation, 157
Anglo-Saxon, 282
Armor, Robert A., 320
Army-Air Force Clemency and Parole Board, 130, 131, 132, 133
Army Correction Program, 121
Arrest pattern, 164
Arson, 287
Ash, Ellis, 175
Assault, 43, 161

aggravated, 202
Assistance of Counsel, 41
Atlas, Bob, 174
Attitudes, 157, 171
Automobile thief—joy rider, 202
AWOL, 122, 135
Ayer, W. A., 149

B

Bailleaux v. Holmes, 117
Ball, J. C., 239, 250
Baltimore, 288
Banning v. Looney, 79
Barnes, H. E., 22, 227, 250
Battery, 43
Becker, Howard, 180, 184, 211
Behavior problem delinquent, 202
Berger, Warren (Chief Justice), 116
Berk, B., 149
Beto, George, 117, 299, 330, 331
Beverly-Grant Opinion Schedule, 208
Beverly, Robert F., 215
Bill of Rights, 39, 40, 44, 55
Bizarre offense, 287
Black Muslims, 113
Blackstone, 7
Bloch, Herbert, 186, 187, 212
Bolden v. Pegelow, 117
Bored, 28
Boston, 288
Boy's girl theory, 227
Brain damage, 157
Brim, O. G., Jr., 149
Brockway, Zebulan, 300
Bromberg, W., 296
Broome, Leonard, 21
Brutality, 103
Butches, 249
Butler, Edgar W., 233, 250

C

California, 109, 210, 233, 288
California Youth Authority, 109
  Community Treatment Project, 205
Capone, Al, 20
Career (Criminal), 158
Case, J. D., 149
Cash bond, 45
Caucasian, 322
Cavan, Ruth Shonle, 174, 186, 188, 212, 245, 250
Challenge of Crime in a Free Society, 21
Chaplins, 103
Chicago, 288
Chicago's Wright Junior College, 301
Chicano, 262
Chilton, Roland, 224
Christian Science, 262
Christmas, 265
Churchill, Sir Winston, 19
Civil Rights Act, 65
Clark, Ramsey, 30, 31, 280, 331
Classification Committee, 258
Clemency, 126
  Initial, 130
Clements, Hubert M., v, 82, 117
Clemmer, Donald, 137, 147, 149, 173, 175, 193, 213
Cleveland, 288
Clinard, Marshall B., 173, 187, 188, 212
Cline, H., 149
Clinical psychologists, 294
Cloward, R., 149, 150, 202, 219
Coffin v. Reichard, 80, 81
Cohen, Albert, 222
Cohen, A. K., 227, 250
Cohen, Frank H., 250
Cohen, Fred, 117
Cohen, Neil P., 280
College Programs, 317
Colvin, Craig R., v, 298
Common law, 39, 282
Community, 99
Community based programs, 105
Community Treatment Project (CTP), 202, 208
Conflict gang delinquent, 202
Conforming, 207
Conformist, 207
Con men, 168
Connecticut, 14
Conquest of England, 6
Conrad, John P., 214
Conspiracy, 43
Constitutional Guarantees, 32, 34
Constitutional law, 50
Contributors to the crime problem, 5
Cool Cat, 167
Cooper, Robert, 250
Coppedge v. United States, 22
Correction Division, Chief of the, 129
Correctional
  administration, 62, 82
  client, 16
  processing, 157, 170
  programs, 101
  programs within institutions, 102
  systems, 82
Correctional Training Facility (CTF), 119, 120, 123, 124, 125
Corrections, history of, 82
Corruption, 103
Cote, Ernest A., 299, 330, 331
Cottrell, Leonard S., Jr., 21
Court martial, 129
Covert manipulators, 233, 234
Cressey, Donald R., 149, 150, 173, 174, 175, 186, 212, 213
Crime and Delinquency, 81
Crime and Personality, 158
Crime in America, 30, 280
Crime of Punishment, 30
Crime
  causes of, 23
  cultural aspects of, 5, 19
  motiveless, 287
  professional, 8
  white collar, 8
  without victims, 8
Criminal, 188, 189
  behavior, group support of, 156
  behavior, senseless repetitive, 287
  justice system, 12, 33
  law, 32, 34, 50
    basic principles of, 32, 42

procedures, 32, 50
  Texas Code of, 44
  professional, 8, 159, 188
  professional *heavy*, 202
  semi-professional property, 202
  typology, 155, 181
  white collar, 188, 202
Criminologists, 158
Criminology, Field Studies in, 313
Crippling diseases, 157
Cross-tabulation typologies, 155
Cull, John G., v, xvii, 23
Curley v. Gonzales, 80
Czajkoski, Eugene H.

D

David v. United States, 296
Davis v. Lindsay, 81
Dean, Mary L., vi, 216
Death Cell Row, 254
Defending, 207
Deformities, 157
Delaware, 14
Delinquency, 216, 221
  types of, 217
Delinquent, 172, 219
  casual, nongang, 202
  criminal role career, 158
  female, 202
  habitual gang, 219
  juvenile, 216
  middle class, 217, 218
  occasional, 218
  overly aggressive, 202
  predatory gang, 202
Demanding, 207
Demographic variables, 156, 165
Dependents, 108
Deprivation model, 139, 142, 144
Dession, George, 194, 297
Detroit, 288
Detroit House of Corrections, 300
Dickens *(Oliver Twist)*, 20
Disciplinary Barracks, 119
Double jeopardy, 40
Disorganized acting-out, 189
District of Columbia, 87

District of Columbia Reformatory, 163
Dormitories, open, 96
Downers, 166
Dressler, David, 239, 251
Drug Pusher-Pimp Pattern, 155
Drug pushers, 168
Drugs, 166, 167, 169, 287
Drug users, 166
Drunkenness, 161, 166
Dunham, H. W., 212
Durham, 283
Durham v. United States, 55
Durkheim, Emile, 180

E

Eastern Michigan University, 301
Eckerman, W. C., 297
Eclectic approaches, 155
Education, 318
Educational level, 156
Educational program, 307
Educational Testing Services (ETS), 325, 326
Educational TV, 311
EEG, 157
Ehrmann, W., 251
Eighth Amendment, 41, 57, 70, 71, 72, 113
Elliott, Mabel, 241, 251
Emancipation of women, 232
Embezzler, 202
Emotional sensitivity, 230
Empey, LaMar T., 117
Empirical typologies, 155
Encephalitis, 157
England, R. W., 251
English Criminal Law, 7
Entrapment, 43
Epilepsy, 157
Ethnic minority, 51
Ex Parte Hull, 113
Ex post facto laws, 42
Eysenck, H. J., 158

F

Facilities, 293

installation confinement, 119
Family relations, 216, 220
Federal Probation, 331
Federal services agencies, 29
Female offender, 96, 225, 276
Ferdinand, Theodore N., 173, 180, 183, 184, 185, 189, 190, 211
Fernald, M. R., 225, 251
Fifth Amendment, 38, 40, 55
Fighting, 189
Finks, 255
First Amendment, 39, 43, 56, 73
Fitzgerald, Maurice, J., 174
Fleming, Ian, 25
Florida, 288
Floyd, C. M., 150
Forgery, 202
Foster homes and group homes, 105
Fourteenth Amendment, 38, 39, 43, 55
Fourth Amendment, 56
Fox, Vernon B., vi, 5
Frustration, 230

G

Ganey, Judge T. Cullen, 8
Gangs, 202, 219
Garabedian, Peter, 194, 213
Garrity, Donald, 149, 193, 194, 213
Geis, G., 186, 187, 212
General Educational Development Program (GED), 123, 308, 322
Germany, 177
Giallombardo, R., 149
Gibbons, Don C., 149, 173, 180, 181, 182, 185, 187, 195, 197, 200, 202, 203, 204, 205, 211, 224
Gibbons' typologies, 200
Glaser, Daniel, 116, 117, 149, 299, 315, 332
Glickham, Sylvia, 174
Glueck, E. T., 149, 222, 226, 251
Glueck, S., 149, 222, 226, 251
Glue sniffers, 221
Goffman, E., 144, 150
Gordon, N. J., 332
Goldberg v. Kelly, 80
Goldstein, A. S., 296

Grand Jury, 40
Grant, J. D., 206, 214
Grant, M. Q., 206, 214, 215
Grau v. United States, 53
Gray, John Morris, vi, 119
Green Dragon, 254
Griffin v. County School Board of Prince Edward County, 76
Gross, L., 210
Group typologies, 155
Grusky, O., 150
Guarding procedures, 72
Guided group interaction programs, 105
Guilt feelings, 275
Guttmacher, M. S., 297

H

Habeas corpus, 65, 70
Halleck, S. L., 249, 251
Hancock v. Avery, 80
Hardman, D. G., 251
Hardy, Richard E., vii, xvii, 23
Harris Poll, 9
Hatfield v Bailleaux, 117
Hayner, Norman A., 175, 193, 213
Hazelrigg, L., 150
Head injuries, 157
Heat bringers, 168
Hegelian, 177
Hempel, Carl G., 173, 211
Heroin, 166, 168
Hewitt, Lester, 174
Heyns, Garrett, 117
Higher Education, 298
Hirschkop, P., 80
Hobgood, Martha, 297
Hoehne, Charles W., vii, 32, 55, 58
Holt v. Sarver, 76, 80, 81, 113, 117
Homosexuality, 232, 250
Housebreaking, 161
Huber Law of Wisconsin, 106
Hughes, P. H., 150
Hugo, Victor, 20
Humanitarian ideals, 136
Humiliation, 230

Index 337

I

Ideal typologies, 155
Identifying, 207
Idleness, 103
Illinois State Penitentiary at Menard, 302
Immature-impulsive, 233, 234
Importation Model, 139, 143
Impulsive, 189
Incarceration, continued, 98
Incarceration, effects of, 103, 270
Incorrigibility, 225, 236, 237, 238, 247
Incorrigible girl, 225, 236
Individual advising, 323
Inmates, dangerous, 72
Inmate Hierarchy, 270, 277
Inmate population, 146
Institutional setting, 306
Institutions, 82
Instruction, special techniques of, 325
Instruction, types offered, 310
Interpersonal Maturity Level Theory (IML), 205, 208, 209, 210
Intervention, 10
Involuntary manslaughter, 43
IQ, 172, 309
Irwin, J., 150

J

Jackson v. Bishop, 80
Jackson v. Goodwin, 81
Jacobs, B. R., 80
Jails, 281
James, Jesse, 20
Jealousy, 230
Jenkins, Richard L., 174
Jesness Psychological Inventory, 233
Johnson v. Avery, 70, 81
Jordan v. Fitzharris, 80, 81
Judicial reluctance, 63
Judicial role, 62
Judicial system, 77
Jurisdiction, 44
Juvenile Delinquency Control Act of 1968, 10
Juvenile Delinquency Prevention and Control Act of 1961, 10

Juvenile delinquent, 96, 216

K

Kanno, C. K., 297
Kansas, Fort Riley, 122
Kassebaum, G., 150
Kay, B. A., 227, 228, 245, 251
Kennedy, Robert F., 19, 22
Kirby v. Thomas, 117
Kluckhalm, F., 229, 251
Konopka, G., 231, 251
Korn, Richard, 193, 213
Kraft, L., 80

L

Larceny, 43
Law Enforcement Assistance Administration, 13, 14
Law of Criminal Corrections, 67
Lawson, Robert G., vii, 270
Lawyer, jailhouse, 33
Lay public, 270
Lazarsfeld, P., 210
Lee, R. E., 235, 550
Leeke, William D., viii, 82, 117, 118
Legal challenges, 82
Lesbianism, 241
Les Miserables, 20
Levy, R. J., 150
Liberties, 73
Library coordination, 307
Library facilities, 323
Life imprisonment, 266
Lindner, R., 150
Lindsmith, A. R., 212
Liquor, 57
Logan, Nell, 239, 250
Lombroso, C., 185, 186, 225, 227, 250
Loveland, F., 195, 214
LSD, 168

M

Maine State Prison, xv
Males, 96

Malum in se, 42
Malum prohibitum, 42
Mandamus, 66
Manipulator, 207
Manpower, 293
Manual of Correctional Standards, 69, 72, 78, 306
Marijauna, 168, 291
Marital relations, 222
Marital status, 156
Martindale, D., 210
Masked behavior theory, 227
Mathiesen, T., 150
Matthews, Richards, 62
Mattick, Hans W., 22
McKinney, John C., 177, 179, 180, 181, 182, 184, 211
McKorkle, L., 193, 213
McWilliams, J. P., 332
Mempa v. Rhay, 80
Menninger, Karl, 30, 31, 280
Mental deterioration, 49
Mental disorder and crime, 281, 284, 286
Merrill, F. E., 241, 251
Menton, R. K., 21, 147, 150, 174
Messinger, S. L., 150, 213
Methodology, 157
Middle ages, 5, 6
Middle-class, 28
Military Occupational Specialty (MOS), 124
Military prisoners, 119, 120
Military records, 122
Milleman, M., 80
Miller, M. J., 151
Miller, R. W., 212
Minnesota Multiphasic Personality Inventory (MMPI), 157
Mirando v. Arizona, 59
Mischievous indulgent, 189
Mixed pattern, 164
M'Naghten's Case, 36, 283
M'Naghten Test, 36, 55
Model cities program, 10, 104, 116
Modus operandi, 156, 162
Montesquieu (*The Spirit of the Laws*), 20

Moonlight, 159
Moral deterioration, 103
Morris, Delyte W., 299, 306, 332
Mothers, 232
Multiple pattern, 164
Murphy, Maribeth, 309
Murphy, Melvin L., 309
Mulligans, 254
Murder, motives for, 230

N

Nagel, E., 210
Napoleonic Codes, 7
Narcissism, 135
Narcotic addict—heroin, 202
Narcotics, 37, 57
National Council in Crime and Delinquency, 88
National Jail Census, 13
Negro, 322
Neighborhood, 216
Neurotic, 189, 207
 disturbed, 233
New Jersey, 288
Newman, C. L., 251
New York, 109, 288, 300
New York Reformitory for Women, 225
Ninth Amendment, 41, 57
Nisbet, Robert, 174
Norris, G., 150
North Carolina, 289, 311
Northern Illinois University, 301
Novick, A. G., 241, 251
Nye, F. I., 236, 240, 241, 252

O

Objectivism, 177
Occasional offender, 188, 225, 227
Offender
 normal, 23
 occasional, 188, 225, 227
 one-time, 202, 218
 property, 202
 situational, 225
 violent sex, 202
Offender of opportunity, 225

Offense behavior and interactional setting, 165
Ohlin, L. E., 140, 150, 202, 219
Omnibus Crime Control and Safe Streets ACto of 1968, 10, 83
Oregon State Penitentiary, 315
Organic variables, 157
Organized crime, 8, 188
Orientation and reference groups, 157
Origins of Crime, 5
Overholser, W., 296

P

Parole, 108
    conditions of, 133
    failure of, 17
Parson, T., 179
Peer groups, 26, 233, 270, 277
Penal code, model, 112
Penologists, 272
People v. Gitlow, 81
Perrow, C., 150
Personality, 270, 271
    disorder, 292
    profile, 157
    unsocialized, 207
    structure, 172, 157
Petersen, David, viii, 135
Petty criminals, 188
Ph.D., 172
Philadelphia, 288
Physical deterioration, 49
Pierce v. LaVallee, 81
Pilot Intensive Counseling Organization (PICO), 197, 198, 199
Pimps, 167, 168
Pittsburgh, 288
Piven, Herman, 118
Placement Tests, college, 325
Pleas
    guilty, of, 46
    nolo contendere, of, 46
    not guilty, of, 46
Policeman, 51, 216
Police power, 34
Pollak, O., 226, 227, 251
Polsky, Ned, 174

Pratt, L., 230, 251
Pre-prison variables, 146
Pre-release program, 106
Pre-sentence Diagnostic Procedure, 288
President's Commission on Law Enforcement and Administration of Justice, 88
President's Task Force on Corrections, 95
President's Task Force on Prisoner Rehabilitation, 287
Presidential Task Force Report: Organized Crime, 9
Principal to a crime, 42
Prison conditions, 72
Prison Education Program, 305
Prisoners, 123
Prisonization, 137, 138, 142, 143, 146, 147
Prisons, 281
    contributions to crime, 23, 29
    minimum security, 96
    obsolescense of, 97
    services of, 307
Probation and Parole, 98, 101
Probation, Chief of, 95
Probation violation, 246
Probation-violator, girl, 225, 243
Process I (LL), 191, 192
Process II (UL), 191, 192
Process III (LM), 191, 192
Process IV (UM), 191, 192
Professional *fringe* violator, 202
Professional thief, 202
Professionalism, 28
Professor, 310
Prohibition Era, 7, 9
Project New Gate, 315
Property offender—"one time loser," 202
Prostitutes, 166
Protestant Ethic, 24
Pseudo-social and asocial, 194
Psychiatric-oriented approaches, 155
Psychiatrist, 216
Psychiatry, 281, 282
Psychological aspects, 23
Psychologist, 216
Psychopathic assaultist, 202

Psychotics, 26
Public Law 90-377, 119
Puerto Rico, 87
Pusher-pimp, 166

Q

Quinney, Richard, 173

R

Rape, 43, 202, 204
Rap sessions, 27
Receiving stolen property, 43
Reception center parole, 109
Reckless, Walter C., 173, 174, 227, 251
Redl, F., 174
Reedy, Corbett, xiii
Reformation, 84
Registration, 323
Regulations, 67
Rehabilitation, 75, 87, 100
Rehabilitation counselor, 32, 33
Re-imprisonment, 99
Reinemann, J. O., 244, 252
Reintegration, 84, 86, 87
Released, 108
Research and Development Programs, 109
Restoration Board, 128
Restoration Policy, 128
Restoration to Duty, 127
Restraint, 84, 85
Revenge, 84
Rhode Island, 14
Richmond, M. S., 118
Rickert, H., 177
Riemer, Svend, 180, 181
Rivkin, Dean Hill, 280
Robin Hood, 20
Roebuck, Julian B., viii, 155, 173, 174, 183, 212
Role career, 172
Role lag, 228
Role models, 26
Rorschach Test, 157
Rosenheim, F., 252
Rosenthal, Jack, 22

Rosenwald, R. J., 235, 250
Rowdies, 168
Royal Oak, Michigan, 111
Rubenfeld, Seymour, 189, 190, 191, 213
Rubin, Sol, 67, 79, 81
Ruffin v. Commonwealth, 79
Running away, 235, 246, 247

S

Sampilner, Robert, 22
San Quentin, 312
San Quentin Project, 318
San Quentin State Prison, 302
Satutory rape, 202
Scheidemandel, P. L., 297
Schack v. State, 80
Schnur, A. C., 150
Schrag, Clarence, 147, 150, 175, 193, 201, 213
Schuessler, Karl F.
Second Amendment, 40, 56
Scholastic Aptitude Test (SAT), 165
Self-concept, 157, 171
Self-incrimination, 40
Self-understanding and adjustment, 23
Self-worth, 232
Selznik, Jerome, 21
Sentence, length of, 309
Seventh Amendment, 41
Sex, 232
 crimes, 287
 delinquent girl, 225, 226, 238
 factors, 275
 offender, 202
Sexual
 interaction, 169
 offenses, 246
 techniques, 169
Shakespeare *(Romeo and Juliet)*, 20
Sheldon, William, 157
Short, J. F., 236, 240, 241, 252
Silva, G. E., 150
Single Pattern, 163
Sixth Amendment, 41, 56
Smith, Charles E., ix, 281, 296, 297
Smith, H. C., 228, 237, 252
Snell, J. E., 235, 250

Index

Social adjustment, 16
Social education courses, 104
Social order, 277, 278
Social Security Number, 322
Society, 277, 279
Sociologist, 216
Solitary, 71
Somerville, Dora B., ix, 225
Somototype, 157
Sostre v. Rockefeller, 69, 80
South Carolina, 89, 107
South Carolina Department of Corrections, 89, 107, 110, 114, 118
South Carolina Probation, Pardon and Parole Board, 89
Southern Association of Colleges, 315
Special education, 307
Speed, 166
State vs. Jones, 50
Stockades, 120
Stoned, 166
Strawberry, K. B., 297
Street Corner Society, 218
Street crime, 8
Street, D., 150
Stubbs, Wright, ix, 253
Studt, Elliot, 118
Study time, 324
St. Valentine's Day Massacre, 7
Sudden release, 324
Sullivan, Clyde, E., 214
Sutherland, Edwin, 138, 147, 150, 174, 175, 181, 186, 187, 188, 212
Sutter, Allen G., 175
Swindling, 43
Sykes, Gresham, M., 139, 150, 175, 193, 213
Symptom, 5
Synopsis of Texas Legal Rights, 58
Synthetic typologies, 155

T

Taliaferro, Maryann, Mrs. xvii
Tangled pathology, 219
Task Force Report, 13
Task Force Report: Corrections, 79
Teenage girls, 230

Tenth Amendment, 41, 53
Texas Code of Criminal Procedure, 44
Texas Department of Corrections, 253, 256, 258
Textbooks, 323
Theft, 43, 189
The Walls, 256
Third Amendment, 40, 56
Thomas, Charles W., ix, 135, 151
Thomas, W. I., 226, 227, 250, 252
Thompson, G., 296
Thugs, 168
Tittle, C. R., 151
Tittle, D. P., 151
Tompkins, Dorothy, 211
Treatment of Military Prisoners and Administration of Military Correction Facilities, 119, 120
Trese, L. J., 229, 252
Triangle, 235
Tricks, 166, 167
Trop v. Dulles, 80
Truancy, 217, 246
Trusty Shack, 257

U

Unadjusted girl, 226
Uniform Crime Report—
  1968, 21
  1970, 12, 17, 18
United States, 15, 40
  Army
    Clemency Branch of the Correctional Division, 133
    Clemency and Parole Board, 130
    Correctional Training Facility, 124
    Provost Marshall General, 124
    Secretary of the, 130
  Board of Parole, 94, 95, 176
  Bureau of Census, 14
  Bureau of Prisons, 7, 75, 78, 94, 95, 107
  Constitution, 35, 38, 39, 43, 48, 64, 73
    Amendments to:
      First, 39, 43, 56, 73
      Second, 40, 56

Third, 40, 56
Fourth, 56
Fifth, 38, 40, 55
Sixth, 41, 56
Seventh, 41
Eighth, 4, 57, 70, 71, 72, 113
Ninth, 41, 57
Tenth, 41
Fourteenth, 38, 39, 43, 55
Court Cases
  Bailleaux v. Holmes, 117
  Banning v. Looney, 79
  Bolden v. Pegelow, 117
  Coffin v. Reichard, 80, 81
  Coppedge v. United States, 22
  Curley v. Gonzales, 80
  David v. United States, 296
  Davis v. Lindsay, 81
  Durham v. United States, 55
  Goldberg v. Kelly, 80
  Grau v. United States, 56
  Griffin v. County School Board of Prince Edward County, 76
  Hancock v. Avery, 80
  Hatfield v. Bailleaux, 117
  Holt v. Sarver, 76, 80, 81, 113, 117
  Jackson v. Bishop, 80
  Hatfield v. Bailleaux, 117
  Holt v. Sarver, 76, 80, 81, 113, 117
  Jackson v. Bishop, 80
  Jackson v. Goodwin, 81
  Johnson v. Avery, 70, 81
  Jordan v. Fitzharris, 80, 81
  Kirby v. Thomas, 117
  Mempa v. Rhay, 80
  Mirando v. Arizona, 59
  People v. Gitlow, 81
  Pierce v. LaVallee, 81
  Ruffin v. Commonwealth, 79
  Schack v. State, 80
  Sostre v. Rockefeller, 69, 80
  State v. Jones, 50
  Trop v. Dulles, 80
  United States v. Cruikshank, 56
  United States v. Durham, 296
  United States v. Robinson, 54
  Washington v. Lee, 81
  Weems v. United States, 80
  Williams v. Field, 80
  Wright v. McMann, 79, 80, 81
Department of Defense, 119
Department of Health, Education and Welfare, 83
Department of Justice, 94
  Federal Bureau of Investigation, 7, 12, 83
Department of Labor, 10, 83
Department of Social Welfare, 94
Disciplinary Barracks, 120, 123, 127, 131
Military Justice, Uniform Code of, 119
Navy, 119
Office of Economic Opportunity (OEO), 315, 316, 317
Office of the Provost Marshall General Correction Division, 128
Supreme Court, 11, 13, 60, 114
University of Chicago School of Law, 62

V

Vedder, Clyde, B., x, 225, 246, 251
Venue, 44
Vice, 9
Villa, Pancho, 20
Vining, Joseph E., 118
Vinter, R. D., 150
Violence, 28
Virginia, 163
Virginia Commonwealth University (VCU), 298, 299, 302, 318, 320, 321, 322, 323, 325, 327, 328
Vocational Rehabilitation, 10
Vocational Rehabilitation Services, 281, 29, 292
Vold, George, 212
Voltaire (Henriade and Oldeipe), 19
Voluntary manslaughter, 43
Volunteers, 111
Vukcevich, S. U., 301, 332

W

Waldo, Gordon P., 118, 304, 332
Walker, Nigel, 22

Ward, David A., 150, 175
War of 1812, 6
Warren, Earl (Chief Justice), 60
Warren, Marguerity Q., 173
Warren, M. G., 215
Washington, D. C., 109, 288
Washington v. Lee, 81
Wattenberg, W. W., 252
Weber, Max, 177, 178, 179, 180, 211
Weems v. United States, 80
Weiss, Herman R., 22
Wellford, Charles F., x, 151, 176, 213
Wheeler, Stanton, 147, 151, 194, 213
Whyte, William T., 218
Wickersham Report, 8

Williams v. Field, 80
Willie, W. S., 297
Wilner, D. M. 150
Wilson, John M., 118
Winch, Robert, 211
Winters, Glenn R., x, 62
Wisconsin, Welfare Department, Corrections Division of the, 111
Wolfgang, Marvin, 211
Women, 276
Work program, 102
Work program for inmates, 102
Wright v. McMann, 79, 80, 81
Writ of habeas corpus, 65, 258
Writ of mandamus, 65